Mirror to Dan

Described by the author as 'simply a work of love', *Mirror to Damascus* provides an enthralling and fascinating history of Damascus from the Amorites of the Bible to the revolution of 1966, as well as being a charming and witty personal record of a city well-loved.

In explaining how modern Damascus is rooted in immemorial layers of culture and tradition, Colin Thubron explores the historical, artistic, social and religious inheritance of the Damascenes in an amusing and perceptive manner, whilst interspersing the narrative with innumerable anecdotes about travellers of bygone days.

Mirror to Damascus is a unique portrait of a city now obscured by recent upheavals, by one of the most indefatigable and popular of travel writers.

Born in 1939, Colin Thubron is a direct descendant of of the poet, John Dryden. He was educated at Eton and worked for four years in publishing in England, before touring Europe. He has since travelled extensively, from the High Atlas Mountains of Morocco to New York and the South Seas. He is the author of many travel books, including *Jerusalem*, which will be reprinted in the Century Classics series in 1987, and was awarded the major PEN award in 1985.

The cover illustration is taken from the collection of paintings at the
Mathaf Gallery, 24 Motcomb Street, London, SW1

Mirror to Damascus

Colin Thubron

Century Publishing
London

First published in 1967 by
William Heinemann Ltd

© Colin Thubron 1967
All rights reserved

This edition first published in 1986 by Century Publishing, an imprint of
Century Hutchinson
Brookmount House, 62–65 Chandos Place, London, WC2N 4NW

Century Hutchinson Publishing Group (Australia) Pty Ltd
PO Box 496, Hawthorn, Melbourne, Victoria 3122

Century Hutchinson Group (NZ) Ltd
PO Box 40–086, Glenfield, Auckland 10

Century Hutchinson Group (SA) Pty Ltd
PO Box 337, Bergvlei 2012, South Africa

ISBN 0 7126 9456 0

Made and printed in Great Britain by the
Guernsey Press Co. Ltd., Guernsey, Channel Islands.

For my
Mother and Father

Contents

Acknowledgements

I WISH TO acknowledge the kindness of the following for help in preparation of *Mirror to Damascus*: Mr Chafic Imam, Director of the Museum of Folk Art and Traditions, Azem Palace, Damascus; Mr Assouad of the Department of Antiquities, Damascus; and the staffs of the Institut Français de Damas, the School of Oriental and African Studies, London, and the Oriental Department of the Public Library, New York. Above all, I am grateful for the perseverance and sympathy of Rae Jeffs in helping me with the manuscript.

None of the above mentioned is responsible for any opinion expressed in this book.

Maps

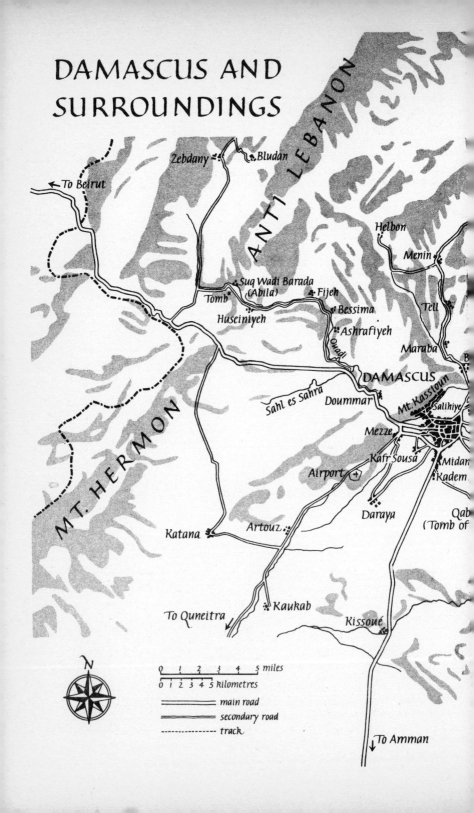

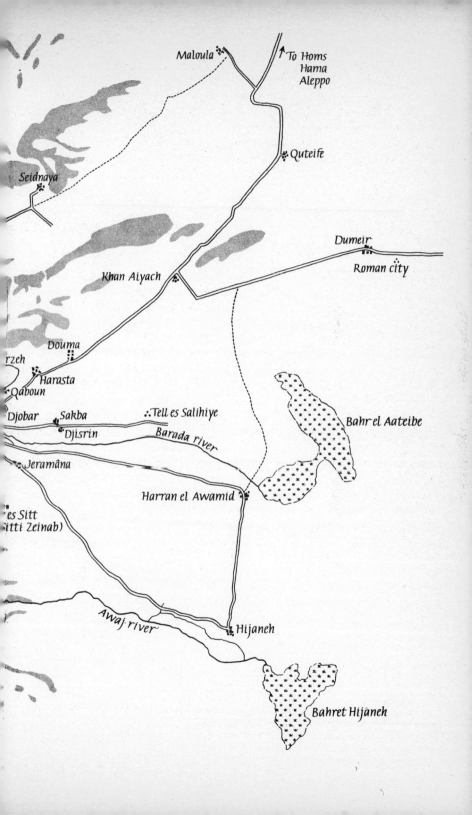

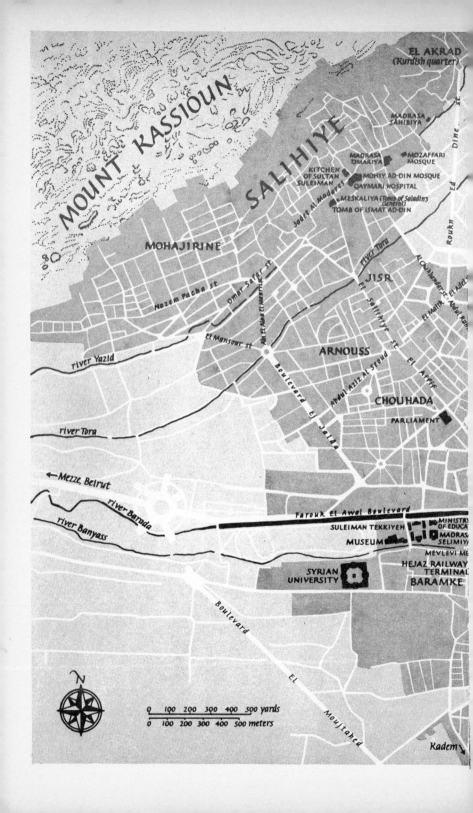

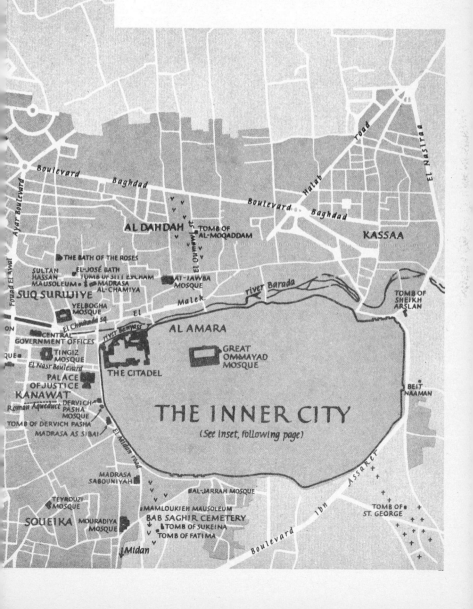

DAMASCUS
with
SALIHIYE

Boulevard

Baghdad

Ayar Boulevard

Fouad El Awal

Boulevard

Halab Road

El Nasitaa

Boulevard   Baghdad

AL DAHDAH

El Otmawi St.

TOMB OF
AL-MOQADDAM

KASSAA

THE BATH OF THE ROSES

SULTAN
HASSAN
MAUSOLEUM

EL-JOSÉ BATH
TOMB OF SITT ESCHAM
MADRASA
AL-CHAMIYA

AT-TAWBA
MOSQUE

river Barada

TOMB OF
SHEIKH
ARSLAN

SUQ SURUJIYE

YELBOGHA
MOSQUE

El
El Choukada sq.

Malek

river Banyasi

AL AMARA

ON

CENTRAL
GOVERNMENT OFFICES

QUE

TINGIZ
MOSQUE

El Nasr Boulevard

PALACE
OF JUSTICE

KANAWAT

Roman Aqueduct

TOMB OF DERVICH PASHA

MADRASA AS SIBAI

THE CITADEL

GREAT
OMMAYAD
MOSQUE

BEIT
NAAMAN

DERVICH
PASHA
MOSQUE

El Midan Road

THE INNER CITY
(See inset, following page)

Assaret

MADRASA
SABOUNIYAH

TEYROUZI
MOSQUE

SOUEIKA

MOURADIYA
MOSQUE

AL-JARRAH MOSQUE

MAMLOUKIEH MAUSOLEUM
BAB SAGHIR CEMETERY
TOMB OF SUKEINA
TOMB OF FATIMA

Midan

Boulevard

Ibn

TOMB OF
ST. GEORGE

DAMASCUS: THE INNER CITY

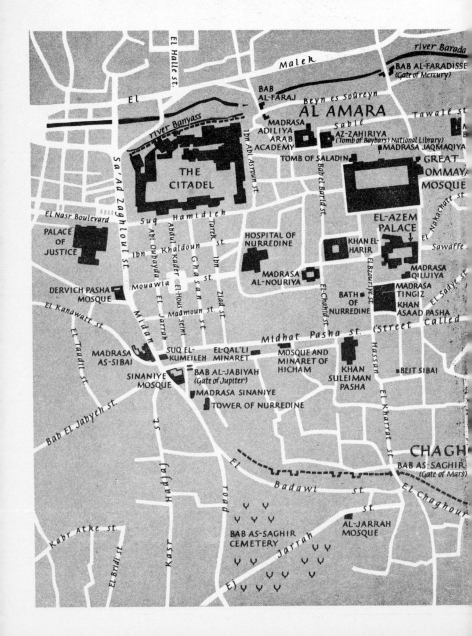

N

0   50   100   150   200   250 yards
0   50   100   150   200   250 meters

El Farrayne st.
BAB AS-SALAM
(Gate of the Moon)
Ancient wall from Bab as-Salam to Bab Touma

El Joura st.
Cheikh Rislan st.
BAB TOUMA
(Gate of Venus)

TOMB OF
SHEIKH
ARSLAN

IRID st.
El chatti

Rabia El Adawye

Bakri

El Nahawi st.

El Deire st.

RASA
AIYA

El Keimariye

El Hammam st.

El

st.

BAB TOUMA
(Christian quarter)

ST. ANANIAS
CHAPEL

KEIMARIYE

El Knisst st.

El Dawame

st.

Azaryeh st.

Kassabé

Dja afar

Hananiya st.

Boulevard

Bab Touma st.

BAB CHARKI

EL Na 3ce st.

EL Na 3ce st.

(traight')

Bab   Charki   st.

BAB CHARKI
(Gate of the Sun)

HARET AL YAHOUD
(Jewish quarter)
Tell

El Hadjara st.

DAHDAH
PALACE

Amine

EL

Ibn

BAB KAYSAN
(Gate of Saturn)

Assaker

Jaramana Road

+ +
+ + +
+ + +
+ + +
+ + + +
+ + + + +
+ + + + + +
+ + + + +
+ + +

Introduction

Mirror to Damascus was written twenty years ago in a flush of enthusiasm for an alien and exotic world. To me the inland cities of Syria—Aleppo, Hama, Homs and, above all, Damascus—held a fascination more complex and opulent than the desert ever could. I find this still.

But like all the great cities around it, Damascus has changed startlingly since the time I first came there. The fall of Beirut has seen the rise of the Syrian capital both materially and politically. Damascus's population has tripled, but the tide of rural immigrants has rejuvenated rather than smothered it. An upsurge of residential suburbs on all sides (despite a countervailing sprawl of shanty-towns) announces a metropolis both more sophisticated and more confident than the one I knew. A wealthy middle class has displaced the older Damascene families, and the international and military influence of this once rather provincial city (soldiers and their families, numbering half a million, now nestle in the suburbs) lends it a new tension and a new pride.

There are changes even in the Old Town (buildings cluttering the Citadel and the Great Mosque cleared away.) Yet here the ancient flavour persists. A café society still hums and confabulates along the Barada river. The traditional courtyard houses remain, and the suqs still flare with colour.

Damascus, in fact, has fared better than any other great Middle Eastern city. Istanbul and Cairo have both been subsumed by peasant immigration until they have become culturally unrecognisable. Jerusalem has changed both physically and politically, doubtless forever. Baghdad has been distorted by war. Beirut is a city only in memory. Yet Damascus remains: its essence preserved, but its stature heightened.

C.G.D.T.
London, 1986

1. First Fruits

This is the paradise which the righteous have been promised. There shall flow in it rivers of unpolluted water.

Koran xlvii. 11.

WE KEPT CLIMBING up and up. Soon, it seemed, I would be able to stretch out a hand and touch the cloud above the hill. Every now and then the man's foot disturbed a stone, which escaped down the slope in ugly leaps, drawing a dust of pebbles after it. Saffron butterflies fidgeted among the rocks and settled on shrubs whose substance had been blown out by wind and sun.

Everywhere up the hill these ghosts attended us: clumps of colourless thistles; filmy-leaved plants whose violet stalks fingered each other obscenely over the stone; bushes which threw up thorns and noxious berries. The sun had drunk up almost all life. The weeds themselves only flowered by miracle. Men had left rubbish behind, familiar objects which assumed a curious importance among the rocks: tendrils of rope, warped shoes, tins, shreds of cloth, corn cobs, broken plates decorated with sad flowers.

The man's hand was suddenly extended above me. We had climbed Mount Kassioun. He squinted down the hillside with the blindness of long familiarity. Some Syrians would have lingered over the sight with lustrous eyes, and bestowed wild similes on it; but the sheikh was tired and old; and anyway, this was Damascus, defying men's words.

In the west I could see the red-veined slopes of Anti-Lebanon. The shadows of clouds were sliding over them like waves of creeping shrubbery. The hills grow troubled and chaotic here. They bump against one another among the clouds and seem in perpetual strife to reach the skyline.

'*Jebel es Sheikh*,' the man said, and pointed. Behind his arm stood the three peaks of a mountain: the psalmist's Mount Hermon, which reaches nine thousand feet into the sky. Its base is smothered by foothills; its summit shines with perpetual snow. '*Es Sheikh,*' the man repeated, and thumped his head. 'It is the grey-haired mountain. *Abyad!* Its turban is white.'

On its further slope the river Jordan rises in a bright spring, and trickles away unnoticed to the south. Beyond it the Lebanese mountains descend gradually to Tiberias. Its south-east crown looks towards Gilead and Jerusalem, and to where the Moab Hills glow over the Dead Sea. Moses, from Mount Nebo above Jericho, must have seen its white tip as he gazed at the country in which he was not granted a grave.

A long way to the west of where we stood, poplar trees well up in the hills. Like the lances of an unseen army, they move along the course of the Barada river, the Abana of the Bible. In the distance they pass between pastel ridges and are almost thinned away. Then they gain strength, countermarch through dry defiles and burst into the plain. For mile upon mile the orchards push back the desert to the horizon, and nudge at the last foothills of Lebanon. In the nearest fields I could discern the dark tones of walnut or the silvery crests of olive trees; but further away they grew into a jade harmony, splintered by houses or the white minaret of a village mosque.

At the river's watershed rests Damascus. The orchards draw themselves around in a protecting cushion. Beyond, the hills of el-Aswad and Mania—the Black and the Inaccessible—drift in bare folds. Still further, blue-grey mounds lie like volcanic islands in a sea of mist, and drop away where the desert burns into the sky.

'Will you not be going down to the city?' the man asked suddenly. He had joined me as I was climbing the hill, and his curiosity had not been satisfied. 'How long do you stay in Damascus?'

'I don't know. Several months.'

'*Wullah!* What would one do in Damascus for months? What is wrong with New York?' (A foreigner is always an American here.)

'I'm English,' I said.

He mumbled a welcome. Then, why was I not going on to Lebanon? In Damascus I could see the Great Mosque and the big bazaar in an afternoon. Then I could go to Beirut. He had heard something about the women in Beirut. 'You know that in Damascus you sleep alone. . . . But the orchards here; look at the trees. You don't find trees like this anywhere, God be praised. It's a paradise. . . .' He said good-bye, saluting with a hand whose skin was cracked like tree-bark, and his legs, as he started down the edge of the hill, were wire-drawn and repulsive, like the sinews of Signorelli devils.

To gaze down on Damascus is to view confusion. The streets are artefacts from different ages, contorted and overlapping. Even from a height the city takes pains to conceal her identity; enmeshing the eye with walls, enigmatic trees and alleyways curling in irrational directions; for here it is the custom that beauty be veiled.

But the western mind, with its love of order, wishes to know how things have become what they are, and demands a discipline. The wish can only be fulfilled, and the discipline imposed, by history. If the city is engaged in her entirety, she evades and bewilders. Encountered age by age, she may be a little understood. The past may be lured back into sight, figures stand as men of their time instead of staring out of chaos, buildings be explained.

So the discipline becomes a search into time. Often the clues lie thick and flagrant. Sometimes a legend or a few stones must suffice. And as the evidence piles up, the city should grow from within, like a fruit, and at last emerge full-formed. The starting-point must be here, on this mountain-haunt of half-legendary patriarchs, for the earliest days of Damascus are blurred in myth. One must begin with Genesis.

Moslems, who believe in early Christian tradition, have for centuries thought of Damascus as the original Garden of Eden.* God fashioned Adam from the clay of the Barada river, and Adam had roamed over the mountain where I stood; here Abraham built an altar to the Lord; Moses and Lot and Job prayed on its summit; Christ Himself came. The hillside is riddled with tombs and robbers' dens, with the sepulchres of forty martyred Greeks and the bones of Moslem prophets: places of pilgrimage for Turks and Pakistanis, who scribble their names over the walls.

I started to walk along the ridge. A hawk spread sail above me, and remained crucified in some vacuum of the upper air. Giant boulders clustered along the slopes, as if, in some twilight time, rock-hurling Titans had battled over the hills. I kicked against fossils as I tramped across the mountain, but in

---

* The paradise legend was widespread long ago. Out of Shakespeare's *Henry VI* comes Winchester's angry cry:
> 'Nay, stand thou back; I will not budge a foot:
> This be Damascus, be thou cursed Cain,
> To slay thy brother Abel, if thou wilt.'

the caves I stumbled only on troughs of sharp limestone rocks and the crusts of goats' droppings.

Once or twice I touched the city's suburbs, scrambling along walls which flaunted bougainvillaea, and powdery gardens crammed with roses. The only movements were those of little girls in ill-fitting shoes, labouring uphill with petrol-cans of water.

I had been walking for half an hour before the suburbs were behind me. The mountain stretched northward, broken by many clefts. Two miles in front, bare against its side, stood the village of Burzeh. Eight hundred years ago the Arab traveller Ibn Jubayr wrote of it as the birthplace of Abraham and the site where Cain had hidden the corpse of Abel in a grotto. 'The blood reaches from about half-way up the mountain to the cave, and God has preserved red traces of it on the stones. . . .' A few centuries ago this crimson stratum of rock crumbled away, but it remains in blotches all over the mountainside, in hollows and in the glyphs of stray stones.

By now the orchards were held off a mile away by the flanks of Kassioun. As I walked, I watched the trees shift and regroup themselves. And I thought about Eden.

Men once located paradise in mysterious antipodes of the world. The Chinese imagined theirs at the Himalayan source of a perfumed river. The Greeks envisaged the Garden of the Hesperides at the axis of the earth. Homer and Strabo dreamt of a continent beyond the Pillars of Hercules; among the remote seas of North Britain, fiends and heroes dwelt in the Isles of the Dead. Seneca imagined heaven beyond Thule in the frozen north and Virgil placed his Elysian Fields beneath the earth itself. Moslems have written of a place in Persia or Samarkand or Ceylon, or in the garden of a sea-girt mountain. Only the Damascenes till and irrigate their Eden, live in it and die there and still link it with paradise.

I reached a ravine above Burzeh. At its entrance, say the Syrians, Abraham turned back, sated with blood, from his pursuit of the four kings. For in the Book of Genesis Abraham 'divided himself against them, he and his servants, by night, and smote them, and pursued them unto Hobah* which is on the left hand of Damascus'.

There was no sign of the cave of Cain. A beautifully constructed mosque had once been built over it, enclosed by a wooden lattice. Now there was no mosque, and no ruins. The

* Modern Djobar.

[4]

only grotto appeared to be one in which seventy prophets had starved to death, passing their last loaf of bread from hand to hand until they died. Burzeh was asleep in the afternoon furnace. There is a military camp here, determined to hold the breach which Abraham won. Slowly I felt the absurdity of it all. Here was I, looking for the cave of man's first victim, crushed with a stone or a cudgel; and all around, in the aegis of barbed wire and bayonets, lay the guns and tanks of his descendants.

Two small boys, sitting among rocks, held up a bunch of green-pink grapes to me and made money signs. One of them kept calling something out and I heard the word *Hâbîl* several times, Arabic for 'Abel'. He began to climb up the hill, pointing with a fistful of grapes. I followed. They both grew excited and cheerful, and pranced ahead of me repeating '*Hâbîl, Hâbîl*' as if the words were magically drawing me after them. Up a track where goats grazed, we came to a building which stood among olive trees. The upper courses of its walls had crumbled away, leaving a jagged skyline, like the ruined adobe of a Pueblo Indian.

'*Marhaba!* It is hot! Welcome to the house of Abraham.' A clump of men had quickened into welcome at our approach. I felt bewildered. The house of Abraham? What of *Hâbîl*? They said that Abraham had lived by the cave of *Hâbîl*. It lay beside us.

The house of a patriarch by the cave of a murderer?

'Is it not strange? *Ma baqulsh hage*. But God knows all things.'

An amphitheatre of faces enclosed me, and a kettle was soon murmuring on a portable stove. It is common knowledge among Syrians that Englishmen are as addicted to tea as Frenchmen to wine. They talked in a garble of Arabic and French.

'Abraham was king of Damascus,' said one.

'He founded Damascus,' declared another. 'But then he moved on. He didn't stay here.'

'He bought Damascus,' swore an old man with an urbane twinkle.

'And is it not written in Genesis,' added a man who must have been a Christian, 'that Eliezer, the steward of Abraham, was a Damascene?'

I remembered a passage from Josephus: 'Abraham reigned at Damascus, being a foreigner, who came with an army out of the land of Babylon. But after a long time he got up and removed from that country also with his people, and went into the land of Canaan. Now the name of Abraham is even still famous in the country of Damascus; and there is shown a village named from him "The Habitation of Abraham".'

They all said that the site was beside us. The *Masdjid Ibrahim*. A holy place. But he had not died in Damascus.

'Where then?'

'In Jordanie.' They nodded in unison, as if he had passed on only last week.

The teacups were filled again. Except for their belief that Abraham was born here, they had confirmed the Old Testament and the ancients.

The boys beckoned me into the courtyard of the house. The blueness of the sky sprang in on us, and from a trellis across the roof light green vines cascaded onto our shoulders. A cat rubbed itself over my shoes, and because cats usually run away, I thought this must be a good place. A woman dressed in a white skirt and *tannoura* pantaloons stood at the far end of the yard. For a moment I thought she must be some sort of nun. The boys had become suddenly subdued.

'*Masdjid Ibrahim*,' she said. We went into the room beyond. It was high and dark and very spacious. For the first time I recognised that I was in a mosque, by a static fountain, under arches painted black and pale orange.

We mounted stone steps to a gallery. Two candelabra were lit above me: garish things, oddly touching. Silks had been draped along the railings of the gallery and the walls were encrusted with charms and inscriptions. In the rock at the top of the stairs a passageway entered the side of the hill. It was so narrow that only one person at a time could squeeze into it. Somebody handed me a taper.

A few yards into the dark, my feet felt the edge of a cavity. The walls around it were greenish and laced with scratchings. I felt cramped and slightly faint. The smell of candle grease sickened the air. I held my taper over the hole. It was small, about the size to hold a man. The cat came and purred reassuringly at my ankle. I knelt and fixed the white candle to the rock. One of the boys squirmed in beside me. He spoke in a harsh whisper, pointing at the sides of the hole, which were smothered in wax. He laid his fingers on red blotches around the bottom of it, and brought the side of his hand violently against his head. '*Dahm!*' He pointed to the veins in my arm. 'This is where he laid *Hâbîl*.' It was the red rock again, more scarlet in the gloom.

I emerged into sunlight. The boys seized their coins and scuttled down the path. The woman would not take anything, only drew the palms of her hands against the courtyard wall and smiled confusedly. I made my way back to the road, trying to remember simple things: the hanging vines, the men caressing their cups of tea, the shy woman, even the cat. But under my feet the ground rang hollow with imagined caves, the sky exhaled candle grease, and like Agag I walked delicately, trying to avoid the blood along the track.

Then I started back across the Kassioun Mountain. It did not matter how long the walk would be, for in front of me the orchards of paradise were beginning to close in again.

*　　*　　*

Ten miles east of Damascus the mound of Tell es Salihiye stands a hundred feet above the orchards—a hill of bricks and bones piled on top of one another. With an unquestioning respect for its holiness, people of successive religions have fed the hill with their dead, era after era, until it has become a confused mansion of races and beliefs. Thorn bushes stubble its lower slopes, and shreds of artemisia carry on the ascent until they mingle with Moslem graves on its summit. But it supplies the clue to the birth of Damascus, for here archaeologists found traces of Chalcolithic men who had lived by her rivers in the fifth millennium before Christ.

The city is even older than legends tell. Moslem historians believed her to have been founded by Demschak, a slave of Abraham given to him by Nimrod. But by the time Abraham came, Damascus was ancient. Josephus attributed her foundation to Uz, great-grandson of Noah, and son of Aram, who possessed himself of Syria and whose descendants were the Arameans. Yet in the base of the tell are buried layers of brick baked by short-skulled Chalcolithic men who had settled three thousand years before the Arameans came.*

Almost nothing is known of these first Damascenes. In a beautiful ivory panel in the Damascus Museum they march with narrow-hilted swords and javelins, and wear Egyptian hairstyles: bas-reliefs which only accentuate the rupture of time. An Egyptian tomb-painting gives a rare glimpse of them: brownskinned men on a peace-mission to the pharaoh. They are leading a baby elephant with mammoth tusks, a chariot, jars of

* The el-Amarna tablets record that Damascus was the capital of a state called Ube.

[7]

oil, copper ingots, weapons, horses and aromatic shrubs. The king of Syria is giving his son as a hostage, and the boy, who is sitting on his father's hand, looks back at him resentfully.

I tried to climb the cleft on the north side of the tell, and blundered among the wreckage of sixty centuries. The bones were so riddled of substance that I treated them as carelessly as the shards which tinkled under my sandals. Every stratum of brick or pottery marks the graves of an era. When the lowest tier of basalt was new on the ground, Tuthmose III seized Damascus for the eighteenth dynasty, and the effeminate pharaohs Amonhotep III and Ikhnaton released her to the Amorites. The Amorites were the first Semitic people to have settled: elegant men in elaborately woven clothes; grey-eyed, long-haired women with faces like domestic fowls. A century later Ramses II recovered the city, but was beaten out by the Hittites.

Along miniature paths among the bones flowed slender black beetles, and lizards threw themselves away over the shards. I walked across the formless ground which somewhere marked the arrival of the Arameans in the thirteenth century. They made Damascus the capital of a wealthy land, developed the irrigation of her orchards and remoulded her streets after the grid-system of Babylonia. They gave her the worship of Haddad, the Thunderer, and in other tumuli they left behind the clay figurines of a fertility goddess, and blotchy-eyed horses and hogs.

A hand's breadth of earth accumulated on the tell while King David conquered and garrisoned Damascus, and while Rezon, 'adversary to Israel all the days of Solomon', recovered her for the Arameans. A jumble of pottery marks the sanguinary reign of the Damascene king Ben Haddad, of his servant Hazael who murdered him in accordance with the prophecy of Elisha, and of the wars of the Books of Kings and Chronicles.

As I neared the summit I dislodged a clump of earth which burst in the cleft below leaving a glistening white bone on the ground. The dust flared up in a suffocating pall. I leant back against the hill and watched brown-speckled butterflies tumble like falling leaves down the storeys of mankind. A missionary from Damascus, wandering over the tell, discovered on its northern slope a limestone slab carved in the likeness of an Assyrian priest. His face had been mutilated into that of a sick lion, his feet to unshakeable plinths. Yet Assyrian soil is still young on the mound. Ninth-century tablets record that Shalmaneser III slaughtered a coalition of twelve monarchs, headed by the king of Damascus. In a high-flown passage of Assyrian chronicle, he scattered their corpses and blood all over the valleys, styling himself 'King of the Universe'. But in reality the battle was indecisive. The Assyrians did not capture Damascus until she had been deserted by her allies in 732 B.C. Then Tiglath Pileser III desecrated her orchards and deported many of her people. The palaces were plundered* and the Aramean gods were dethroned by Ashur and the cult of Assyrian kings.

> So fire I sent in Hazael's house,
> And it eats the palaces of Ben Haddad
> And I shall break the bars of Damascus.

Except for a luckless rebellion in the reign of Sargon II, a long silence falls, and by 717 the city had become so depopulated that two Hittite tribes were settled there.

I had reached the pinnacle of the hill. A long way below me a man cantered his horse along the fields. I looked down at the meaningless earth. To a more skilled eye it would have proclaimed: after the Assyrians came the Babylonians, after the Babylonians the Persians. The sun gods of Persepolis were set up beside Haddad. Artaxerxes II built a temple to the sacred prostitute Anahita. And Damascus arrived at the gates of classical history so hoary with centuries that her foundation was already traced to giants among men.

I sat down, exhausted by the growth and waste of dynasties. Moslem graves were already adding their thimblefuls of dust to the hill. Mourners had laid sprigs across the tombs, and bleached flags flapped stiffly in the pores of the brick. What sensual places the Moslems give to their dead! Throughout Islam they sleep in gardens of dark trees or occupy delectable viewpoints. Across the western view of the grave-mound the desert and the mountains meet in a skirmish of foothills. Northward run the ranges of the Tiniyeh, with gulfs like white rivers running down their flanks. Towards Jordan glow the hills of Bashan, and to the south, in every shade of green, lies the prospect of Eden, and the grey majesty of Hermon.

* A part of the palace furniture was discovered in Upper Mesopotamia in 1930.

*   *   *

A tempest of multi-coloured pigeons blew over my head. Damascus lay almost within reach. Now I could pick out some of the places below: the twin roofs and dome of the Great Mosque; the honey-coloured citadel; the minarets of Suleiman's lovely sanctuary in its grove of conifers and plane trees. The steepness of the streets and the yellow walls reminded me of sea-villages in Italy. Cauliflowers and water-melons the size of beach-balls were spilled out onto the pavements. Children were wandering home from school: jubilant boys with insubordinate grins; girls in regulation blue and white check frocks—little Murillo Madonnas.

I crossed a district of foreign embassies and expensive flats; then across strands of the Barada, already cumbered with autumn leaves. I entered the city walls without being aware of them. The houses were piled so thick against and on top of one another that it seemed as if nobody could be living there.

The Suq Hamidieh is a giant corridor of a market. Its corrugated-iron roof is perforated with stone and bullet holes, which throw ringlets of sunlight against the windows over the shops. Beneath it walks the chimera of today's Syria: peasant women in full-length *festan*, foreheads circled in gold coins; countrymen, splay-footed in black and dark blue *cheroual* pantaloons*; shopkeepers with scarves and brocades; slight-moustached men whose *keffiehs* fall dashingly over their shoulders; black-coated, black-veiled women; elderly, tarboushed sheikhs, solemn as owls; businessmen in styleless suits; Saudi Arabians in long *qumbaz*; brown-cloaked Iraqis; Druses, Alawi, soldiers, priests.

At the market's end a skeleton of Roman columns reflects the sun in a pale glare. In two steps I had walked from the flesh of a city into its bones. I turned into a *suq* of shoe-sellers. It was very dark. Cataracts of footwear descended from frames on all sides: like a subterranean garden in which darkness is necessary for the growth of shoes—a boscage of Moroccan leather slippers, wooden and gold sandals glittering with cut glass; bobbled tartan boots.

Beyond the bazaar the wavy walls and houses half embrace you. Here and there grow trees and vines. If a door is left open a courtyard always lies beyond; a fountain brims with water, and the shade of lemon trees stains a tessellated pavement.

* The distinctive bagginess between the legs of the *cheroual* is a masterstroke of sartorial foresight. It is thought that the second Messiah will be born of man; so every wearer of *cheroual* goes in readiness for this parenthood.

Near the eastern gate the Barada river was frittering away the Roman walls. I heard the cries of the Christian quarter— invitations to see mosaic factories, buy silks, drink coffee, look at brasswork. Was I not American? And my money, like the desert, as good as boundless? Innumerable hands were twisted into that compound Arabic gesture which asks 'Where-have-you-come-from-Where-are-you-going-to-What-are-you-doing?'

'Have you seen the Gate of St Paul?' demanded the most clamorous, his face divided by a grin. 'What about the Chapel of Ananias?' I told him that I had not seen anything, that I wanted only to trace an Old Testament tradition. Had he heard of Naaman the Syrian, who was healed of leprosy by Elisha? He frowned and jerked back his head, which is Arabic for 'No'.

'There used to be a building called the House of Naaman the Leper,' I said, '*Bêt Naaman.*' He frowned and jerked again, murmuring about chapels and mosaics. His name was Razouk, he said. He was a law student at the university. He could show me all Damascus in an afternoon. Would I meet him the next day by those old bicycles over there?—he pointed to a tiny shop. We shook hands and he gave me a bemused grin. I believe he thought Naaman was a friend of mine.

A hundred years ago the House of Naaman was a lodging-house for lepers. They were locked outside the city walls, and would go to the *Bêt Naaman* to die. The story in the Book of Kings is steeped in Levantine duplicity. Naaman was general to Ben Haddad, the king of Damascus; but he was a leper. During one of his campaigns he captured a Hebrew girl who told him of the prophet Elisha. But when he went to Elisha, he received a message to bathe seven times in the Jordan, 'and was wroth, and went away, and said . . . Are not Abana and Pharpar, rivers of Damascus, better than all the waters of Israel? may I not wash in them, and be clean?' But Naaman reluctantly obeyed, and he was healed. When he tried to press gifts on Elisha, the prophet refused; but Elisha's servant Gehazi extorted a reward from Naaman under false pretences. Then Elisha, with one of the most chilling curses in scripture, trans-ferred the blight of Naaman to Gehazi and his posterity for ever. 'And he went out from his presence a leper as white as snow.'

Naaman's house had stood where the two rivers, for a few hundred yards, flow side by side. Nobody seemed to have heard of it. One old man, a scissors grinder, was very angry.

There were no lepers in Damascus now. Did we have lepers in America?

He started grinding a knife and I went away.

I asked another man, who worked at a near-by factory for handloomed brocades. 'Ah,' he sighed. 'There is nothing there now. An arch. Some trees.' But he agreed to show me the place.

A hundred yards north-east of the Roman Charki Gate, a big depression in the ground is filled by a timber arsenal, and a fragile arch stands among a tumult of shacks. I slid down an embankment and into a courtyard, where planks had been heaped against a mud hut. The door was locked. A man and a boy fetched keys for me, but would not go in. To begin with I saw only bales of paper. Then my eyes adjusted to the dimness. The tomb filled up half the room and looked like the gigantic shaft of a half-buried column. On it stood a candle and a broken plaque of Kufic script. There was no notice, no pious curio, no hint of identity; but I remembered a tale that the grave of Gehazi lay in Naaman's house.

I felt as if I had violated the place. The man and the boy were waiting outside the entrance and neither tried to explain anything. I came out and they locked the door. Whose tomb was it then? The man's reply sounded like 'Zrass Azouar', but he knew nothing more.

As I walked back through the courtyard, I noticed something among the trees at its far end. At first I thought that five or six people were huddled among ruins, but when I walked closer I only saw three graves. What I had mistaken for people were posts, whose tops were bound in blue muslin, standing at the head and foot of each mound. Above them stood an Arabic arch, striped angry orange and blue, and its foundations were of Roman stones. The graves were still ornamented and cared for.

Later I came here with Razouk. The place bewildered and disturbed him and he said: 'These are the tombs of very poor men.' He did not know the English, and I did not know the Arabic for 'leprosy', so we talked no more of them. They had probably been the last to die. The ruins were so deserted that the place still seemed tainted; and a child had scribbled on one of the walls: 'We cannot get to God by any way, because nobody knows where he is.'

2. The Tomb of Abel

W E WERE SITTING, by accident, in a restaurant of shabby
repute. Out of curiosity, I had asked for *arak*, the Arabic wine
flavoured with aniseed. Razouk had been too polite, and his
brother Suhel too hungry, to tell me that a plethora of *hors-
d'oeuvre* was included with the wine. Our table was soon enveloped by increasingly undesirable little dishes: red peppers,
something masquerading as an egg, sodden chips and radishes;
yoghourt, sheep's livers and a sapless fish; eggplants stuffed
with something pernicious, a plate of milk and submerged
beans, very fried bread, an indeterminate grey paste, frogs
in cold batter and a crowd of objects lurking in dark sauces.

Suhel was a short, sallow-faced youth crowned with a stack of
black hair. We had been talking about the orchards of Damascus
and the best way to travel round them. He was in favour of buses,
Razouk muttered taxis, and I insinuated a horse.

'Horses are too expensive,' said Suhel, 'and you'll be sold a
bad one and lose too much money when you try to sell it back.
Have you ever seen a horse market here? By God. . . .'

I said that buses never went to many of the places I hoped to
see. I needed something which would move along tracks and
footpaths. Suhel was gnawing a frog. Razouk suggested that I
use a bicycle; I could go to the Friday bicycle market and buy
an old one, but it would disintegrate in a week; he knew where
I could hire one. It would not be beautiful, but it might last a
few months.

It was a tiny shop in the Street Called Straight. The owner
appraised us with a pinched expression and pointed to three or
four machines which here pass for bicycles. Lamps and pumps
and gears are rumours from Europe; brakes are laughable
luxuries.

The bargaining began in mild tones. Was this not a poor
foreigner, Razouk said, waving a suppliant hand at me. What did

[13]

the man mean by six lira a day? Had he no soul? The man said he had a wife and five children. For *five* lira a day he would make any repairs to the bicycle.

Razouk looked at the bicycle as if he had worked in the trade all his life. 'Your bicycle is not fit for a muckworm,' he said.

The man's reply came too quickly for me, but it sounded like a round Islamic curse, which included not only the person concerned, but his ancestors and posterity, his wives, donkeys, crops, cat and everything that is his.

Razouk smiled.

'It is a moon of a bicycle,' the man persisted. He kicked the front tyre which emitted a faint hiss. Razouk criticised the steering, the chain and the handles. The man pointed to the soundness of the spokes and came down to four lira. After Razouk had started to leave the shop and the man had affected disinterest and they had both niggled over piastres, the deal ended. Razouk's ancestors were restored to their natural bliss and I had a bicycle for a month.

Bicycling, even in the modern part of Damascus, is a specialised art. No notice need be taken of traffic-lights or one-way streets; but a floppy hand dangled out of a car window is a common signal meaning that its owner will, some time soon, do something outrageous. The width of tramcar ruts has been exactly measured for the overthrow of cyclists, who may at the same time suffer mule-bite or be fouled by a camel.

But, as the bicycle-vendor murmured, we are all in the hand of God.

*   *   *

The Barada river is born in the mountains of Lebanon. Without it, there would be no Damascus, and this alone tempted me to explore its valley. But there was a second, stranger reason, for on a precipitous peak above the river stands the tomb of Abel.

Religious men trace much of the world's evil to that murder. Adam, it is true, sold innocence for knowledge, but his sins were pride and curiosity—two Arab traits. But Abel's death revealed the violent and unnatural in man, and from it, one could claim, flows all that is calamitous and historical. So my journey had two destinations: the source of the Barada, the watershed of the city's blessings; and the tomb, the parent of her evils.

The road is steep and beautiful. By late October the wind blows sharply, but the sun still strikes hard and the dust is unappeased. Damascus disappears behind white hills, and the mountain shelves of the Anti-Lebanon circle warily round. The Barada gurgles on every side, splashes into the road or dribbles down attenuated cliff-side weeds.

It is a tiny river to have engendered so much—the size of any English woodland stream—and it carries its green train through hills which are merciless to life. Nowhere does it touch on a tree or flower which is not its own. Purple-capped thistles accost it with stiffened arms. Water-beetles pirouette through glittering bubbles, and underwater weeds trail along the current like the plumes of drowned warriors.

Several miles beyond Doummar, which the Romans once made rich, the road parts with the river. The dust and heat are choking and blinding. Gawky crows, bodiced in soot-grey, clap among the rocks. Then the way descends through cypresses to the village of Judeideh, and the sounds of water rise again.

A few miles further and the road enters a senate of mountains, where a dazzling minaret betrays Bessima among its spinney of poplars. The Damascenes come here to cheat the summer sirocco, but in autumn it is deserted. The villagers have pilfered columns from ruined classical cities, and lain them on the house roofs where they are used to roll away the water after rainy nights.

It was evening by the time I reached Fijeh, the major source of the Barada. The last traveller to have written of it, a hundred years ago, had seen the river gushing from a cave beneath the ruins of two temples. I saw a huge restaurant, equipped with every seaside offence: vermilion railings, mock-brick walls, canopied swing-chairs. Rows of jet fountains, mercifully extinct, had been piped round the stream and a chimney-stack of stones wavered above it: the swan-song of a Roman temple.

A fat and very happy man emerged from the restaurant and asked me if there was anything I wanted. Nothing, I said. For a while I leant over the wall and wondered if there was another Fijeh.

The sun had crept round to the west and was poking yellow fingers through the hills. I bicycled back in the direction of Damascus, not knowing where I would spend the night. At the village of Ashrafiyeh a pale youth, about seventeen years old asked me if I would have supper at his house. His name was Mustafa. His father was ill, but I would be welcome. The naturalness of his invitation put me at ease. To entertain a guest is a spontaneous obligation—a legacy from the desert, which insists on law or extinction.

We walked across a bridge and past a mosque to a house which looked half-built or half-destroyed. The door was opened by a heavy-bodied woman with a guileless face. 'My mother,' he said. She moved with unexpected grace, and apologised that her house was untidy. I saw a single room with cemented ceiling and walls, and a floor partly covered by coarse carpets. Clay shelves contained blankets and a few jars. Mustafa went out and picked two roses, flowering alone in the garden, and gave them to me.

The room was full of people squatting against the walls, and children stalked each other along the floor. Mustafa's father lay on an iron bed which occupied one quarter of the room. He seemed a very old man indeed, the flesh withered to paper-thinness round his bones, the bristles on his cheeks as stiff as corn. When he saw me, he raised his hand in a military salute and smiled wanly. His eyes were grey and very bright. I said I did not wish to disturb him. He did not understand, but nodded and grinned.

Hayat, his wife, brewed up tea and murmured to her relatives: silent men and ashen-faced women with shy smiles. There was a married daughter, called Saliha, and a brother of the old man, with the same grey eyes. They had come to enquire about the old man's health and to offer help, for a big family is a man's only insurance. Most of them lived in a village fifteen miles further into the mountains, and they left before darkness.

I sat between Mustafa and two children. One of them wheezed bronchially every time she bent down, and the other was blotched with iodine all over his face and legs.

'I have eight brothers and sisters,' Mustafa said. 'I had more once, but God took four of them in sickness. My father was hit by a taxi in Damascus. He has been in bed a month now. They say that in another month, if God wills it, he will be walking fine.' How long ago had any doctor seen him? Mustafa could not remember. Twenty days perhaps, or more. Every time I looked in the direction of the bed, the old man would catch my eye and stiffen into convulsions, moaning weakly, grimacing and grasping the bed-rail over his head with both hands. When he thought I was not looking, he relaxed, chatted to himself, and pulled the threads out of his pullover; and I came back from the fountain with Mustafa to find him sitting up smoking a cigarette, with his horny feet hanging over the bed.

Hayat carried in a tray of beans, salted olives and yoghourt, which we ate on torn-up strips of flat *markouk* bread. The women eat the scraps which the men leave behind, a system which at first destroys any appetite. But later, when the mortified host detonates into cries of 'Eat! Eat!', the women are forgotten.

Hayat fed the younger child at her breast. Then she shovelled bread and beans alternately into her own and the boy's mouth. The old man mumbled to himself under the blankets, but if either of the children played too near his bed he would thrash out at them with a broken stick, beat it against the wall or run it over the iron railing like a militant xylophone.

Before the accident he had earned good money: equivalent to six pounds sterling a month. Now he was given nothing. 'It wasn't his fault that the car hit him. Cars should look where they're going. And they should have taken him to the hospital.' Mustafa fumbled with the medicine which the doctor had left. It contained morphine and opium, *Sédations des douleurs intenses*. The man pulled his jersey over his head and pointed to a rainbow hump across the base of his spine. A plaster encased three broken ribs. He eased himself back and started to moan again, from habit.

Suddenly Mustafa pulled out a knife and bolted through the doorway. Hayat was screaming from the courtyard. But we were all too late. By the time I came out she was locking the remainder of her chickens into a pen. They were spare little birds, and three of them, bloody at the throat, lay like bundles of old rags over a dried-up patch of sweet-corn. Mustafa cursed and clenched his hands. 'It was the dog again. It got away over the river. By God, next time I will kill it!' Now they only had five chickens left.

Hayat came back and smiled, told me not to be disturbed and asked me to eat some more. She lit a paraffin lamp and hung it from an iron hook in the ceiling. In its amber light the fissures under the old man's cheekbones darkened and ran down into the stubble of his jowls, and his eyes looked unnaturally bright. He was, I thought, a rather beautiful old man. The girl was wheezing again and Hayat, who could not eat any more because of the chickens, gathered her onto her lap. Saliha crouched in one corner and talked with a lilt which tripped always along the brink of laughter; but the shadows thrown by her *ratouy* obscured her eyes. Hayat kept looking at me and smiling, mumbling welcomes and *'Sharraftena'* and asking pardon of God for the poor meal.

Blankets were thrown down, and they prepared to sleep. As there was no room for us all, Mustafa said he would take me to his eldest sister, Refaiyeh, who lived further up in the village and looked after two of the children for her mother.

Electric bulbs pricked the village with light and people were walking near the river. Everybody seemed to be a relative of Mustafa. 'That was my uncle's eldest son,' he said. Then *'Salâm 'alêkum.* My sister's husband's brother.' We walked a long way before we reached the house. The news had preceded us and a woman was already standing in the doorway holding a lamp. Two small children clung round her knees.

We squatted in the room by the glimmer of the lamp. Somebody had gone to connect electricity to the house. I could only make out a spinning-wheel and a paraffin stove in one corner of the room, and clay shelves piled with more blankets and jars.

I offered the woman some tea which I had bought in the village. At first she refused, but we had taken her unawares, and she had nothing in the house, so eventually a hand hovered out of the gloom and took the bundle. The stove flared up. People filtered into the room: robust men swathed in *keffiehs*, awkward and formal at first, but soon smiling. A joke that they were all fools was spreading among them in squibs of laughter. They hailed me, through the dimness, as 'Mr Colin', and each one asked me to pardon the behaviour of the rest.

Then the electric bulb lit up and we saw each other. They had mild, honest faces—except, perhaps, for the village intellectual, whose eyes were shining and close-set, like a pair of tempered daggers. Refaiyeh was a handsome girl with full features and the upright figure of a Bedouin. Her room was larger than I had thought, and was backed by a recess stacked with amphorae. A large chest stood in one corner—of the kind which Moslems give to their daughters to hold their trousseaux —and there was a cupboard draped in netting to keep out the larger insects.

As the hours ran by in talk, a tric-trac board was produced, fondled and put away. Then the men began to sing in the long, impassioned cries of Arabia, old songs which I could not understand, but which were 'very wonderful'. The joke about fools was revived. I was asked to sing too. *The Duke of Plaza Toro* evoked bewildered silence, but fierce applause greeted *Stranger in Paradise*. Again the wild Arabian songs filled the night. The phrases would sometimes begin 'Mr Colin . . .' and would dance from mouth to mouth until they cascaded into assurances that the words were welcoming.

Soon the room was exploding with noise and I thought the village policeman would enter and demand my passport. Later I saw that he was sitting at my elbow, his head thrown back in song. Passers-by squatted in the doorway and chanted under the stars. Refaiyeh, sitting apart, tried to read stories aloud to herself, sometimes smiling at us remotely. After a long time she put the children to bed, but for almost an hour the little girl Majida fixed me with a hazel stare from between her blanket and her tangled curls.

The intellectual moved to my side and monopolised a silence. 'What are the British doing in Aden?' His demand fell on our friendliness like a policeman's hand on a criminal's shoulder. He must have been listening to a wireless. Even the others appeared to resent the intrusion, though every Syrian's mind is a honeycomb of political notions. Nobody else expressed interest in Aden, so I professed ignorance of it. What was Aden? Did you eat it, smoke it, blow bubbles with it? (Since the Arabs pronounce it Ah-den, I felt quaintly justified.)

Somebody began to sing, someone resurrected the joke about fools, and the moment passed.

*   *   *

'You beautiful in sleep,' said Refaiyeh in English.

For a happy moment I thought she had been looking at me during the night, then realised that she had been thumbing through the children's English school books and was trying to ask me if I had slept well.

'Yes,' I said. 'I beautiful in sleep.'

We drank sweet coffee and chewed the salted olives. At seven o'clock Mustafa had to take a bus to Damascus, and we left Refaiyeh in the doorway, with a child under each hand.

I bicycled back to Hayat and the old man. He was in pain, and lifting a hand in his military salute, half-turned. When he saw me, his flair for drama revived, and he became ossified into a peculiar shape. I tried to say good-bye and take his hand, but his fingers felt like the prongs of a fork and he only moaned.

I gave Hayat some cigarettes for him and wedged a little money between them—equivalent to a week of the old man's wages—saying that it was to buy medicine and that I could reclaim the sum from the health ministry in Damascus. For a moment her eyes glittered, then she refused. I looked hurt and pressed her, and in the end, perhaps thinking of her chickens, she clasped it against her, smiled confusedly, and touched her breast.

*　　*　　*

My shadow, in the early morning, wrinkled over the rocks like a circus freak on a penny-farthing bicycle. Far in front of me, crowning an insurrection of cliffs, a great bird seemed to have laid a snow-white egg. '*Hâbîl, Hâbîl*,' nod the people of the valley, 'The tomb of Abel'. And at its foot the ancient Greek city of Abila bears witness, by its name, to their tradition, and speckles the mountainside above the river with the doors of tombs.

Abila once lay on the important road between Heliopolis, the modern Baalbek, and Damascus. Lysanias, who was king of Chalcis shortly before the birth of Christ, made it his capital. Some time after his murder at the instigation of Cleopatra, it passed to a second Lysanias, whom St Luke mentions as being tetrarch of Abilene during the ministry of St John the Baptist, and it is mentioned again during the last years of the Byzantine emperor Heraclius, who yielded Syria to the Arabs. Nomads plundered it and raided its religious fair (or *suq*) and the Arab village which grew up on its site has been called Suq Wadi Barada ever since. The friezes and capitals of the old city are reborn, in dizzy guises, in the houses of the new: Doric capitals for footscrapers, architraves for cornerstones, the leaf-whorls of volutes and modillions in many orchard walls.

I crossed the bridge where the river falls in three sheets under a tumult of maple trees. Even the most accessible tombs lie high up in the hill. Birds have chafed out nests where the rock is softest. Where it hardens, the early Greeks hewed out stairways which offer a sure footing. At the entrances to some of the sepulchres stand figures carved in relief. From a distance they seem to be substantial and to look confidently across the valley. But nearer, this essence dissolves. The limestone chips stare out harshly and the figures lose all character. The wind has eased away chunks of head and body. Only the long Ionian chitons are distinguishable, and the feet planted squarely apart.

Inside, I found long, deep shafts, harbouring broken stone, dust, and occasionally fragments of bone. They were family graves. In every vault four or six shafts had been sunk in the rock. An arch had been carved over the recess of each one, or of each pair. In such a sepulchre, perhaps, Joseph of Arimathaea laid the body of Christ. Corpses were probably lowered into the clefts in linen robes and wooden coffins, and wealthy men, in the days of Ptolemaic ascendancy, were entombed in anthropoid sarcophagi carved with the faces of classical Greeks, their chins tufted like pharaohs.

I sat by the Roman road to Abila and ate pomegranates. It had once been an important road, but only a few hundred feet of it were recognisable, where it stabbed through the knee of a hill. Six feet above my head I saw two inscriptions, and felt a surge of homecoming as I recognised, not the fetters of Kufic nor the bravado of Arabic *naksh*, but the firm hand of Imperial Rome: 'Emperor Caesar M. Aur. Antoninus. Aug. Armeniacus, and the Emperor Caesar L. Aurel. Verus Aug. Armeniacus, restored the road which the force of the river broke away; the mountain being cut through by the direction of Julius Verus, legate of the province of Syria, at the expense of the people of Abilene.' A niche, emptied of its bust, gaped above, and a second carving testified to the constructions of 'Lysius Maximus'. Once the road was carried to Abila along a viaduct, but now it ends in a precipice. Peering over the edge, I saw the tombs again; and far below writhed the Barada, which the ancients, grateful for its richness and beauty, called Chryssorhoas, the River of Gold.

The tomb of Abel had vanished behind the sheerness of its mountain. It must have stood a thousand feet above me and I could see no way of approaching it, for its summit erupted into an almost vertical wall of rock. I started to climb across fields pitted with limestone. The view below resolved into simpler lines: white mountains, a thread of green. On a hill opposite, boulders leaned along the furrows of the scarp, like rocks in a Japanese dust garden. There were no more green noises. Things rustled and whirred; I listened to the valley and heard nothing but the dry click of insects' wings, the painless rub of frazzled scrub, airy stems grating on stones. Clusters of a faded yellow plant rasped in the wind: wraiths of flowers. Down in the valley a donkey moved on its shadow like a sleepy fly, and people had become Utrillo figures, scorched into the fields and walls.

Above me weaved a track marked with the print of goats' feet. A way was beginning to open up in the rocks on the summit.

For fifty feet I climbed on hands and knees, in and out of the shade of dwarf oak trees—nature's last gesture in the wilderness. Below me, as the view extended, the poplars multiplied in the valley, and seemed to be marching through the unfriendly hills with a set purpose to Damascus.

All at once I had reached the top of the mountain. Between my fingers I felt the sudden fragility of tiny violet flowers. The ground sloped away evenly among a proliferation of dandelions, and a white dome surged against the sky.

The place was deserted. I was faced by a long building with shuttered windows. I opened a wrought-iron gate and walked into a courtyard. The gate clanged behind me. I peered down through a hatch and met my own gaze thirty feet below in the sanctuary well. I rattled the door of the mausoleum, but only an echo sounded. On the far side of the building, a track ran for miles along a ridge, showing that somewhere there was an easier ascent than mine.

Less than a century ago, the two Doric pillars and architrave of a Roman church stood on the mountain. St Helena was supposed to have built the church where Cain and Abel offered up their sacrifices; but there is no sign of the ruins now, and the columns of the portico have tumbled down the mountain. The people say that Cain slew Abel in the village of Zebdany ten miles to the north, and that for forty years he carried him on his back, not knowing what to do with him. On the slopes of this mountain he noticed a raven which was digging a hole to bury one of its kin; so he copied the bird and interred his own brother here.

I walked round the tomb. Three narrow windows pierced the back wall, and I wedged my head as far as I could into each of them. Through the first two I saw only an empty floor, mottled with light from chinks in the shutters. Beyond the third, startlingly close, lay a monstrous grave—twenty feet long and disproportionately narrow, like the grave of a serpent.

I drew back my head into the sunlight, remembering the Book of Genesis: 'There were giants in the earth in those days.' I recalled other tombs. At Beitima, near Hermon, sprawls a sepulchre thirty feet long which legend claims as the resting-place of Nimrod, the mighty hunter and rebel against God; for his sins the dew never falls on his grave. And on the mountain of Shiit in the Lebanon rests a long, slender tomb which the inhabitants say is that of Seth, the third son of Adam.

Sitting under the dwarf oaks, I contemplated giants. Ten or

twelve thousand years ago, the land must have been filled with them. They would have used poplar trees for crutches and lived by picking out the birds which nested in each other's hair. At dusk, after the sun had set beyond their vision, they slept with their tapering wives in elongated caves. The last of them, weary and wifeless, dwindled into his grave at the cock-crow of history. Then came men. They found the megalithic dolmens of Palestine and western Europe, and cave-tombs, sometimes hundreds of feet in length.

I gazed back at the walls of the sanctuary. Perhaps the legends of giants were grounded elsewhere. The Book of Deuteronomy asserts that Og, King of Bashan, was the 'remnant of giants; behold, his bedstead was a bedstead of iron; nine cubits was the length thereof, and four cubits the breadth of it, after the cubit of a man.'* The Books of Chronicles record the last days of ogre-kings, the Titans of Gath and Gezer, whose spear-shafts were like weavers' beams. The sons of Anak made the spies of Moses look like grasshoppers; the Emim and Zamzummin strode among the crags of Moab and the Land of Lot; the Rephaim groaned under the waters. And Amos declared that the Amorites were tall 'like the height of cedars' and 'strong as the oaks'. So perhaps the bones of an Amorite king or a Philistine colossus lay under the dome of Abel.

But an inhabitant of Suq told me that a Roman emperor was buried here. His words stunned me. Which emperor could it be? Was it the body of Caracalla, murdered on his way to the Temple of the Moon at Carrhae? Or the corpse of the cunning emperor Macrinus, who was slain near Antioch? Or were Gordian's ashes smuggled from the Euphrates, or the flayed remains of Valerian from Persepolis? Perhaps they had even dredged the mutilated carcass of Heliogabalus out of the Tiber and cast it back at his homeland.

As I descended to the foot of the Mountain of Abel, the sun alighted onto the hills and the moon was countermarching over Lebanon. I heard an American voice. I looked round, but saw only a benevolent old man in a white *ratouy* headscarf. His name was Ahmed. He said he had taken a boat to the United States as a young man and had been a train driver in Michigan for thirty years. God had delivered him safely back in his home village with some money, a Mid-West accent and the respect of many

* The word 'bedstead' probably means 'sarcophagus'. Since the average length of a cubit was eighteen inches and the king would have been at least a foot shorter than his coffin, Og may have measured twelve feet.

friends. We walked to his house, which looked across the valley at the face of the mountain, and passed mounds of rubble collected by the villagers for the base of a road. Pillars and entablatures from the Greek city mingled with the debris as incidentally as tin cans. Classical roof-rollers appeared again.

Ahmed's wife had a long, humorous face and looked much younger than her husband. From under her open veil her hair fell in a scrawny pigtail, at the end of which she had fastened the key to the house. Ahmed was seventy years old, and his many childen included a daughter of six, whom he offered to me if I could wait so long, and laughed. Like many Syrian children she had beautiful fair hair, which the old man kissed with entrance-ment.

We sat on cushions along the verandah. Dusk insinuated itself down the aisles of the mountains and blew flights of late pigeons over the sky. We could see the tomb of Abel directly above us, its dome still glinting with sunlight.

'It is the Druses who go there,' he said. 'They come in groups from around Hermon and Lebanon. You have heard about the Druses?'

I had thought they lived mainly in southern Syria. I had seen them in the markets of Damascus and had been surprised by the thunder-blue eyes and porcelain beauty of the women. Their religion embraces belief in Adam and Christ as incarnations of God, and there is a discredited theory which traces their ancestry to the Crusaders.

Ahmed said he knew nothing of their faith, except that they kept it as dark as a railway tunnel, and that their belief must extend to Abel. He looked up at the mountain-top again. 'At night we sometimes see their fires from here,' he said, 'and hear them dancing and firing shots. They first come to the tomb in daylight. A man calls down from the summit to the keeper of the shrine at the toe of the mountain, and he climbs up and unlocks it for them.'

I looked at the mountain. It was unbelievable. 'How can he possibly hear the cry?'

'He always hears the cry.'

'What if he is sleeping? Or listening to Radio Cairo?'

'He always hears it. Then they give him part of their meat as payment—the kidneys of a sheep or something, to take back to his family.'

The dome of the tomb had vanished like a light extinguished.

Now we could only make out the lines of the ridge, black and strangely level, usurping half the sky.

Ahmed went indoors to pray. After a quarter of an hour he came out again and read me the story of the conception of the Virgin Mary from the Koran. It is a devout story, for the conception is ministered by an angel, second only to a gift from God. We sat out in semi-darkness for a long time, and talked about the Koran and the Bible and the succession of the prophets. His mind went back to his years in America, to the Michigan Express, the Dutch engineers and the cold winters. Beneath the blackening mass of the Mountain of Abel, we compared memories of New York and Pompeii. He admired the works of the ancients, and told me how Yugoslav engineers, piping the Barada river through a near-by mountain, found that the Romans had anticipated them eighteen hundred years before.

Soon the coldness of the verandah tiling was eating through our stockinged feet. Inside it was warm and the children were asleep, tumbled together like dolls. Ahmed's wife brought us home-made crystallised fruits, but Ahmed ignored them and again took down his prayer-mat from where it hung among a cloud of flowers around his Koran. He faced the wall, interspersing his *suras* with gurks and wheezes: such prayer, I thought, must be the zenith of contentment. His eldest son asked me about England and America and how he might find a more lucrative job. '. . . fifteen dollars a *day*? . . . *Wullah!* That's fifty-five Syrian pounds. . . . How much is a wife out there? . . .' My replies were muttered, because Ahmed was praying, but soon he trundled away to bed, leaving us to discuss piastres and pounds and, I feared, Aden.

I shared my room with thousands of beans laid out to dry, and a cupboard inlaid with mother-of-pearl. And I dreamt of Ahmed kneeling punctually to his prayers while the Michigan Express crashed all its gates from Grand Rapids to Detroit.

*   *   *

The air in the mountains is hard and bracing on autumn mornings. You wash in ice-cold water and feel that the sun will never be warm again. In the valley above Abila the trees still clustered along the train of the river. I thought that perhaps, after all, its source lay beyond the borders of Lebanon. But as I followed it upward it grew bright, and was distracted by every rocky spur.

I bicycled past the station which pumps water through the hillside in the wake of Rome, and moved through a valley wild with thistles and tumbled rocks, to a skyline of crippled olive trees. A black-backed snake which had been coiled on the road like a broken fan-belt, flickered into the scrub.

Soon the slopes of far ridges lifted austerely in front of me, and I emerged into the fertile plain of Zebdany, which spreads into Lebanon. On every side surged the fawn and sunset hills where Noah grazed his flocks. The fields were puckered with prostrate vines, and here at last I found the source of the Barada, in a meagre lake. By a bewitching illusion, it appeared to be flowing uphill across the plain. I threw a leaf into the river and watched it hesitate a moment, then seem to move, very gently, against the laws of nature. But this, I remembered, was haunted country, the retreat of gangling ogres, of wyverns and demiurges.

Back in the seclusion of the mountain river, I sat down and ate the succulent grapes of Zebdany. Greek tombs squinted at me from the rocks. A herd of goats tinkled over the edge of the hill. Beneath musky fir trees, sacred to Pan, I looked along the line of the river and thought myself in Greece. Beneath my hand sprang crocuses, which blessed the marriage bed of Zeus and Hera. Beside me shimmered an olive tree, Athene's gift to mankind.

Naiads must dwell here, I thought—half-mortal nymphs of springs and rivers. They scattered themselves throughout the Roman Empire for their sculptured likenesses have been found as far away as India. For centuries they would have lived undisturbed beneath Abila. If I waited long enough, one might appear, frail and gossamer-haired as a waterfall. The last of them, fathered by wandering centaurs during the closing years of Heraclius, could only have retreated here; for higher up the river ran through the plain and fields and villages.

Frogs examined me from along the sides of the river. Upstream some Druse women were watering their donkeys. After a minute they went away, and after a long time the clop of hoofs died. A bird cried from a plane tree. And there slowly came a thought that the naiads might have mingled with the mountain men. Their span of years had contracted, but they had kept lovely shapes and blue eyes. They had survived on honey and shish-kebab, washed down with *arak* and Chalybonian wine. By day they would conform to Islam and go in heavy robes, but travellers at night must hear the distant sounds of ancient merriment. Then, airy-bodied, the naiads trip down to the waters of the River of Gold, and dance to the mingled harmonies of Grecian lyre and Arabic lute. . . .

3. The Roman Peace

> . . . the city which in very truth
> belongs to Zeus and is the eye of the
> whole East—sacred and most mighty
> Damascus.
>
> *The Emperor Julian*

DARIUS III FLED so precipitately from the battlefield of
Issus in 333 B.C. that he left his baggage behind him in the royal
palace at Damascus. When Alexander the Great sent horsemen
to capture the city, the gates were treacherously thrown open to
them. Their booty included the royal harem, a handsome
treasury, and the sister of the Great King who, in accordance
with the Achaemenian custom, was also his wife.

For the first time, Europeans ruled Damascus. They found
the well-ordered city which the Arameans had laid out centuries
before on the north bank of the Abana. Already the orchards
were rich and the underground irrigation systems intricate.
Year after year the Arameans tunnelled through the limestone
in the sodden darkness to bring the river to a few more miles
of desert. And the whole Syrian army could hide in these tunnels
today.

Near the place where the Great Ommayad Mosque rises, the
Greek colonists built their own town. With its agora, gymnasium and the symmetrical design of its houses and arcaded
streets, it might have been built in Attica or Ionia. Some
Damascenes adapted themselves and their gods, changed their
clothes and learnt Greek, but Hellenism was never more than a
fragile ship on a deep Semitic sea.

Damascus knew no peace. No sooner had Alexander died
than Syria was tormented by the wars of his successors—the
Seleucids in Asia and the Ptolemies in Egypt. Damascus lay on
the fringe of the Seleucid power. Far Eastern trade began to
by-pass her and move through the upstart city of Seleucia on the
Tigris. Then it would follow the Euphrates to the newly-built
capital of Antioch, and to the military camps of Apamea, filled
with the trumpeting of six hundred war elephants.

Damascus was shuttled between Seleucids and Ptolemies and
became, for a few months, the capital of the Seleucid Empire.

But as the empire began to contract before its more united and energetic neighbours, the trade routes were diverted again through quieter inland ways, which brought wealth to the Nabatean Arabs of Petra. Finally Damascus placed herself under the protection of the Petraen king, and a Nabatean quarter sprouted up east of the Greek city.

Fourteen years later, Tigranes of Armenia overran all Syria; but his kingdom began to encroach on that of Rome, and so disorderly was his gigantic army that the Romans claimed to have killed a hundred thousand infantry for the loss of five men.

In 64 B.C. the Damascenes greeted, with unrecorded feelings, the strange northern legionaries of General Marcus Aemilius Scaurus.

*　　*　　*

For days I walked through the old city without noticing a grain from its Roman past. Its aspect is mediaeval: crushed and confused; streets wrapped in sudden belts of din and silence. Men seem to have lost the battle against their environment, to have wedged themselves against the jumbled architecture of their fathers. Streets which at first move confidently, strident with voices and the crash of hammers, disintegrate into lanes which twist along discreet walls, past closed doors. Often you can stretch out both arms as you walk, and stroke the sides of an alley until it dies beneath a dwarf arch and is succeeded by an anarchy of passageways.

But after a while I began to recognise the bones of another city: the pattern first imposed by the Greeks, and confirmed by the Romans. It is Roman works which remain. The level of the ancient city lies fifteen feet beneath the present one, but here and there a plastered-up column leans out of a wall, the base of a broken pillar is used for a seat or a doorstep, hewn stones support a minaret. It is typical of Damascus that she has absorbed them without fondling or jealousy, simply propped herself against them with an Arab indifference to antiquity.

Once, on turning to leave the mausoleum of a sheikh, I realised that two Roman columns, daubed in paint and plaster, supported half the building. Another time, lost in a web of alleys, I came upon carvings in basalt round a merchant's doorway, and a pitted monolith of a pillar, used for announcements of wrestling competitions. And on the hospital of the mediaeval sultan

Nureddine, under a gush of stalactite carving, rests a superb classical pediment.

Today the Street Called Straight is only one quarter of its original width, but it still follows the course of the famous Roman *decuménus*. Many things proclaim the classical route. I found three columns mewed up in the walls of a near-by khan, shielded by trees and vines. In the centre of a printing factory stood a pillar whose base plunged beneath the cellar of the building. Electric switches had been stapled to its side, and its faded capital supported the belt of a Heidelberg printing press.

A few years ago, workmen demolishing houses in another part of the street came upon a pale-stoned arch which had once looped over the northern portico of the road. It has been reconstituted at today's ground level, and now attains a delicacy which its architects could never have given it, flanked by fluted columns, rising from the lean congestion of the Arab street, magnificently redundant. Near by, two pillars in the back wall of an ironmongery point the course of the old road, their shafts festooned in brasses and chains, their pediments dimpling and cracking the ceilings. The street ends in the east at the sole survivor of the seven great Roman gates of Damascus—the northern entrance for the Gate of the Sun.

There are subtler signs of vanished things. The curves of alleyways even define the position of a theatre, but warehouses and enshrined holy men now crowd the site. The plays which colonial Greeks and Hellenised Arabs watched under the glare of a Syrian afternoon were generally equal to the theatre's coarse Herodian architecture. The citizens laughed themselves sick over the hoary histrionics of Plautus, cheered for simpering actors with painted faces or female masks,* and heaped abuse on a *stupidus*. Occasionally a travelling troupe of Hellenes must have found its way to the city; but probably there came only a puzzled silence from a half-empty auditorium as the voice of the dying Alcestis faded into the camel-roar of the Street Called Straight.

Around scattered pillars and the insinuations of streets, the Roman city begins to draw breath. Sixteen hundred years ago, walls of hewn limestone, fifteen feet thick, rose along the banks of the Barada, and were buttressed by a *castrum* in the west. From the Gate of Jupiter to the Gate of the Sun ran the Street Called Straight, ribbed in wax-white porticoes, flanked by a

* The donning of women's masks was an undignified reversion to the antique Greek custom.

theatre and the governor's palace, and embellished at inter-
sections by marble tetrapylons. The centuries-old sanctuary of
Haddad had been stamped into the ground by an enormous
temple to Jupiter. A forum had succeeded the agora. In the walls
stood triple entrances, the gates of Saturn, Mars and the Moon,
the temple and portals of Venus.

Because it is known where each of these gates stood, the lines
of the great colonnaded streets between them can be accurately
drawn. Sunken columns confirm their routes; their width can
be measured and their style gauged. In the central thorough-
fares went the chariots and horses of officials, the carts of the
coloni, and the dapper white mules of upper-class ladies, mimick-
ing the fashion of Antioch. Macedonians, Phoenicians, Armenians and Jews shuffled through the shadow of the porticoes
among the orchard peasants. Sheikhs whose fathers had been
mere brigands strode in from the desert clothed in purple,
and civil servants hitched their togas out of the gutters and
sighed to be back in Rome. The markets were cluttered with
slaves, and Bedouin in skins and sandals; country women in
cotton dresses and strings of many-coloured beads; Palmyrene
merchants with stubbly beards and fringed togas; purple- and
gold-vested priests effeminately crowned in tiaras; here and
there a mendicant troupe of flute and castanet players, a Par-
thian horse-dealer with divided hair and Medic dress, or
Hellenised Syrian ladies flaunting Chinese silks and glistening
at the throat with strands of gold, earrings tinkling down
around their veils in miniature bells.

Europeans were submerged by this peacock world; only in the
castrum the javelins of the Fourth Legion Scythica glinted with a
threat of Roman discipline; and occasionally the carts would be
cleared off the streets as Aramean recruits for the Third Legion
Augusta were marched to Numidia in a whirl of doltish faces and
scarlet paludaments.

In those days the gates sucked in and spewed out the commerce of the world. Damascus courted every passing caravan,
bought, transported and resold any kind of ware, profiting from
the western Roman empire's craving for eastern luxuries. Two
great trades converged on her: the incense routes of Arabia and
the silk traffic from China.

Out of the country of the Sabaeans in southern Arabia—'the
land of Secret Mystery'—the enormous caravans rambled up
through Arabia Felix and Petra. Sometimes they reached the
Mediterranean at Gaza, but often they journeyed north along

the limestone and basalt paved road of Trajan, and blocked up
the streets of Damascus round the gates of Saturn and the Sun.
Negro slaves trailed their manacles among the camel-loads
of ivory, tortoiseshell and animal skins from Abyssinia, and the
apes and scented gums of the East African coasts. Myrrh and
frankincense passed through the city to the temples of Ionia or
the Palatine Hill.

Indian and Arabian ships, which had evaded the pirates on the
Red Sea, docked at the ports of Petra. Some unloaded only sugar
and cotton and slandering parrots; others were pungent with
spices, nard and styptic of olives for the curing of wounds, and
brought beryls or the pearls which criminals were forced to
gather off the shark-troubled coasts of Malabar and Ceylon.
From Petra herself came iron and gold and ingots of silver, with
sesame oil and many perfumes.

The eastern trade followed the Euphrates in a great arc
towards the sea. In dangerous times as many as three thousand
camels might march together. Commerce lay in the hands of the
Palmyrenes, who carried the traffic of the Persian Gulf from
Babylon to Syria, and received the silks and jade for which
Persians had bartered in dumb show with Chinese merchants far
to the east. The Palmyrenes often took the Strata Diocletiana to
Damascus—a highway which linked the Euphrates to the
Mediterranean, cutting across the desert for almost three
hundred miles. Wells had been sunk every twenty-four miles
along the route, and it was watched over by forts and patrolled
by a Roman dromedary corps.

Later, the convoys straggled out of Damascus over the
mountains to Sidon and all Phoenicia. Here the finished silks
were shipped westward and the raw silk was woven into garments. The most beautiful found their way to the shopping
arcades of Rome, where fashion-conscious patricians conceived
such a mania for them that the emperor Tiberius forbade their
use by men.

Damascus joined the Decapolis League and transported Syrian
glass, the honey and balsam of Palestine, cassia from Dan and
ebony from Edom. Egyptian trade reached her from across
Sinai and the Plain of Jezreel, while the Phoenicians filled her
with robes of Tyrian purple. Grain flowed in from the Hauran,
and even a little tin came from the island of Britannia, and such
rarities as Spanish silver and lead, or brass from Cilicia.

Damascus herself produced Chalybonian wine, wool, linen
and pale amber. The perfumes of Syria were famous and subtle:

oil of saffron blossom and the damask rose; compounds of cinnabar, honey and wine; unguent of lilies; and the juice of the galbanum, which sold for five denarii a pound in Rome and was sovereign against snakes. Damascene perfume-vendors were responsible for the whiffs of cat-thyme and myrtle and marjoram which followed women all over the Empire.

The city also specialised in cone-shaped baskets stacked with 'pruna' and 'cottana', dried plums and figs which became a luxury. Even in Britain archaeologists have found the distinctive 'pruna' stones. Damascene dates and nuts became famous, and Pliny complained that damson trees transplanted to Italy were wretched beside those of Damascus.

Her citizens filtered into the Empire, settling as farmers in Gaul or traders on the Rhine. Lucian warned Greek servants that they might be 'subordinate to a doorman with a vile Syrian accent', and Juvenal complained that the Orontes was spilling into the Tiber. In the third century, even some of Rome's emperors were Syrian. A phallic stone encrusted with jewels once usurped the pantheon of Latin gods, and senators gazed in disgust at the emperor Heliogabalus with painted face, prancing in ecstasy to the cymbals of Syrian dancing-girls on the Palatine Hill.

The Damascenes took the Romans' gold but refused their culture. The Romans, unlike the Greeks, did not take to oriental ways. In Syria they were always strangers, marked out by their sober dress and absurd honesty, and they mostly shared the dudgeon of the homesick legionary who scribbled on a rock: 'The Syrians are a lousy race.'

*   *   *

The covered Hamidieh market leads to the wall of the Roman sanctuary to Jupiter-Haddad. Momentarily, it is a crossing from dimness and disarray to light and order. The ghost of an entranceway looms at the market's end: thirty-foot columns paled to ethereal colours. Smaller pillars, with elegant Corinthian capitals, lead to the *temenos* of the temple, but you can penetrate no deeper into the Roman sanctuary. Inside the walls, the Great Ommayad Mosque has smothered it. Some of its columns have been pressed into the porticoes, and a few still bear Greek inscriptions from times when men felt honoured to

supply materials for temple buildings. They are simple acknow-
ledgements: 'In accordance with his will, the inheritors of
N. . . .' 'After the will of Zenon, son of Diodore, son of Metro-
dore.'

The ancient temple was a near relation to shrines in Baalbek
and Palmyra. The mosque walls were once merely its inner
court and are superb still: gigantic, mellow blocks and Egyptian
pilasters. Shops lean against their outer façades, and the air is
grilled by the scraping and whirring of furniture-makers, and
pungent with resin. Classical arches curve over a debris of
pillars by the tomb of Saladin, and buildings all around have
picked a few bones from the dismembered leviathan.

While repairing a part of the Great Mosque, builders discovered a three-thousand-year-old relief in the walls. It showed
a sphinx with griffinish wings and a curled tail, which had
been part of a sanctuary still older than the Roman one—the
Aramean shrine to Haddad, the god of thunder and the sun. The
Romans destroyed this shrine to build their own temple, but
Haddad had reigned a thousand years and would not so easily
be usurped; he grafted his own qualities onto those of Jupiter,
and lived on respectably, under a Roman name. Atargatis, his
consort, was associated with Venus or Juno, but no Hellenistic
garb could cover her Semitic earthiness. Temple girls played
flutes and cymbals round her altar, and her eunuch priests
prophesied as far afield as Italy and Greece, and broke into
delirious dances.

On a bas-relief from Dura Europos, the two divinities—
Haddad and Atargatis—can be seen sitting together. The
columns beside them are decorated with bulls' heads, for the bull
was sacred to Haddad. The god's face is framed in girlish locks
and crowned with a tiara; he holds in his right hand a stunted
thunderbolt. Atargatis, a true matriarch, is bigger than her
husband, and a pair of lions shelters behind her thighs.

Along the south wall of the old temple, workmen have been
laying drainage pipes twenty feet under the ground. At this level
they still strike bricks and masonry, but the city hugs herself too
close for excavation. Even in the Museum there are only a few
ancient pieces from Damascus: elusively-glazed glass, some
minor work in pottery and metals, and bronzes whose mock-
Hellenic features are fiercened by pairs of oriental eyes.

Damascene sculpture was rigid and undeveloped. The limestone bust of a woman, found in the orchards, is typical. She is a
crudely-worked, flat-faced matron, and a veil falls over her

severely braided hair to her shoulders. She breast-feeds a tiny, naked child, who clings to her like a puppy. Her frontal pose and vacuous expression were common ware in Damascus, for the city struck an unhappy medium between two arts: to her north and west, Hellenic cities produced marble statues with something of the poise and restraint of classical Greece. But to the south flourished the culture of Hauran, whose black basalt rock fringed the Damascus oasis. It imposed harsh terms on its sculptors, withstanding all attempts at subtlety of form or texture. An ugly, pitted stone, its statues were resolved into exuberant curves, sometimes portraying women with an ebullience of breast and waspness of waist which is almost Hindu.

The city's museum perfectly displays the extremes between which she lay—on the one hand stands a basalt Minerva, sombre, elemental, starkly compelling; on the other a sepulchre-white statuette of Greek Aspasia, born of grace and light.

*   *   *

It was the Roman layout which first bound together the Greek and Aramean towns and enclosed them in walls. A circus was built where the modern Boulevard de Baghdad runs, and a Roman channel still guides drinking-water to the quarters round Kanawat. Its arches are plastered over or sunk under the earth, but I traced its course from where it gushed out of limestone conduits to its disappearance, with the same suddenness, under a police station. Only once, the voussoirs erupted from their clay, polished black by passing hands.

The city walls are maimed and disjointed; mosques and bazaars ate them up in the western quarter long ago. Only the tower of Nureddine pushes silvery stones above the roofs. The south-west part of the old town is quiet, lined with stone-carvers near the Mamloukieh cemetery, chipping out marble flowers. The medieval battlements emerge from houses, garrisoned by pigeons. Their towers slouch behind broken balustrades, minarets and lines of washing like tattered sails. Horses clatter under the mediaeval Bab Saghir, the Little Gate. After a few hundred yards, the houses recede and the walls stop before an expanse of dust, where masons hack at limestone, and bird-sellers gather.

Further east the palisades only half recover and stand bared against the sun at irresolute heights of six or eight feet. Rubble and Roman blocks, they curve to the Turkish Kaysan Gate, which stands where the Gate of Saturn fell. Here they meet the site of the Roman walls, and gain height again. But they have long since passed into senility, puckered with windows and beams. Clay houses dangle over the towers and garland them with vines.

The northern arch of the Gate of the Sun, which the Romans reserved for pedestrians, is scarred every day by the sides of lorries. Its central and southern entrances, sealed up for centuries in the wall, have at last been restored and opened, and the generous triple entrance stands as it did a millennium and a half ago. Beyond it the Romans modified the rectangle of their battlements to follow the wanderings of the Barada. At first, as I walked west, I passed palisades and towers which plait together the masonry of Ayyoubids and Mamelukes and the quarry-stones of the Turks. The Barada flows in front of them, ugly and troubled.

Then I reached the Bab Touma, a mongrel, mediaeval gate which stands on the site of the Gate of Venus. I crossed a demolition site and slid down to the river through willow trees; under a modern bridge I saw the stub of a classical one, for here, even thirty years ago, a man crossed the river by the grace of Imperial Rome.

Beyond Bab Touma, the whole Roman wall seemed to have heaved itself out of the ground. The houses momentarily dispersed and I walked in shadow between the monoliths and the willow-filled river. Broken pillars lay along the base of the parapets, and the shrubs which had tumbled out of the crevices remained there after death, like withered hair.

A hundred yards beyond, I came on the site of the Gate of the Moon. The Moslems built another entrance here in the thirteenth century, and called it Bab as-Sâlam, the Gate of Peace. The consoles of its machicolations are scarcely touched, and a clear Kufic script runs in a bar across the arch: 'In the name of God, the Compassionate, the Merciful. The building of this Gate (may it be a happy portent!) has been restored under the reign of our master the sultan al-Malik as-Salîh, most august lord, the learned, the pious, the champion of the holy war, the assisted of God, the vanquisher, the victorious. . . .'

After the Bab as-Salâm there are no more walls, but originally the mediaeval defences strode parallel to Roman ones. Now only a road called Beyn es Soûreyn, 'Between the Ramparts', remains; and two gates built in the Middle Ages. They appear very suddenly: fusty patriarchs studded and cased in iron. Their hinges flag and their double-folding doors are never closed. One of them, the Gate of the Gardens, is successor to the Roman Gate of Mercury. The other is the Bab al-Faraj, whose doors have lain open for so long that successive layers of tarmac on the alley have wedged them ajar. The last of the great gates, the Jabiya, stands in the south-west corner of the walled town on the site of the Gate of Jupiter. It is a triumph of mediaeval sturdiness, immured in bazaars where the sun never finds it, its consoles shouldering a market roof. Years ago a dead holy man was caged up in the wall near it, and as I stood there a boy bent down and smothered the grille in front with kisses.

The citadel stands in the dust of the *castrum* west of the old town and is constructed on the Roman pattern still. Pompey was perhaps the first to build a camp here, for he arrived in Damascus the year after she passed to Rome, and meted out justice to the petty Hellenic kings who scurried to him with petitions.

The Roman wars only momentarily disrupted the city's long commercial gluttony. Crassus took Syria as his province when the Empire was divided between Pompey, Caesar and him—an avaricious old man, who irritated all Syria with his weights and scales and revenues. But the Damascenes did not have to suffer him long. With an army of over forty thousand, he marched against Parthia in defiance of the omens: at the Euphrates thunder bellowed and a general's horse drowned in the river, and as the army prepared to cross, the first eagle standard turned round. At their victory celebration, the Parthians used the skull of Crassus as a stage prop in a Euripidean tragedy, and poured molten gold down its mouth to sate its avarice. A relic of his army trickled back to Syria under the command of Cassius, the future murderer of Julius Caesar.

Thirty years later the Parthians had overrun the state and were cleaning their armour by the Mediterranean. Mark Antony drove them back. He rode in and out of Damascus recruiting soldiers, and gave the city to Cleopatra, with half Syria. Coins were struck for her in the mint; but after a while the Serpent of Old Nile went away to Judaea and tried to seduce Herod the Great, who thought of murdering her. Herod himself had ridden to Damascus in his youth and been granted territory by the proconsul, and though she lay outside his kingdom, he embellished the city with a theatre and gymnasium.

[37]

Hadrian was legate of Syria for four years, and must often have journeyed to Damascus from Antioch: a striking sight in the oriental streets, with his grey-blue eyes and fair complexion.* As emperor, he returned fourteen years later—on foot and bare-headed as always—and honoured the city with the rank of metropolis. His impressions are unrecorded. Perhaps he felt nostalgic; or retched at Herod's architecture. The broad lips had grown firmer, the eyes deeper set. For the past fourteen years he had travelled all over the western half of his empire, tramped through North Africa and built a wall in the drizzle of North Britain. Now he passed on to rebuild Jerusalem and restore the sea-worn tomb of Pompey at Pelusium.

Septimius Severus and his successors adorned Damascus with her gates and colonnaded streets, and bestowed colonial rights on her. Construction started on the temple of Jupiter-Haddad. In A.D. 274 Aurelian passed through with Dalmatian horsemen on his way to assault Palmyra, and brought back as captive the warrior-queen Zenobia, 'more lovely than Cleopatra', to grace in golden chains his triumph at Rome.

With the death of Palmyra the wealthiest days of Damascus ended; but she was never poor. Diocletian, in darker years, built her military camp into a powerful castle, and equipped her with an arsenal. From this time, perhaps, dates the prestige of the Damascenes in forging blades.

To the men who lived in those centuries it must have appeared as if the Roman power would endure for ever. But catastrophes usually came from the desert. Damascus would be the first to suffer. Even in Antioch, in A.D. 260, the people had no inkling of an incursion from the east. Assembled in the great theatre one day, they saw an actor stare up at the hills and suddenly exclaim: 'Either I am dreaming or the Persians are upon us!' The audience burst into applause even as the javelins fell among them. . . .

* Hadrian's favourite architect was a Damascene, who designed part of the forum in Rome, and threw a great bridge over the Danube.

4. The Cool River

A fountain of gardens, a well of
living waters, and streams from
Lebanon.

The Song of Solomon

ONE OF THE joys of desert travel is the first sight of a
new shape or a green plant. To anyone nearing Damascus from
the east, it is the Lebanese mountains which first throw a
feather of whiteness above the skyline. Then, slowly, the slopes
gather substance and detail, and the luxuriance of orchards
breaks on the vision: 'a city with trees and rivers and fruits and
birds', says *The Thousand and One Nights*, 'as thought it were
a paradise'.

These orchards, which the Damascenes call al-Ghuta, envelop
and feed the city. With the river which bears them, they explain
her existence. The Damascenes are right to be proud of them,
for they are the richest orchards in the Middle East and contain
a variety of trees unique in the world. In earliest spring they are
cloudy with apricot and plum blossom, and summer burdens
them with fruit until their boughs moan. Under the June sky,
women ease up their pantaloons to their calves and crush the
apricots in stone troughs, or pick the kernels from the gruel as
it is laid out in the sun.

The Barada, the 'Cool River', reaches them still cold from the
grottoes of Lebanon and splays out into a million arteries whose
quota of water has been carefully apportioned since Aramean
times.

In autumn the olive trees thicken with fruit, blood-red pomegranates burst their skins and swollen walnuts thump to the
ground. Corn and barley burgeon in the shadows. Month after
month the groves are glutted with mulberries, figs and man-
darines, and grapes which dangle in crocodile teardrops to the
earth, or grow sweet and round on yellowing vines. Exhaustion
only comes with late autumn.

Along the skirt of the orchards, where the fields turn to desert,
are the remains of Greek and Roman towns whose histories have
vanished. Their walls and columns lie in hieroglyphs about the
sand—clues to a thousand years of European domination; and

because the traditions of their builders were smothered long ago, they possess a pathos greater than that of classical ruins in Europe.

I followed the Barada from the neck of the orchards into the desert. It descends swiftly through the Lebanese hills, and reaches the plain of Damascus at Mezze, where it diffuses into four streams and disperses through the city. For centuries the Damascenes thought of this 'parting of the waters' as the centre of their paradise, their river of Eden, which in Genesis 'became into four heads'. They placed near here the grave of the mother of Mary, and the birth and childhood of Christ Himself.*

Families used to squat under the trees in summer, poring over the Koran and sipping tiny cups of coffee. Palaces and villas once looked down on the waters, and the gardens were heavy with fruit trees and famous for their roses. The perfumes of Mezze found their way to all Asia, and the bazaars still sell tiny bottles of its rose water.

I found the special purity of Mezze vanished. The Beirut road crushed the river with noise. Willow trees grew dusty on its banks and the waters flowed along a bed speckled with refuse. The ghost of the earlier village was harboured by a single grove of poplars and willow trees, where old men in tarboushes knelt at the hour of prayer among pots and coffee-cups. They were surrounded by transistor radios and children's swings. If they sat too near the edge of the trees, a passing lorry drenched them in fumes. But they seemed oblivious and contented; and on the other side of the road a trellis showered down wine-red roses, as lovely as any that grew in the gardens of Semiramis.

The streets of Mezze were filled with noise and soldiers. Only the doors of its mosque were beautiful, their copper surfaces engraved with angular birds, and flowers like stars which had burst into bloom.

From here the Barada spreadeagled through Damascus and into the autumn orchards. For miles the trees overspread the road: apricot and apple leaves billowing reddish-gold. From time to time the plantations parted before the tombs of holy men or the walls of a village, and at midday hundreds of school-children spilled into the orchards like elves.

After many miles the trees became jaundiced and stunted,

---

* Koran xxiii. 50: 'We made the son of Mary and his mother a sign to mankind and gave them a shelter on a peaceful hill-side watered by a fresh spring.'

thinning away from fields of aubergines and cabbages. The goats grew lean, the sheep blemished, and in the villages the limestone minarets dwindled to clay towers. At last the trees receded to a hair's-breadth line of poplars.* The fields were downy with cotton, wound in little white turbans amongst its tangle of mauve-brown foliage. Women and children glided about the fields like caryatids with enormous bales on their heads. At this time of year even the vines are spent, and the wheat and barley still infant in the ground.

Further on, only empty-headed reeds swayed in the wind or lay in sheafs where they had been felled for building fences. Camels had invaded the meadowland and nomad tents were pitched out in the scrub. Syrians, who love the concept of subterranean streams, say that the waters of Damascus re-emerge as the Dog River in Lebanon, or flow underground until they reach the Persian Gulf. Yet I could see the rivers faltering in the sand. To the south, the thinnest line of green drew the course of the Awaj, the ancient Pharpar, to its bed in a suffocated marsh. The Barada itself dies here, in an expanse of reeds, the haunt of duck in winter. Beyond, stretches the desert and the humps of tells and long-dead craters, and a mirage shuffles the sky and the land into layers, as if a pall of blue smoke were burning along the horizon.

The meanest building or tree attains significance. I remember the houses of Hijaneh, clustered among basaltic boulders; a mound of graves where camels were eating green boughs which had been placed on the tombs.

These mud-built huts half belong to the desert and their people are semi-nomadic. An odd quiet pervades them. Your feet thump and scrape in the closeness of alleys. In some villages the women wear dresses of aquamarine and flaming saffrons, and their scarves drop from severe headbands in flashes of sequins and magenta tassels. They walk erect and possess more than their share of the lean desert beauty.

'Harran of the Columns' is the most curious of these stricken hamlets, its people ground into listlessness by scorching, malarial summers. Above its roof rise three Ionic pillars, reminders of a time when the desert bloomed into greenery beneath the masterful hand of Rome. They are soot-black, and seem to blight the village beneath them. Most of its people

* Two kinds of poplar: the Persian, which is quick-growing but whose wood is of poor quality; and the silver-leafed Greek poplar which yields the finest timber in Syria.

were too lethargic to talk or move, but a boy led me to the base of the pillars, which are set in the walls of a house; and there was an instant of Bedouin pride in his eyes as he refused a coin.

North of Harran, in the village of Dumeir, stands a finely-preserved Roman temple which the peasants call 'The Castle'. On its eastern façade a Greek inscription dates it at A.D. 245. Its design is austere but unusual: an arch and Corinthian pilasters surround the entrances, with well-moulded pediments above. The outer doors lead to vestibules at each end of an almost square cella, and above one of them the image of an imperial eagle stares out over the desert.

A few miles beyond, a Roman town lies out in the sand. Even its name is unknown. It has fallen into tumultuous mounds, and at some later time its half-buried temples were walled round to give shelter or to form rudimentary defences. Only occasionally the stones throw up a glimmer of order: the line of a courtyard or the wraith of an arch. Underground aqueducts belch out water in spring, and the veins of a theatre wrinkle the hill above.

If you sit quietly, even for a moment, the desert begins to agitate. Lizards flip onto the stones, and beetles trail along the splintered crust of the earth. A gun-shot can raise a storm of sand-grouse or stir the long legs of a desert hare. And in the dusk the ground casts up hundreds of pale-furred jerboas, whose tufted tails fly out behind them like kites.

The mountains behind Damascus possess still older towns. Helbon, whose Chalybonian wine once graced the table of the kings of Persia, stands in a mild valley and looks down at cliffs which are dimpled with sepulchres. The village fountain, mounted on Corinthian capitals, spills into a stone basin bearing in Greek the words 'Great King Markos'.

The mountains above Menin, ten miles to the east, are full of temple-caves. I climbed its northern acropolis among the remains of shrines, and found myself in a theatre of white rocks. Far below, the stillness was pricked by a sad multitude of cock-crows, and the spring-waters of Menin meandered into alabaster hills. I stood on the crest with two crooked walnut trees. In front, an enormous plinth, carved out of the hillside, had survived for two thousand years still upright: a meaningless portal leading only to the violence of flint and thistles. Holes in the cliff, which had once supported beams, now harboured wild lavender, and dismembered buildings were piled up against the mountain.

A temple had been cut twenty-four feet into the cliff-side and was empty, its walls dinted with shelves and niches. These sanctuaries, I thought, must have been carved before the classical orders were invented. Then I saw a second shrine, and round its entrance a frame and cornice of beautifully-carved leaves and stems.

A gasp of evening wind interrupted the heat and silence, and the sun grew faint. As I clambered down the western slope, I felt as if I had caught the titanic blocks in the act of falling, that at my approach they had stiffened in their places, and that the dust still trifled with the yellow flowers.

From Menin, looking south on a clear day, one may see the tip of Hermon. I reached it along the foot of the Mezze hills, and because I rode a bicycle, I was mistaken for a peasant, and arrived unchallenged in the military village of Katana. Not far away the Barada's companion river, the Pharpar of the Old Testament, flows down from its source on the mountain. The Arabs call it 'el-Awaj', 'the Crooked One', for it coils through endless crescents before reaching the southern orchards.

Hermon is a holy mountain, as indefinably as Fuji or Olympus. Its name means the 'Sacred'. Some say it is the mountain of the transfiguration, and it attracted the veneration of men as early as the Amorites, who described it as a breastplate gleaming across the desert. On its crown the stones of a Baalist high place of sacrifice and a Roman temple lie together. Nimrod, the biblical hunter, dwelt on its slopes, and died there from an insect which had crept through his ear and into his brain.*

Southward from Hermon, after the last trickles of the Pharpar have met and gone away, the land is bare. Its plains are only littered with basalt chippings, and even the wild swine here used to make themselves inedible by gobbling liquorice plants.

But in spring, an astonishing bloom breaks across the mountians and through the orchards. Tiny, pastel flowers deploy about the fields, and orange blossom, once gathered for Saracen brides, flakes along the wind. Wherever a knight died, a tough Crusader plant puts out mauve flowers in April, and on the hills grow wild lilies, sown by the tears of Eve as she fled out of Eden.

Strangest of all is the fragile Adonis flower, the scarlet anemone. Aphrodite fell in love with the beautiful shepherd Adonis, but the jealous god of battle had him killed by a wild boar

* Damascenes still call a headstrong man a 'Nimrood'.

in a valley of Lebanon, where the Adonis river, every spring, flows blood-red to the sea.* The women of Lebanon used to go into mourning annually on the day of his death and clutter the water-springs with funerary images or throw them into the ocean. In spring they still point to his blood-red wind-flower as a symbol of resurrection, and invoke the name of Adonis, or Thamuz,

> Whose annual wound in Lebanon allur'd
> The Syrian damsels to lament his fate
>   In amorous ditties all a summer's day,
> While smooth Adonis from his native rock
>   Ran purple to the sea.†

*   *   *

Greek legend, in perplexing disguises, lingers all over the Syrian mountains and desert; but classical remains are always ignored. The country people attribute them to Solomon or to djinns, or (in the case of a church) to St Helena, the mother of Constantine. Old Testament figures, many of whom reappear in the Koran, are often held responsible for unidentified ruins, or phenomena in the landscape.

Ibn Batutta, who arrived in Damascus during the Black Death in 1348, saw in the near-by village of Kadem the 'Mosque of the Footprints', which a holy man declared to be those of Moses. It was even claimed that Moses was buried there. At the height of the plague, and after fasting for three days, the entire population of the city walked to the mosque, the emirs barefooted, the Christians with Bibles, the Jews with Talmuds. All morning they knelt under the July sun, praying for deliverance, and, adds the traveller, 'God lightened their afflictions; for the number of deaths in a single day at Damascus did not attain two thousand, while in Cairo and Old Cairo it reached the figure of twenty-four thousand a day.'

The village of Kadem, which means 'footprint', is linked to Damascus by the long suburb of Meidan. The 'Mosque of the Footprints' still stands, but now the imprint is attributed to Mahomet. For the Syrians say that the Prophet stopped at the

---

* Scientists, innocent of legend, attribute this to red soil at the river's source.
† *Paradise Lost*, Bk. 1.

village on his furthest journey north and gazed enraptured on the rivers and orchards of Damascus; but here, runs the legend, he turned back to Mecca, fearing to enter a paradise other than that of heaven.*

The village is insignificant now. The mosque, where the emirs used to assemble for the annual pilgrimage to Mecca, shies back from the road. I pushed at the door, but it was locked. I walked round its walls, and was faced by bare stone and a resentful woman seated in the shadow on the far side. But a man in a tattered headscarf and an old army greatcoat hailed me as I came away. Did I want to go in? I only had to ask. He laughed at me with pale-grey eyes. A frost of white bristles caressed a face of great gentleness.

'Almani?'

'No. English.'

He spoke slowly, in a French-Arabic patois of his own. 'J'étais soldat avec fransiyîn. *Wullah!* Trois années!' He marched up to the mosque doorway and unlocked it. A tapestry of scarlet vines fell against our heads. The courtyard was larger than I had expected, and overgrown, and a ruined prayer-hall leant against one side.

The old man had become mild again, and secretive. He unlocked a domed mausoleum, which stood alone in the courtyard, and beckoned me in. A green robe and turban covered the grave of a pasha. His family and followers lay round him under raised slabs in the pavement, marked by funerary turbans carved in stone. According to the old man's gestures, the pasha had been a plague on his enemies, had wrung their throats as if he were twisting flannels, then deftly plucked off their heads.

At the far end of the room stood a *mihrab*—the niche which lies towards Mecca in the holy places of Islam. A stone had been set in the paving at its base and the yellow outline of a footprint was worn in the stone. The old man's eyes twinkled. It was hard to know whether he was elated or amused.

'Mahomet!' he breathed. He circled his fingers round his eyes and turned in the direction of Damascus. 'Vers *Dimashk!* Regardez. Paradis! Après il. . . . Allah! . . . J'ai oublié . . . oublié. . . .'

He was determined to tell me in French about Mahomet's return from the outskirts of Damascus, but the words eluded

---

* The site of Mahomet's footprint originally lay on the Kassioun Mountain' where the traveller John Sanderson saw 'a great hudge foote of stone' as late as 1601.

him. He kept muttering to God and repeating 'Mecca' to himself. With his finger he outlined Mahomet's heel where it had bitten into the stone as the Prophet turned back. Then he raised his hands to the *mihrab* to explain how it faced the direction of the footprint.

I remembered other footprints. Mahomet left a faint spoor in the Dome of the Rock at Jerusalem, another in Cairo, and a hammer-toed imprint which the Turks carried away to Istanbul. I murmured a word or two about the earlier tradition of Moses, wondering if it had survived, but the old man only looked puzzled. In the end he scrambled to his feet, stood to attention, and resorted to the last of his French vocabulary. Mahomet, according to the mime, exercised a soldierly right-about turn and stepped off on the left foot for Mecca.

5. Christian Damascus

The watchman said, The
morning cometh, and also the
night.

Isaiah xxi. 12

SIX MILES SOUTH of Damascus, beside the road to Jerusalem,
a Christian shrine stands on a hill. Around it the sand has lightly
covered old foundations, like veins and tumours of the earth, and
the dust slips in drowsy filaments down subterranean cisterns
and tombs.

The hill is called Kaukab, 'Celestial Light', and is the traditional place where St Paul was blinded by heaven on his way
from Jerusalem to persecute the Christians of Damascus.* 'And
as he journeyed, he came near Damascus and suddenly there
shined round about him a light from heaven: And he fell to the
earth. . . .' From the crest of the mound I could see Mount
Kassioun, and the hill-suburbs of Damascus like an avalanche of
rubble fallen to the bottom of its slope. The stones and pillars
marooned on the hill are probably those of a Byzantine church,
and the tombs may belong to Christians who asked to be buried
there fourteen hundred years ago.

The shrine to St Paul is modern, not yet completed, and
resembles a gigantic military drum dropped in the desert, and
surrounded by an arcade of semi-circular arches. It is guarded by
a man and a dog, who live in a concrete hut at the foot of the hill.
The chapel is not beautiful, but its lines are simple and its site
austere; and soon the newly-planted conifers will raise their
ranks around it, and the Lebanese winds begin to work their
changes on its stone.

I returned to Damascus by the Jerusalem road. It probably
runs close to the Roman one, along which St Paul's followers
led him by the hand and into the city. They would have entered
from the south, and the Bible says that they took him to the
house of Judas, who was perhaps a physician. 'And there was a

---

* For the convenience of pilgrims, the site was later localised near the
Christian cemeteries by the east wall of Damascus, and revered with un-
withered fervour and bigotry.

certain disciple at Damascus, named Ananias; . . . And the Lord said unto him, Arise, and go into the street which is called Straight, and inquire in the house of Judas for one called Saul. . . . And Ananias went his way, and entered into the house; and putting his hands on him said, Brother Saul, the Lord, even Jesus, that appeared unto thee in the way as thou camest, hath sent me, that thou mightest receive thy sight, and be filled with the Holy Ghost.

'And immediately there fell from his eyes as it had been scales: and he received his sight forthwith, and arose, and was baptized.'

Nobody in the Christian quarter had heard of any house of Judas. A Greek Orthodox priest told me that it had vanished centuries back 'though of course the Catholics may have invented some place. . . .'

Were there no traditions, I asked, no rumours, not even a picturesque lie?

He chewed a strand of his beard. He admitted that Judas had been unfairly neglected. 'But there's not much left of anything now. You see, the alley has been widened. You could baptise an elephant here!'

Yet traditions, I discovered, had once been numerous and explicit. An ambassador to Turkey from the court of Louis XIV had said that a fountain stood near the house of Judas by a pillar called the Antique Column. St Paul had been baptised at the fountain. It was even whispered that Ananias, his healer, was buried under the pillar.

A month later, while I was examining the Roman arch in the Street Called Straight, a shopkeeper lured me in to look at his brassware. While we were discussing the price of kettles, he mentioned that the house of Judas had stood here. 'A very old tradition. Of course, I would not swear that it was true. . . .' He took me upstairs to a window and showed me the wall of the house next door. 'Old stones!' He had heard that their cellar was full of them. His voice scaled down to a breath of murky confidence. 'Nobody knows how old.' Outside the shop I could see the north column of the Roman arch. I told the man the legend of the fountain and the Antique Column. Had there ever been a fountain there?

'*Ya salâm!* Of course! There was a fountain in this shop where I stand! And old stones all around!' He gaped at me, agog at the conclusive proof. 'If Ananias came in by the back door. . . .' He was immensely grateful to me, for tourists could now be told about the house with absolute authority. In a moment he would be pulling the skull of Judas out of a kettle.

I walked round to the house behind the shop. I could not guess at the age of the blocks in the wall. When I knocked at the court-yard, a woman put a very frightened brown eye to the chink and said that there was nobody called Judas living there. The truth, I think, is that the legendary house stands in the Moslem quar-ter and that a small mosque has been built over it. Its rickety balcony projects into the Street Called Straight, and since the mosque cannot afford a minaret, the muezzin calls from this balcony, facing the wall two feet away.

As I reached the gate at the end of the Street Called Straight, small boys clustered round me shouting 'Anania! Anania!' and led me, armoured in cynicism, to the traditional place of the house of Ananias. A girl took me fifteen feet down to the level of the Roman street. The whole chapel below was perhaps thirty-five feet long, its rough stone walls and ceilings severely impressive. Two grilles in the roof filled it with a remembrance of light. I saw only a few pews, an altar with a scarlet cloth, and ugly wax tableaux on the walls. Some immured fragments of classical pillars stood out by their paleness, and a semi-circular side-chapel lay dark beyond an arch.

This is the only early church to survive in the city, and it echoes in its structure the simplicity of the first brotherhood: the bare, practical stones of saints and ascetics. So I was morti-fied to discover that Saladin had turned it into a mosque and destroyed much of the early work. Excavations in 1921 brought further confusion by uncovering the remains of a classical temple, and from the debris emerged an altar consecrated not to Christ, but to Jupiter-Haddad: 'Celestial God, National and Supreme.' For a time it seemed as if the legend that the place had been the house of Ananias was dead. Then from the form of the Greek letters on the inscription, scholars dated the altar to at least two centuries after Christ. So perhaps the Roman temple had been built to obliterate a Christian holy place—vulgar temples were a favourite means of obliteration—and the tatterdemalions in the street who cry 'Anania!' are right.

The footprints of St Paul do not vanish here. After several years' preaching in Arabia, he returned to Damascus. The Jews picketed the gates hoping to kill him, but 'the disciples took him by night, and let him down by the wall in a basket'. An early church was built near the Kaysan Gate, where Christians be-lieved the descent to have occurred. The Arabs raised a mosque on the rubble of the church. After many hundred years the mosque disintegrated, but bequeathed a single column of the early church, still standing in the dust.

The Bab Kaysan today is a handsome Ottoman gateway with heavy mouldings and big, tawny stones. Beneath its arch the Greek Catholics have built a shrine to St Paul, where I sat under a bas-relief of the apostle gravely descending the battlements in an enormous hamper. In relief it looked a simple operation, but in reality it must have been hazardous. Damascene baskets are unpredictable. They are mostly twined together from reeds, whose frayed ends bristle out in protective quills, and when heavily-laden they are safer carried on the head.

I looked round the shrine of St Paul at a few poor icons. It is simple and full of light, but the intangible aura called holiness is absent. It does not even appear to be a place of worship: only a threshold from which tourists can tramp up to the top of the gate, and look down twenty-five feet through 'St Paul's Window' on its flagrantly Turkish consoles.

The Romans straddled this site with a triple entrance, crowned by a statue of Saturn. St Paul never saw it. In his time there were older walls, but there was almost certainly a gate here. The Bible asserts that the saint was let down by a wall, since the gates were guarded by the Jews; but the Damascenes insist on the truth of the Kaysan Gate legend, and cite in their defence the tradition of St George.

Georgios, they say, was an Abyssinian Christian porter who was guarding the Kaysan that night. He allowed St Paul to escape, and in the morning the governor had him executed.

His tomb, which stands in the Christian cemetery beyond the walls, was a place of pilgrimage for centuries, and pious men would chip off tiny pieces from his marble execution-stone and carry them back to Europe. I went to the graveyard with a friend whose name was Georgios, who visits the tomb every year on his saint's day. A corridor of conifers led us to a church, its copper-plated doors embossed with the carving of a knight in Gothic armour, slaying a dragon; for despite the strength of his legend, the Damascene St George has lingered in a strange disguise—blended irredeemably with the patron saint of England, who was a Roman officer martyred under Diocletian and buried at Lydda. Dragon-slaying has become an attribute of both saints. On icons all over the city, monsters which would have petrified the simple porter die beneath his lance in an uproar of flames. Mediaeval travellers in Damascus were shown a rock from which he mounted his white stallion, and elderly Damascenes can still describe the fight as if the gnarled thews and blazing hiccups had only just subsided.

Georgios and I came to a tiny shrine whose walls were composed only of glass in a wrought-iron frame. A silver dome shone over it. Inside stood an octagonal plinth, which supported an icon and a tray of red earth for candles. The icon was stifled by silver medallions. Underneath, its paint had flaked away. Georgios lit two candles and handed one to me, cramming his own into the red sand without any sign of reverence.

'He is buried under the plinth,' he said. 'It's an old, old grave.'

I asked him about the execution-stone, thinking that it must have dwindled away, but he said, 'That is buried here too. It lies over the body of Georgios.' He took some oil from a bottle which stood inside the plinth, and smeared a cross on my forehead. 'This is a custom. For strength of spirit.'

When we stepped out of the shrine we saw many women standing over a flower-heaped grave like a tribunal of blackbirds, the tears scouring down under their veils. The mother of a dead man was tearing her cheeks with her finger-nails and casting a handkerchief on and off her head with wide, despairing flurries of her arms.

We moved away to the brink of the burial-ground. I asked Georgios to translate what the woman was crying. 'My God, why have you done it? Where is my son? . . . O my son, why did you go away? And you the best of sons. Why . . .?' It was eerie and shatteringly sad, a long Semitic heartbreak from many centuries: the keening of David for Absalom. Self-control is not a part of the scheme for facing death. Mourning is the proper business of a woman, and she will carry it into old age with her, throwing up spidery gestures and sighs at the mention of a man dead thirty years, so compounded and self-perpetuating is the marriage of grief and ritual.

'It is ugly and useless,' said Georgios disgustedly. 'We are moving away from such things. Her son cannot hear what she is saying. Her saint will not help her.' The realities, according to Georgios, were beyond the sphere of St George. One gave the saint a candle out of habit once a year, and hung him up in bedrooms for good luck; but that was all. 'He did not protect any of these,' he said, nodding at the field of graves.

Often the Syrian Christians inset a tomb with a photograph of the dead, especially if a person died young and good-looking. Everywhere these faces stared out at us from the marble.

Georgios stopped at a casket surmounted by the busts of two brothers: comfortable, mustachioed men who looked like company directors. But Georgios said that they had been murdered out of jealousy while they were praying in the mountains. 'And over there is the tomb of a great man. He killed thousands of our enemies, this fellow. Then the Turks—God's curse on them! —hanged him in the Merjeh Square in 1916. He was one of the martyrs. The inscription reads "The tomb of the Arabic world —Razouk Saloum. . . ." You could write books about the people buried here.'

We neared the avenue of conifers again, treading on stale flowers, and passed the grave of a young girl, who Georgios said had committed suicide. 'Her family did not allow her to marry the man she loved. You see the epitaph? She wrote it herself before she died. There's romance for you!'

> I am sorry for the young,
> Because the sand goes over them.
> Janette, you came like the moon
> And you ended like a dream.
> I am very happy that I am near my God now.

We walked down the conifer avenue, the woman's voice following us in wintry skirls, growing more bird-like with distance.

*　　　*　　　*

Christianity drove underground the capricious gods of the Roman world. Jupiter-Haddad was tumbled at last out of his sanctuary in Damascus, which was rededicated to St John the Baptist. The greatest days of commerce were long since over, but the slow death of the western Roman Empire did not cripple the city. The Eastern Empire filled her with churches, and fifteen monasteries dotted her orchards. The streets glowed with the long-bodied, limestone churches of Byzantium. Sometimes their entrances were sheltered by a portico of columns, with capitals of saw-toothed leaves, or acanthus fronds oscillating in an imaginary wind. The finest churches were floored with simple mosaic. Sunlight seeped through their wooden lattices. A triple nave, like the nave of a Roman basilica, lent a gaunt grandeur to the larger churches, and a screen shielded the semi-circular sanctuary.

The streets began to lose the ornament of Rome, but houses perpetuated the old pattern, concealed behind plain walls and turned in jealously on beautiful courtyards.

The school of Damascus resounded with philosophic controversy, and its library shelves were filled with the works of the ancients. Close on the heels of the greater schools at Alexandria and Antioch, the theologians wrangled over the nature of Christ. The corridors reverberated to the dogma of the Monophysites who prevailed in the city, believing that His divine and human parts were inseparable. Between intervals in persecution rose the dissenting voices of Melkites, the bicker of Arians and Maronites, or the bleat of a Nestorian, spinning finer the tangle of dialectic.

The bishop of Damascus was second in Syria only to the patriarch of Antioch, and his school flourished illustriously until long after the Moslem conquest. Several of its alumni are still significant: Sophronius, who became bishop of Jerusalem; Andrew of Crete; St John Damascene.

Of all this activity scarcely a pediment or tessera remains. A few stones linger in the abandoned house of Naaman, and I found a pair of small Byzantine columns supporting the entrance to the latrines of the Sayat Mosque. A few years ago, workmen by the tomb of Saladin uncovered a mosaic portraying two deer stampeding among nonchalant birds, its colours resolved into subtle browns and pinks. These, with museum fragments, represent the city which even the stolid Pachymeres called 'most beautiful'.

But signs of early Christianity, which were smothered in Damascus, lingered in her archipelago of mountains. Villages like Maloula, forty miles north of the city, hugged their customs, incurious of change, and Christianity dwelt on ignored in the cloister of the Anti-Lebanon.

I woke one morning with a plan for bicycling to Maloula; but I kept thinking about the old man at Ashrafiyeh and the plaster round his broken ribs. His village did not lie too far from my route. If I reached it by midday, I might be in Maloula by nightfall.

When I arrived at the house I could not hear a sound. I looked through the window and saw that the room was empty. A hack-saw and a spade lay on the floor. The bed had gone. I decided to go to Refaiyeh in the main village. From a long way away I could see the courtyard of her home, where stood a manikin figure which I thought looked like the little girl Majida.

By the time I had reached the house she had vanished, but the door was open and I could hear voices.

I stepped inside and saw a pair of feet sticking out beyond the end of the bed. They were joined to the most spindly shanks I remember, but as I entered they swivelled to the ground and the old man's bright eyes were looking at me and he was grinning all over his face. 'Mr Colin! By God's mercy! Welcome! Welcome! You have made us lonely! Look at my back! I will be working again in a few weeks, God willing.'

They caricatured my remembrance of them: the old man more mischievous than before, Refaiyeh more quiet and lambent-eyed, Hayat breast-feeding her baby and fighting off the claims of unqualified feeders. Majida's hair had grown like a cotton-bush. Mustafa was making plans for me to meet everybody in the village. And now that their possessions had been united in one place the room looked gay, with rugs and goatskins on the floor.

That afternoon we walked a mile to irrigate the family orchards: a withered half-acre of apricot and apple trees, and a tangle of radishes. The hours were hot and peaceful, guiding the trickles along the crude earth passages, blocking them away from each tree after it had been fed. Now and again we heard a clatter of shot where Mustafa was hunting birds among the rocks. Later he returned, swinging starlings and robins which he was taking home to cook.

It was dusk by the time we started back for the house, and we ate in lantern-light. Refaiyeh had baked a heap of *makrouk* bread which was still steaming. Hayat was laughing softly to herself and making arrangements for me to marry a sixteen-year-old village girl, and installing my parents in her other house. And from time to time the old man would prise himself off the bed to show how well he could walk, each time filling me with a nervous wonder that his ghostly legs supported him.

I tried to smuggle bread to the macilent ginger cat. Every time it sidled near the tray somebody would thrash a stick against the floor and it would vanish. The children fought each other until one of them was ground into tears; then somebody would grab the stick and the flurry of their feet would subside among piles of blankets. Only Hayat could not use the stick. Even when provoked, she prodded about with it, smiling tenderly, and not even the cat took any notice.

Soon the room filled up with friends. I could remember all their faces and their dusty handshakes. We passed round some photographs which I had taken of the family. Each one elicited a gale of comments and laughter.

'Has the son of my wife's brother a squint? I did not know he had such a thing.'

'Salim would have been better upside down. . . .'

'Has Rouayda a squint, Hayat?'

'He squints when he's hungry.'

'By God, what a blessing! Mustafa is out of focus. . . .'

It was late before everyone had departed. I lay awake for a long time. It is a habit among the villagers to sleep with a light on: a leftover from more dangerous years. The old man muttered and scratched himself in his dreams, and two dogs wrangled for hours in the moonlight.

*   *   *

The road to Maloula was steep and deserted. It was midday before I bicycled up the pass of Abraham, where country women worked with their men in the stone quarries, heaving huge boulders from hand to hand; then along the gravestones of Maraba, past Tell and its hollow-trunked plane trees, and beneath the cave-temples of Menin.

After a while the hills unbent into a tableland filled only by scrub and grasshoppers and the obscene leap of locusts. The mountains become elusive here, the ranges of Helbon and Shurabin wasted and ethereal. At midday I reached a notice, standing alone in the desert: 'Couvent de Notre Dame de Seidnaya.' The convent stood in a shallow valley on a citadel of rock. Its white bricks erupted steeply from the stone, and hung towers and cloisters against the clouds. Its limestone blocks were of many ages: some so pale and sharp-cut that they might have been raised that morning; others bitter with sun and wind, like old warriors. Above them rose a clock-tower and a dome of faded silver.

Beneath the convent the village was white with churches, and a dignified Greek Catholic basilica stood at the foot of the rock. Tombs and chapels had been carved in the hills, and a sepulchre tunnelled under the convent; but over its entrance the sculptured saints had been worn into anonymity, and the cave was filled only by empty graves and rubbish.

It is said that the convent was built where Noah planted the first vine. The Byzantine account of its foundation dates it at A.D. 547, during the Persian wars. The emperor Justinian was seeking water for his soldiers, who were encamped near Damascus. He sighted a deer and pursued it to the summit of a great rock. As he drew his bow, he was startled by a torrent of light. The deer had changed to a woman dressed in white. 'You shall not kill me,' said The All-Holy One, 'but will build for me a church and a convent, here upon this rock.'* So Justinian raised for her the dazzling convent of Seidnaya, and installed his sister as its first Mother Superior.

I zigzagged up a maze of steps and stooped through a tiny entrance. This lowest part of the convent is Byzantine still: big, yellow blocks; columns set in the walls; flagstones pitted by generations of pious feet.

The Mother Superior lay on her divan beneath hair rugs, benevolently flourishing a fly-whisk. She talked fluent French, fixing me with intelligent and obscurely humorous eyes. There were about fifty nuns in the convent. . . . Greek Orthodox of course. . . . The village round the convent was mostly Christian, but there were five hundred Moslems where there had once been only three. . . . No, certainly not converts: migration and heavy breeding. . . . Everybody came to the convent—Christians, Moslems, Druses; and each year many were healed. If you lined up all the people cured at Seidnaya over the centuries, they might stretch back all the way to Damascus. . . .

A novice brought me yoghourt and olives in the refectory, and the late afternoon dissolved in indolence among the big, cool passageways of the convent. Such stillness is a luxury anywhere. Among Arabs, who care nothing for silence, it was a miracle. The sun fell angrily on roofs and domes, but the narrow courts were soft with jasmine and shadow. The nuns strode between chapel and refectory, only the swish of their black calico robes violating the quiet.

As the sun vanished below the high walls, I looked for the Mother Superior to say good-bye. When I found her, she offered me a room for the night in the convent.

'Sleep *here*?'

'Why, yes, of course. There is nowhere else.'

A nun led me up a stone stairway and unlocked an iron door. Beyond was a small, tiled room with an iron bed and a view over grey hills: Brother Colin's cell. I realised with a sense of comfort that I was surrounded by representations of people and

* 'Seidnaya' means, in Syriac, both 'Our Lady' and 'A Hunting Place'.

animals again. The Moslems, still haunted by idol-worship, avoid portraying them. But here the smooth faces of incurious saints smiled down from the church walls, and in the curtain over my window glided a lace swan.

I woke to hear the bells ringing for morning Eucharist. It was seven o'clock and the cocks were crowing in Seidnaya. I remembered that the Mother Superior had asked me to join them in prayer.

The church was almost empty of people. Spearheads of flame jutted from trays and lamps, and turned the iconostasis into a mansion of tarnished saints. The vacuous face of the Virgin and the prematurely adult features of the Holy Child looked down from the limestone walls.

The Mother Superior stood among elders, her furry black hood and shawl making her seem homespun and mole-like. Two novices chanted huskily from the lecterns on either side of the aisle, and from time to time a scarlet curtain was drawn back from the screen by an invisible hand, to reveal the *higumenos*, theatrical in blue and gold vestments, bowing and crossing himself emphatically.

The Orthodox service—portentous with the comings and goings of the priest and Sacrament—avoids the personalism of the Western church. Between God and men drifts an esoteric liturgy, brewed up—it almost seems—by the strange, exclamatory priest. The ceremony is performed in histrionic reverie, like the recitation of a magic spell. God hangs awful and unapproachable in a dome of smoke and half-light. His eyes are abstract and his benedictory hand blesses from a long way away.

A blind woman entered on the arm of a child and remained half-leaning against the pulpit. Then fifty orphans from the convent school pattered in, with a line of tiny, solemn-faced village girls dressed in black smocks and white collars. For a long time the priest shook incense round the church, the coals grating fiercely in their silver thurible. The chanting died away in a sad *glissando*. Many figures crossed themselves fumblingly in the dimness.

The procession of the Sacrament was faltering and leisurely. An ancient nun fell to the ground on her elbows, her creased hands curled upwards on the marble floor. The chanting began again, and lingered in the bowl of the dome among frescoed saints. '*Ye holy Apostles, plead before our Merciful God, that he would grant forgiveness for the frailties of our souls.*' The blind woman threw back her head and answered in a strong, stony voice. The nuns responded. She chanted on and on, crossing herself with uncanny precision at the same time as they did. Others had been cured of blindness at Seidnaya; perhaps the Holy Mother and her saint would look also on her. *'Thou shalt make me hear of joy and gladness: that the bones which thou hast broken may rejoice.'*

After the service the sisters ushered me into the sacristy. It was half-lit by candlelight, and lined by icons, many of them Byzantine, but immensely faded; here and there I could distinguish the hand of an obliterated saint, the stance of a horseman, the colour of a dress. Jewels glittered in the dimness and gold lanterns clustered the walls. The Mother Superior opened a small pair of silver doors behind the altar. She drew away festoons of wafery gold crosses and I saw, through an iron grille, the lid of a silver casket. It is said that the casket contains the first picture of the Virgin and Child painted by St Luke the Evangelist.* Mediaeval travellers wrote that the kisses and caresses of pilgrims had worn away all but a symptom of paint, but it is the treasure of the convent. Once its Virgin wept, and the Knights Templars sent back the tears to Europe, believing them to be magically possessed. The liquid was, and still is, sovereign against sterility and ophthalmia, and a phial hung in the stern of a boat would calm all tempests.

In the shadows the nuns were crying and kissing the icons. Two of the paintings were streaming fluid. On one of them the water rose directly from the eyes of the Virgin, which looked away, abstracted and languorous, into the candlelight. I accepted these tears without surprise. Syria is the country of miracle.

The Mother Superior smeared away some liquid from the ikon with a cloth and dabbed it against my forehead and eyelids murmuring 'Dieu vous garde', and on my wrists: 'Dieu vous donne la force, l'intelligence, la santé.'

Later she told me not to bicycle to Maloula as I intended, for there were only a few villages along the track, and they were Moslem. She smiled sadly at my remonstrances, sighed that she was afraid for me and gave me a medallion of St Luke's picture 'pour vous garder'. When I left her, she was swinging incense in the lady-chapel and the courtyards, keeping everything pure, everything holy.

* * *

* St Luke's works are legion. Four portraits are attributed to him by the Greek Orthodox Church, and many more by Roman Catholics.

Beyond Seidnaya a track skirted the Shurabin mountain and covered me with a fine white dust. To the west, extending into the haze, it seemed as if some primaeval Hadrian had built a wall across the lower slopes of Lebanon to hold back the desert; for along the top of the ridges an insurrection of rock dispersed the sand in cataracts beneath it, stretching into the distance, mile after mile, in bastions of cinnabar and pink.

I bicycled through a village whose people had locked themselves away from the noon sun. Eight miles later I saw a man riding a donkey on the skyline. Soon after, the village of Jubb 'adin peered down from the end of a gorge, and the road ran above a valley of mulberry and walnut trees. Maloula covered the mountainside beyond in a screen of domes, caves and white and mauve-blue houses.

The village was full of life and flowers. Buxom, open-faced women tramped along its paths, and water flowed down its broad street. The sheer crags behind it were riven on either side by outlandish ravines, cracks in the mountain from some diluvian miscarriage of nature. A Malouleen legend says that St Tekla, who had sat at the feet of St Paul, was fleeing from the fury of her pagan father when she found herself trapped before the solid mountain; but she prayed so ardently for safety that the cliffs split apart and let her through.

St Tekla's convent lay under a mull of the mountain on the northern side of the village. The church was modern, filled by unlovely paintings, but the convent foundation is said to be the oldest in the world. The saint is buried in a tiny chapel in a cave above, and Christians and Moslems alike come to take away the sacred water which drips from the ceiling. Sterile women swallow oil from the sanctuary lamp, and paralytics pray for two nights in the convent, before climbing up the steep stairway to drink the healing waters.

A few steps beyond the convent I reached St Tekla's pass, which winds through the limestone mountain for a quarter of a mile. Sometimes the gorge measured only a yard in width, while on each side the cliff climbed vertically for two hundred feet. Water trickled along its floor. At first the sun felt its way between the rocks and drenched my cheeks. Then the owl-light thickened and the bed of the cold stream narrowed to a labyrinth, whose sides might insensibly creak together again, a haunt of minotaurs.

I heard, with silvery distinctness, some villagers talking on the cliffs above me. I leant with my back to the rock and listened, for the natives of Maloula are among the last people on earth to speak Aramaic, the language of Christ. Five hundred years before His birth, it became the tongue of the whole Middle East, and the *lingua franca* of the Persian Empire. Now Arabic has almost obliterated it, and even the Aramaic of Maloula has suffered corruption.

By the time I reached the end of the gorge the villagers had gone away. I noticed an aqueduct running along its edge, and many shaft-graves sunk along fissures where the passage yawned open.

Above the gorge stands the monastery of Saint Sarkiss. Only a Greek Catholic priest, Father Theodor Abou-Hanna, lives there now, with a cellar-full of home-fermented wine. His monastery church is small and dignified, but pagan clouds lurk in the Christian sky: the lovely marble altar is shaped in a half-oval, reminiscent of the sacrificial tables of the Jews or the fertility symbols of Baalbek; SS. Serge and Bacchus gallop across an icon; Roman foundations line the crypt. The Byzantine cupola fell some unknown century past, but has been rebuilt in its former style.

Father Theodor pointed to a picture which hung alone in an alcove. 'This is the earliest copy of St Luke's first painting of the Virgin and Child,' he said. 'The original was stolen by Crusaders from the convent of Seidnaya, and taken to Rome. You can still see it in the Church of St Maria Maggiore. You know Seidnaya? The nuns still think they have the picture.' I remembered the weeping sisters and the Mother Superior. Father Theodor's Virgin was decorative, almost coy, too informal for an early Syrian painting even by a Greek freedman. I showed him my facsimile from the convent. 'Rubbish!' he grunted.

We sat in the Father's sitting-room with the head man of Maloula. He was a delightful old man, dressed in black *cheroual* and keffieh, and his Semitic features were classics of facial *mise en scène*: the ridges of his cheeks pouring down into triple jowls, his nose a monstrous, wind-pitted promontory, eyes like sudden bright lagoons.

I asked him if he would speak Aramaic for me. He smiled and looked confused. What should he say?

Anything.

So he began to speak, in deliberate tones, about the affairs of the village.

'Linguists call it Western Aramaic', muttered the priest. 'It's closely akin to Arabic. In fact any Syrian would understand a little.' This, I thought, must be why Arabic had destroyed Aramaic so easily. 'Our villagers all learn Aramaic; they take a pride in it, because it is the language of Christos. But it is only a dialect. Nobody can write Aramaic here. I'm trying to gather money to start a school for teaching it. If you have any friends with money. . . .'

The old man had finished speaking and was chewing figs. I asked him to say the Lord's Prayer. He looked uncertain again, then coughed and licked his lips. Each word disembarked with effort from his mouth. Like Arabic, it is not a language which simply happens; it is hard-working and agile, one sound singing from the tongue-tip, the next stirring down in the throat.

'Obo*ch* tee bishmo lyit kad dash ishma*ch* theyla malakoo tha*ch*. . . .' I can transcribe no more of the Lord's Prayer as it was first spoken, for here the old man's voice, steeped in mortification, faltered and died. He had forgotten the rest.

We stood on the terrace looking down at Maloula. It can not have changed much in the last two thousand years. Nor can the pale road from Seidnaya. A Byzantine monk might trudge to within sight of the dome of Saint Sarkiss before realising that he had stepped out of time. The undernourished animals and stunted crops would not surprise him, nor the shuttered villages. Beside him would stretch the ruptured hills of his fathers, and fields of red poppies, ancient symbols of eternal sleep.

6. The White Banner

... take heed and ere thou movest
Rashly against us learn
That still our banners go down white to battle
And home blood-red return.
Amr b. Kulthum's *Mu'allaqah*

ONE NIGHT EARLY in A.D. 632, Mahomet woke suddenly and called a slave to him, saying that he had received summons from the dead who lay in the graveyards of Medinah to pray for them. The two went out into the night to the cemetery, and after he had prayed, Mahomet said that soon he would die.

For some months he had been racked by head-pains and delirium. A Moslem army, poised to invade Syria, awaited his recovery, but soon afterwards he collapsed while trying to officiate at Friday Prayers. The people became alarmed, but he raised himself and addressed them: '. . . has any prophet before me lived forever, that ye think I would never leave you? . . . I return to him who sent me; . . . My life has been for your good; so will be my death.'

Later, believing him to be recovering, his companions left him with his favourite wife, Ayesha. He lay with his head in her lap. Now and again he weakly sprinkled his face with water. But soon he began to anticipate death, and asked that his slaves be freed and his money given to the poor.

At last, staring into the air above him, he gasped 'O Allah, be it so! Henceforth among the glorious host of paradise.'

Ayesha laid his head back upon the pillow, and Medinah, waking to her first screams, knew at once that the Prophet was dead.

*　　*　　*

There is a mosque near the Little Gate by the southern walls which was said to enshrine the body of Mahomet's beloved disciple, Abu Obeidah, who captured Damascus for Islam. Now that the tomb has vanished—nobody could tell me how—there is a single tangible evidence of the famous siege. Opposite the north-east palisade of Damascus, a peacock-green dome shines fiercely over the creases of plastered walls. A Moslem saint, called the Sheikh Arslan, is buried beneath it, and the grilles of its windows are so decked with the strips of rag tied to them by worshippers, that they have come to resemble dying creepers.

This is one of the quiet places of Damascus, precious for their scarcity. The Barada flows beneath the tomb, mephitic and oil-coloured, and the willow trees droop like tattered clothes.* A witch-hat minaret hangs over it with a mellow jauntiness, and chickens scratch among the graves of men who wished to be buried by the saint. A few twelfth-century arches which lean against the sacred place are labelled 'The Mosque of al-Walid', and here, it is said, the Moslem army, marching on Greek Damascus in A.D. 634, first fell on its tired knees and prayed.

The army numbered almost forty thousand men, and was commanded by Abu Obeidah and the vicious Khaled. The emperor Heraclius was licking his Persian wounds in Antioch. Hearing of Arab attacks to the south, he imagined them to be nomad raids and despatched five thousand men to strengthen the Damascus garrison. But soldiers on the city walls watched the Moslem force with mounting alarm. There came no groups of predatory horsemen, sifting through the farmhouses. Instead, threading along the orchards, marched bunched columns of soldiers, whose lance-heads glinted in hideous constellations which stretched far back into the desert.

Under the pens of Moslem chroniclers, who supply the only detailed accounts of the siege, Greek and Arab leaders attain Homeric stature, their triumphs or defeats governing every battle.† The Damascenes deployed into the trees with Roman discipline, and the Arabs charged them, throwing away their lives with a native sense of theatre, curveting in and out of the Greek lines until the glitter of their scimitars was extinguished.

Soon Damascus was tightly surrounded. Half the Moslem

---

* Damascene lore has it that a temple to Serapis once stood here, and later housed the grave of St Simeon Stylites, the Byzantine hermit who squatted for thirty years on a sixty-foot pillar in the desert. But as far as I can discover, the saint's body was taken in pomp to the Church of Constantine in Antioch, and there buried. The head was later carried about by the Roman armies in the East; an undignified substitute for the Imperial eagles.

† The Arab accounts of the siege are corrupt, but there is little else to go by. Scholars think it probable that Khaled captured the city in 635 and withdrew, and that Abu Obeidah recaptured it a year later.

army, under Abu Obeidah, camped near the walls on the west side by the Gate of Jupiter, while Khaled's forces sprawled along the River of Gold to the east. Damascene foray-parties rode back through the gates with half their saddles empty. They tried to bribe Khaled, but the Arabs were not only looking for plunder, and Khaled's replies were prefaced by a demand that the Greeks embrace the faith of a deceased Arab prophet.

The snows came to Lebanon and the Pleiades fell, but the besiegers remained. Heraclius, who had at last realised the danger to his Syrian provinces, sent an army of a hundred thousand from Antioch, but it was ignominiously routed.

A few months later a second force of seventy thousand Byzantines advanced more cautiously from the north. Under most of its helmets flickered the eyes of fresh recruits. The Moslems were veterans and instinctive warriors, but Khaled formed up two battalions of women, Amazons of the Hamzarite and Himiar tribes, who were used to handling bows and javelins, and who were ordered to slay any man who fled.

Werdan, the Greek commander, sent a messenger offering to discuss peace, but the messenger himself warned Khaled that ten Greeks would be posted in ambush near the meeting-place. After dark, ten Arabs set out into no-man's land. There they found the Greeks asleep, their swords under their heads, killed them and changed into their armour. The next morning Werdan rode out before his army, bedizened in gold and mounted on a white mule. Khaled trotted out to meet him. They dismounted and insulted one another, each certain of his position. Then Khaled drew his sword. Werdan, imagining all to be as he planned, did not move as the ten men in Greek armour rushed towards him.

The Damascene ranks watched the little band approach them, bearing a head on a lance, and thinking they saw the face of Khaled, they burst into rapturous shouts. But as the dust cleared and the party drew nearer they fell suddenly silent. The ensuing battle scattered the Greeks all over Syria. They limped into Caesarea, fled to Antioch, and a few thousand reached Damascus.

The Damascenes repaired the breaches and lined the battlements with catapults, and the first Arab assault fell back in shreds. But they were so closely surrounded that they could scarcely step from their gates, and Thomas, a son-in-law of the emperor Heraclius, had to steel them to a last counter-attack.

'Let no man sleep,' ordered Khaled, seeing the lights moving along the ramparts. 'We shall have rest enough after death. . . .' At dawn the bishop of Damascus raised the cross at the gate which is now called Bab Touma, the Gate of Thomas. As Thomas passed under it, he laid his hand on the Bible and prayed, 'If our faith be true, aid us, and deliver us not into the hands of its enemies.'*

In the battle he picked off many Moslem chiefs with his poison-tipped arrows, but the wife of one of his victims, a woman of the Himiar, shot him through the eye, and he was carried back into the city. After two days' fierce fighting, the Damascenes were again confined within their walls.

The fall of Damascus remains an enigma. Moslem tradition tells that the city surrendered to Abu Obeidah, who entered the Jupiter Gate in peace; while Khaled's men floated over the Barada on inflated water-skins and broke down the east gate from within. Arab historians delight in the improbable concept of Khaled, his black eagle banners shuddering over him, bursting into the Church of St Mary and finding there the meek Abu Obeidah in procession with priests and Islamic dignitaries. And the blood of John the Baptist was seen to bubble up through his tomb and flow in torrents through the sanctuary.

Abu Obeidah permitted Christians to leave the city and travel three days without molestation. Among those who left were Thomas and his wife, the emperor's daughter; and Eudocia, a heroine in the classical tradition. She had loved a young Syrian nobleman called Jonas, but her family did not favour the union. During the siege the lovers attempted to elope from Damascus by night, but Jonas was captured outside the Kaysan Gate. Eudocia, imagining him to have been executed as a Christian, took the veil; but he, in the hope of finding her after the city's fall, became a Moslem and joined the besieging forces.

The terms granted to the Christians infuriated Khaled. After the three days' grace, he and Jonas galloped in pursuit of the refugees with four thousand horsemen, disguised as Christian Arabs. For miles they crossed the desert, following hoofmarks and discarded baggage, until the tracks entered the Lebanese mountains and petered out in glens and defiles, which disturbed the Arabs. Their horses cast their shoes and at dusk the echoes of their hoofbeats sounded like the shout of djinns. There were

* From Washington Irving's *Mahomet and his Successors*, taken from the Arab historians.

rumours of a Byzantine army in the mountains. But Jonas, desperate for his fugitive bride, urged them on through secret passes.

They came upon the Christians in a mountain meadow, and descended on them in bands through the hills. Even the women of the Greeks fought—among them the daughter of the emperor, whom Arab historians portray as a woman of extraordinary beauty, crowned with a diadem of jewels. Only one Christian escaped, and brought to Constantinople the news of the disaster. Thomas was killed, and Eudocia stabbed herself at the feet of Jonas. Khaled recompensed him with the daughter of the emperor of Byzantium, but a few days later she was released to a deputation from her father. So Jonas renounced earthly love and became a devout Moslem, falling like a hero at the Battle of Yermouk. And Allah, he declared in a vision, rewarded his worldly labours with seventy black-eyed houris, more dazzling than the sun.

*　　*　　*

The Arabs settled in Damascus with awe, delight and suspicion. They left the delicate machinery of her government undisturbed, and although their aristocracy imposed itself on Greek bureaucrats and Aramean peasants, the city for a while retained her classical-Syrian features.

Yet the whole Mediterranean world was changing. The dispirited Byzantines were thrust back against the Taurus mountains by armies half their size. Antioch herself fell. Egypt was overrun with ridiculous ease, and to the east the palaces of the Persian kings were turned into mosques and stables. The Arabs' religious zeal was abetted by a hunger for fertile land and plunder, and desert warriors, seeing in the distance the orchards of Damascus, hailed her as the place which Mahomet had promised to his faithful, where cool waters flow through an eternal shade.

While foreign conquests were shearing Byzantium and Persia, domestic quarrels rankled among the Arabs. But tribal vendettas were no longer confined to deserts or obscure Arabian cities. Now they stretched across half civilization, and the world which had been brought together by the personality of Mahomet, and rounded out by the saintliness and vigour of his brief-lived followers, began to disintegrate.

The caliphate (the word 'caliph' simply meant 'successor') was laid open to the scheming of the two great aristocratic tribes of the Koreish—the powerful Ommayad, and the Hashimite, the clan of the Prophet. The natural successor to the caliphate was Ali, the Hashimite cousin and son-in-law of Mahomet. But after the intrigues of the election in Medinah, it was a disarmingly feeble old Ommayad, Osman, who was made master of Islam.

Ommayad favourites were insinuated into the government of provinces. The caliph's foster brother, whom Mahomet had outlawed, was given command of Egypt. His half-brother, who had once spat in the Prophet's face, was made governor of Kufah in Mesopotamia, and the Ommayad leader Muawiya had already secured a hold on Syria by being appointed governor in Damascus.

Ali's supporters grew impatient and fanatic. In April 655, Osman's palace in Medinah was besieged by rebels. They murdered the eighty-two-year-old caliph as he prayed over his Koran, which tumbled from his hands at the verse: 'And if they believe even as ye believe, then are they rightly guided. But if they turn away, then are they in schism, and Allah will be thy protection against them. . . .'

Ali now became the fourth caliph of Islam, and the palace at Medinah was cluttered with nervous provincial governors tendering him their oaths. But at Damascus, the Ommayad governor Muawiya climbed into the pulpit of the city mosque and brandished the severed hand and the blood-stained shirt of Osman, shouting for vengeance.

Ali marched north against Muawiya and met him on the battlefield of Siffin, west of Rakka. After three days' fighting, the Syrians, on the verge of flight, fixed leaves from the Koran to the tips of their lances and demanded the arbitration of Allah. Both armies shouted for the judgement of God. Ali returned to Kufah, and Muawiya to Damascus, and after a prolonged debate, in which the Syrians won a moral victory, nothing was resolved.

Two years later Ali was murdered while on his way to public prayer, which has been a favourite moment for Moslem assassinations ever since. After his death, his followers only grew more bitter and devoted, and they still form the great dissenting sect of Islam—the Shia—with their strongholds of Iran and Iraq. To them, Ali is almost as holy as Mahomet—a true *futawah*, the Galahad and Lancelot of Islam. His wisdom and eloquence have grown proverbial, and for his bravery he was called 'The Lion of God'. The Arab failing of petty vindictiveness was foreign to him, his humanity extending to his deathbed as he insisted on a painless execution for his murderer.

With the lapse of years, the rather stout, mild Ali of history, whose qualities had been those of a faithful follower rather than a leader of men, became almost a god. He grew from the light of Allah in the middle finger of Adam, and his name is inscribed eternally across the sky. He brought men back from the dead, mastered alchemy, and slew eighty thousand djinns. Trees and rocks bowed to him, and in war Gabriel attended him at his right hand, and the angel of death walked before him.

Ali's burial-place was kept secret through the dangerous years of Ommayad supremacy. In 791 Haroun al-Rashid is supposed to have stumbled on it at al-Najaf in Mesopotamia. Every wealthy Shia wished to be buried there. Horse-carts, heaped with the pious dead, shambled to his sanctuary from distant provinces. Marble graves blossomed round it. And cars still speed along the Euphrates every day, carrying the coffins of Tehran businessmen who have spent their lives at conferences and oil disputes, but who wished to be buried as their fathers were.

Yet in 661 Ali was not yet a god. Muawiya proclaimed himself caliph and chose as his capital the ancient city of Damascus. The Shia in Iraq favoured Hasan, Ali's eldest son, but Muawiya descended on him with an army and extracted an oath of allegiance from him in a letter which typifies his politic frankness: 'I admit that because of thy blood relationship thou art more entitled to this high office than myself. And if I were sure of thy greater ability to fulfil the duties involved, I would unhesitatingly swear allegiance to thee. Now then, ask what thou wilt.' And he enclosed a sheet of paper, signed only with his name, by which Hasan secured a huge revenue and retired to Medinah. Eight years later Hasan died there with the nickname *mitlaq*, 'the great divorcer', having taken and dismissed a hundred wives.

Thus, only a few years after the disciples of Mahomet had governed Islam with puritanism, their office fell to the irreverent rule of the Damascus caliphs. Muawiya showed many of the traits of the dynasty he founded, but the quality of *hilm*—of subtle, unruffled statesmanship which the Arabs particularly admire—was his to a high degree. 'I apply not my sword, where my lash suffices,' he remarked, 'nor my lash, where my tongue is enough. And even if there be but one hair binding me to my fellow-men, I do not let it break. When they pull, I loosen; and if they loosen, I pull.'

He would bestow lavish gifts on potential enemies, murmuring to his bemused friends that 'A war costs infinitely more', and he humoured his parliament with the pretence that he was only a first among equals. By patronising the poets, who were the journalists of the time, he forged himself a flattering public image, and in his hands the circulation of a barbed verse became a delicate instrument for calling some wilful emir to order.

Insult and verbal lampoon enlivened his court.* His friends jested with him about his name, which meant 'a barking bitch', addressed him as the brother of a bastard (which was true) and accused him of having outsize buttocks. So long as his detractors were not powerful, the caliph's face flickered into an indulgent smile.

He greeted religious dogma with benevolent scepticism. Perhaps he had lived too close to the 'Companions of the Prophet' in Arabia to have respect for the saintliness of men's motives. But he knew how to turn piety to his own use. After secretly poisoning Ali's governor in Egypt with a draught of honey, he announced it from the pulpit as the vengeance of Allah, as God's answer to the prayers of the people of Damascus. 'The Almighty God,' one of his lieutenants was heard to mutter, 'has armies of honey.'

Yet Muawiya performed his religious duties punctiliously. Every Friday, according to the custom, he climbed into the pulpit of the Great Mosque, dressed in white, and preached a sermon; but to the fury of the orthodox, he would address the congregation while seated, sighing that he was too old and pot-bellied to stand. On other matters he gave way. An outcry ensued when he intended carrying the pulpit of the Prophet from Medinah to Damascus. He had never wished to remove it, he remarked in laconic vein, only to treat it for wood-worm.

Muawiya's reign lasted twenty years—almost the longest the caliphate ever knew. In the east his armies despoiled wandering Turkish tribes, and carried the white banner of Ommaya into the remotest provinces of Persia. To the west they groped along the southern Mediterranean shores towards the Pillars of

---

* An impudent spirit animated Damascene official life throughout Ommayad times. Even Walid I, most powerful of caliphs, was not free from it. While reading out the Koran from the pulpit of the Great Mosque one day, he arrived at the verse 'O that death had made an end of me'; and some worthy standing at the foot of the pulpit exclaimed, 'By God, I would it had.'

Hercules, and with the help of Graeco-Syrian sailors they mastered the sea and drove the tried Byzantine fleets against the Hellespont.

The supporters of the Ommayads, many of Yemenite stock, crowded into Damascus around the Roman citadel. Gradually the Christians and Jews were pressed into the eastern sectors which they occupy today, and the original population was outnumbered. Fifty years after Damascus had become the world's first city, two hundred thousand Moslems lived within her walls.

Yet Christians still held most of the minor administrative posts and comprised the bulk of the doctors, lawyers and scribes. Three generations of a Christian family organised the caliph's finance ministry and were paymasters general to the army. The third was the last 'father of the church', St John Damascene, whose hymns are sung throughout Christendom, and who was the childhood friend of Yezid, the second Ommayad caliph.

Yezid assumed his father's throne by right of heredity, for Muawiya had demanded oaths of allegiance to his son six months before his own death. Thereafter the caliph's brother or his noblest-born son succeeded him, and the assent of the 'whole body of the faithful', which had verified the early elections, became less than a formality.

Yezid belonged to the desert. His mother was a Christian Bedouin and had reared him as a warrior. Muawiya had divorced her for writing rude verses, expressing her preference for a desert tent over the mansions of Damascus.

> And more than any lubbard fat
> I love a Bedouin cavalier.

In the ancient feud between the settled and the nomadic tribes, Ommayad sympathy lay with the nomads, and the desert became the accustomed training-ground for the princes of the royal house. Here they grew hardy and resourceful, and learnt an Arabic untainted by the Aramaicisms of the city. When they arrived at the court in Damascus, stifled with audiences and paper decisions, their minds wandered to hunting and the desert. At every opportunity they abandoned their green-paved palace. The streets were patterned with the clopping of delicate-looking horses and the prance of salukis, groomed silky as damask, their feet bangled in gold. Falcons stooped from the wrists of courtiers, and on the croup of the caliph's saddle, sinuous and superb, sat a cheetah. Behind trotted half the court of the capital, booted

and robed for the chase, their baggage flowing in noisy filaments towards the Gate of the Moon.

Then this half-Bedouin court—surely one of the most eccentric and romantic in history—would vanish into the wastes for
weeks at a time, and there pitch its tents. The falcons spiralled
through a mercilessly blue sky. Some speck, some faintest
shuffle in the sands, would fix their clarion gaze. Then the lords
and ministers of Damascus, in a tide of streaming robes and
flowing hair, would gallop over the stone-dappled ground,
leaping fissures and wheeling through sharp rocks. Far ahead
of them, the salukis coursed over terrain which might have
snapped the legs of a greyhound. The gazelle was always
fleeter, but the falcon had been trained to attack it by circling
and swooping, until the deer became exhausted through jinking,
and the tireless salukis closed on its flexuous course like ribbons
of light.*

The Ommayads built pleasure-castles in the desert, to which
they would resort on the slightest excuse, eluding the plagues
and intense heat of Damascus in summer. Their gates and tur-
rets still scatter the Syrian wastes. Archways bend freakishly
out of the sand, and limestone walls, convoluted with towers
like the Romans built, enclose a flood of green in spring. For a
few extraordinary years the palaces of Qasr el-Hair, Mshatta
and Qusayr 'Amra touched the desert night with music and
singing. Terra-cotta dancing-girls leant from their entablatures
with prurient smiles, and their audience halls were frescoed with
cupids and undisguised Greek muses.

Beside these expeditions into the desert, the nobles revelled
in the old Persian game of polo (*jukan*), in occasional cock-fights
and in horse-racing. (One of the later caliphs held a race in
which four thousand horses took part.) And they matched their
love of sport with a passion for poetry and music, several of the
caliphs priding themselves on their skill with the lute or the
rabeyby.†

* The salukis were often bred so that their colour blended with the terrain
in which they hunted. The Arab, traditionally contemptuous of dogs, admires
the saluki, whose history is ancient and glorious. An ivory saluki-head from
Egypt has been dated at 5000 B.C. Mummified salukis have been discovered
in the Theban Tombs of the Kings; the early Greeks knew them and the
Crusaders emulated the Arabs in hunting with them. Their pedigrees are
chanted in the tents at night, and so handed down by memory.
† The European lute is descendant from the Arabic *'ud* (hence the name).
The *rabeyby* is a single-stringed viol, a plaintively expressive instrument
still popular with the Arabs and Berbers.

Arab historians, who are violently anti-Ommayad, colour the Damascene court in the shades of their own imaginations; but the truth was horrifying enough to orthodox contemporaries. Not thirty years after the Koran had forbidden wine, the joyous glug of the Taif grape could be heard in the palaces of the faithful. Yezid, who was a compulsive poet and musician, alternated his artistic pleasures with drinking-bouts on the Roman scale. He came to be known as 'Yezid of the Wines'. After a day of audiences, ministerial decisions and perhaps a solemn-faced appearance in the Great Mosque, the doors of the palace would close on his disconsolate figure.

Muffled music floated out under the stars. There was a swish of ostrich-feather fans, and the odours of Hadramut rose in a night balm. A lute-player, brought from Medinah at great expense, might excite the company into sudden applause, or a story-teller recount the deeds of south Arabian heroes, stressing their passions with the eloquence of his hands. As the night paled, the aesthetic sense gave way to drunken rapture, the incense stagnant, the goblets dry. Then the nobles would grope back to their harems, surrounded by slaves and preceded by lantern-bearers, and assume their duties next morning like solemnities incarnate.

Some of the caliphs were almost perpetually drunk, but for most of them debauches were well-regulated. The fourth Ommayad caliph only caroused once a month, and then cleansed himself with an emetic in the Roman manner, so that he appeared fresh the next morning. His son drank every other day, and Hisham, one of the most austere rulers, restricted his bouts to once a week 'after the divine service'.

Yezid's favourite drinking-companion was a monkey called Abu Qais, whom he pretended was an old Jew who had been metamorphosed for his sins. The monkey would clamber round his shoulders and drink out of his cup, and he claimed it as the most interesting of his friends:

> My drinking-companion is Abu Qais for he is
> ingenious and intelligent
> When the wit of the company stands mute.

The monkey followed Yezid everywhere, dressed as a divine to annoy his religious ministers. Once, when crowds were clustering round his palace to watch the caliph ride out, he sent the monkey out instead, perched on a horse. Finally he decided that Abu Qais must take part in a race. It was dressed in costly

black silks and a multi-coloured hat, and a donkey was specially
trained to carry it. But the donkey butted it and broke its neck.
Yezid, inconsolable, gave the monkey a state funeral and it was
buried with all Moslem solemnity; but drinking-bouts were
never the same again.

7. Armies of Honey

Never has lord of our race died
in his bed. On the blades of swords
flows our blood, and our blood flows
only over sword-blades.

El Samaoual

THERE WAS A dark side to the reign of Yezid I. Husain,
the youngest son of Ali, rose against him and was slaughtered
with a mere two hundred men at the battle of Kerbela. Even now
the Shia mourn Husain's death in an annual passion-play, and in
remoter parts of Iran and Iraq gash themselves with knives in a
frenzy of anger and love.

Yezid, it is said, wept when his followers brought the head
back to Damascus, and cried: 'Ill-luck to you! I should have
been pleased with your obedience without the murder of al-
Husain. . . .'

A second rebellion, under the rival caliph, Ibn Zubayr, disrupted the Hejaz, but Yezid quickly sent an expedition to crush
it. An apocryphal story describes the Ommayads rampaging
through the holy city of Medinah for three days; Korans are
trampled underfoot, Companions of the Prophet slaughtered and
Koreishite women ravished. In fact the Syrians received the
surrender of Medinah, but marched on immediately to Mecca,
hoping to quench the last of the rebellion by killing Ibn Zubayr,
who had taken refuge there, believing its precincts to be inviolable. But the Syrians catapulted rocks against the holy Kaabah,
which fell in flames (probably lit by the besieged) and split the
sacred black stone into three parts—a blasphemy without equal
in the annals of Islam.

They raised the siege of Mecca suddenly. Yezid of the Wines,
at the age of thirty-nine, had died in the desert near Palmyra,
where he was buried.

He was succeeded by confusion. His sons were incompetent
for the caliphate and it seemed as if the Ommayad power would
be extinguished. Ibn Zubayr was acknowledged by the Hejaz, by
Iraq, and even by a part of Syria. Then Merwan, the doyen of
the Ommayads, crushed his Syrian rivals in a battle on the edge
of the Damascus oasis. But he had married Yezid's wife in the

hope of reconciling her to his usurpation of her son, and one night, as he lay beside her, she took a pillow and smothered him.

The throne of Merwan fell to his son, 'Abd-al-Malik, who had cultivated a reputation for piety; but when the news of his succession reached him, he laid aside his Koran with the words, 'This is where you and I part.' He inherited the family energy and tolerance, a love of poetry and a flair for mixing intrigue with outspokenness. 'Please to remember,' he growled at the people of Medinah, 'that I am not the weak caliph [Osman], nor the flattering caliph [Muawiya], nor the stupid caliph [Yezid], and that I shall not cajole this nation except with the sword. . . .'

For his stinginess he earned the nickname 'The Sweat of the Stone', but the family sense of theatre was extravagant in him. He once lured one of his rivals, Amr ibn Said, into his palace for a parley. After a while he ordered Amr's sword to be removed; for one surely did not wear a sword among friends? Then he mentioned that in the days of their enmity he had sworn to keep Amr in a cage—and a caliph could not break his word. Would Amr mind if he momentarily fulfilled his promise? A cage was produced and Amr was put in it, before the caliph killed him.*

More dangerous enemies were disrupting the empire of 'Abd-al-Malik, and he chose as his punitive instrument the general al-Hajjaj, who has become a bogy for Arab school-children. (Hajjaj was, curiously, an ex-schoolmaster, and propounded a thesis that the caliph was more important than the angels.) He cornered the anti-caliph, Ibn Zubayr, in Mecca. Once more the catapulted boulders looped out of the hills, and crashed through the roofs of the sacred city. Ibn Zubayr's followers, weak with famine, slipped away.

'My friends are deserting me,' he said to his Bedouin mother, 'and my enemies are offering me good terms of surrender. What do you advise me to do?'

She answered: 'To die.'

'But if the Syrians take my body, I fear they will avenge themselves upon it.'

'And what of that? Does the slaughtered sheep suffer, then, if she be skinned?'

* This, in the reign of a just and intelligent caliph, is the only reliable instance of pure treachery. He had already granted Amr a deed of pardon, which he demanded from Amr's widow; but she retorted, 'It is in the grave with my husband so he can accuse thee before God thereby.'

Ibn Zubayr's fears were just. His head was paraded at Medinah and sent to Damascus,* and despite the pleas of his mother his body was nailed upside down on a gibbet—the first crucifixion recorded in Islam—and buried in a Jewish cemetery.

Al-Hajjaj restored the Hejaz to order, before the caliph directed him against Iraq, which was rumbling with discontent again. He pressed across the desert from Medinah to Kufah with a handful of men, and arrived unexpectedly one day at the dawn prayer. Lifting his turban from over his brows, he addressed the astonished people:

I am he who scattereth darkness and climbeth summits.
As I lift the turban from my face, ye will know me.

'O people of al-Kufah. Certain am I that I see heads ripe for cutting, and verily I am the man to do it. Methinks I see blood flowing between the turbans and the beards. . . .'

Invidious historians have mushroomed his monstrosities into 120,000 murders, and have made room in his prisons for 50,000 men and 30,000 women. But whatever the harsh schoolmaster may have done, he coupled it with irrigation schemes and financial reforms; and the people were silenced.

'Abd-al-Malik died in the desert in 705, leaving his throne to Walid, his son, whom Arab historians describe as 'short in stature with a running nose, proud, and self-conceited in his gait'. The Damascenes, however, think of him as the greatest of their caliphs, for behind his childishly arrogant façade seethed tireless energy, and he was, for his time, humane and just. He built prodigiously—mosques, schools, hospitals, forts, roads, wells; he introduced allowances for orphans, and asylums for lepers and lunatics, 'gave every lame person a servant and every blind person a leader'.

Poetry, which to nomad tribes had been an archive of thought and history, revived under the Ommayads. A pleiade of Bedouin poets attended their court. Men still wrote and thought with freedom, and found stimulus in their pagan past. The desert's frugality of word and strength of idea were unimpaired; even the verses quoted at the death of 'Abd-al-Malik were those of a fifth-century nomad:

* The posting of heads to the caliph was a conclusive proof of deeds done, and the parading of them a warning to would-be rebels. In the royal palace there was a special storehouse for skulls, which were kept in baskets, scrupulously labelled.

Now am I, that have passed the space of ninety years,
   as though
   on a day I had stripped off the cheek-straps of my
   bride; . . .
Yea, I perish: but of Time I cannot kill even a night;
   and that
   which I slay of him amounts not even to a thread for
   stringing beads upon.
I am slain by looking forward to day and night, and
   looking onward to year after year.*

By the end of the Damascus caliphate, the desert inspiration
was wilting. Poetry was being throttled by the courtly game
of flattery, which promoted only extravagant metaphor. Perhaps this was inevitable. The language of Arabia, virile, taut
and emphatic, was bastardised by the languages of the conquered. In urban surroundings the memories of the desert faded
and the old songs took on an archaic ring. Finally came Islam,
to strangle speculative thinking.

Yet for a few decades the Ommayads nourished a poetry which
remembered the desert, but applied itself to civilisation. The
general al-Farazdaq and the Christian poet Jarir attacked each
other in libellous verse, and Damascene armies whiled away the
night-watches with recitations of al-Akhtal and Jamil. When al-
Farazdaq rebelled against his caliph, he even couched his threats
in poetry, swearing to

. . . destroy Damascus the town built by *jins*,
Who brought the stones from snow-clad mountains.

Soldiers—hardened by forty winters perhaps, who had shed
Greek blood or slaughtered Berbers in the desert—squatted
round the camp-fires at night and surrendered to words and
cadences; for they inherited the spirit of their Bedouin past,
in which three things could bless a tribe: the birth of a son, the
foaling of a mare, and the emergence of a poet.

The caliph Walid encountered a poet with an artistry of his
own. His wife, while in Mecca for her pilgrimage, fell in love
with Waddah, an Arabian gallant who had made the verse-
plagued beauties of Mecca blush behind their lattices. Waddah
followed the caliph's wife back to Damascus, and composed some
famous verses to her. Soon he gained access to her bedchamber
and whenever she feared a visitor, she would hide him in her
mother-of-pearl-encrusted wardrobe.

* *Poems of 'Amr B. Qamī'ah.* Trs. Sir Charles Lyall.

By now Waddah had become a well-known figure, accustomed to celebrating his own daring and the strength of his love in poetry:

> . . . She answered: The waves separate us.
> I rejoined: Indeed! I swim well.
> She answered: My seven brothers guard me.
> I replied: I am a hero full of courage.
> She said: Between us is a lion.
> I replied: I, too, am a lion when in anger.
> She said: Consider! God sees us.
> I answered: God is forgiving and merciful.
> She replied: I warned thee in vain! but
> Be ready, when the guards are asleep,
> Remain here, like the dew of the night, when no one
>   is watching or looking after.

Rumours of his wife's paramour reached Walid, and one day he visited her at an unaccustomed hour. For a while he talked affably to his wife, who remained perfectly composed. Then he asked if she would allow him to choose a piece of furniture in the room for himself. Of course, she replied, everything she had was his. He looked pensively round before his eyes strayed to the wardrobe. He ordered his servants to take it to his apartments, but he did not open the doors. He had a deep hole dug in the floor of his room.

'Something came to my ears,' he said. 'Is it true? I bury with this wardrobe for ever the object of my suspicion. . . . If, however, the report is false we merely bury a wooden wardrobe.' So the chest was thrust into the ground and a bright carpet spread over it. The incident was never mentioned again, and the poet of Mecca vanished from Damascus.

*　　*　　*

The Damascenes remember Walid as the builder of their Great Mosque, which is perhaps the most interesting Islamic building in the world. The Moslems classify it, after Mecca, Medinah and the Dome of the Rock at Jerusalem, as the holiest place on earth.

During the reign of Walid I, Moslem immigrants and converts overflowed the early mosques at the hour of prayer, while the diminished Christian community trickled into the enormous Church of St John. The covenant of Khaled had promised the

Christians the tenure of their churches, but Walid suddenly repudiated this and announced that he would pull down the Church of St John and build a mosque inside the Roman *temenos.* *

'O Commander of the Faithful,' the bishops warned him, 'we find in our books that whosoever shall demolish this church will go mad.'

'And I am very willing to be mad with God's inspiration,' replied the caliph, 'therefore no one shall demolish it before me,' and he seized an axe and brought the uppermost stone of the chancel crashing down onto the Altar of Martyrs. The emirs hacked down every Christian edifice inside the square, until only the enormous rectangle of Roman walls remained.

The mosque which Walid built in its place became the most magnificent in Islam. Christians from the schools of Damascus provided much of the skilled labour. Twelve thousand craftsmen, assert the Moslem traditions, were brought from Byzantium (the estimates mushroom with the years) and some records of Egyptian artisans still exist. Men may even have been summoned from India, Persia and West Africa.

Ancient columns were brought from near-by towns and a rage for lead-collecting began over half the empire, to provide a light, durable roof. The caliph's men pilfered leaden coffins from tombs, until they were terrified by a corpse whose head fell to the ground and foamed blood at the mouth. 'This,' adds the chronicler darkly, 'is said to have been the burial-place of King Saul.'

As the convoys wound their way back to Damascus, they encountered an old woman who refused to sell her lead except for its weight in silver; but when Walid consented, even at this price, she replied: 'Now that you have agreed to my proposal . . . I give the weight as an offering unto God, to serve for the roof of the mosque.' So they stamped on her quota of lead the words: 'This is God's.'

It is claimed that the people remonstrated at Walid's extravagance—he had even tried to build a chapel of pure gold. But

* For a long time, mainly due to the eleventh-century historian Ibn Asakir, it was believed that the building had been partitioned between Moslems and Christians, since half Damascus was said to have been taken by force and half by treaty. (There were similar arrangements at Cordoba and Homs.) But scholars now consider this a myth, invented to justify Walid's seizure of the church, and that the Moslems used only a mud-built structure against the south wall of the church courtyard.

he replied by emptying the entire treasury into the mosque, so that one half of the building was cut off from the other by a pyramid of gold and silver. This alone was found to suffice for three years' public expenditure. 'O people of Damascus!' he exhorted. 'You boast among men of four things; of your air, of your water, of your cheerfulness, and of your gracefulness. Would that you would add to these a fifth, and become of the number of those who praise God, and are liberal in his service.'

Walid eventually spent seven years' income on the mosque—about five and a half million pounds sterling—as well as many shiploads of gold and silver from Cyprus. And when the accounts came in, laden on eighteen camels, he refused to look at them, for 'Verily we have spent this for God and we will make no account of it.'

The caliph's Greek architects built the mosque sanctuary in three naves against one wall of the Roman courtyard. Six hundred lanterns hung from chains of pure gold, and the courtyard was paved in white marble. Variegated marble panels, which only the Ommayads used in Islam, sheathed the Roman walls for twice the reach of a man. Above them, all round the courtyard, glittered some twenty thousand square feet of tesserae—the greatest mosaic composition ever conceived.

The capitals of the columns were coated in gold, and the *mihrab* was described by Ibn Jubayr as the most wonderful in Islam. Golden vines writhed around the arches, and the dome was likened to an eagle in flight.* In mediaeval times the Roman *temenos* was still enclosed by its outer wall, which was ringed by a gallery filled with jewellers, book-binders and craftsmen of enamelled glassware. Public notaries sat by the Jairun Gate and astrologers squatted on its steps. The mosque vestibule was surrounded by perfumers' shops; paper merchants had their quarter under the painted ceilings of the inner yard, and bread-sellers clustered round the Door of Increase.

In the western minaret dwelt ascetics and holy men. Its lower cells accommodated a multitude of pious unknowns, but as storey chased storey into the sky, they grew oblivious and attenuated as storks. Hair became more matted, limbs more fakir-like, until the topmost chambers housed skin-and-bone hermits, who must have thought the moon itself would one day drift into their fingers.

* The dome was said to be the head of the eagle, the aisle walls its wings. But the simile was invented to explain a misunderstood term of the Greek architects.

At sunset the reading of the Abundance of God was given in a mosque in which men sat dense as ants under the glimmer of the mosaics. 'We have given you abundance. Pray to your Lord and sacrifice to Him. He that hates you shall remain childless.' And the six hundred golden-chained flames filled the hall with their incredible twilight, and burnt in Titian sheens against the polished black pillars of the arcades.

The mosque became invested with wonderful properties. It contained the first Koran, handwritten by the caliph Osman, and a curtained sanctuary where Ayesha had lived and recounted the sayings of Mahomet. One prayer spoken here, swore a holy man, was worth thirty thousand said elsewhere, and here men will continue to worship God for forty days after the end of the world. In one of the towers was kept a pair of beryls called 'The Little Ones', which glowed in the dark after the candles were put out, and every night, after the great doors were closed, St George came there to pray. Talismans left in the mosque from Christian times preserved its precincts from all harmful creatures. No spiders or swallows ever entered. No pigeons or sparrows nested there.

In 1069 the Great Mosque was gutted by fire during a fight between Damascenes and the mercenary troops of the Fatimids. It was many years in rebuilding. In 1150 a mechanical clock was installed in the vestibule of the east gate. Every hour one or other of two brass falcons would drop a weight from its beak into a vase, and a shutter would close over one of twelve openings in the small arches above them. As each hour passed at night, a lantern inside the clock would be turned round by a water device, and would shed its light through a circlet of red glass.

The gate where it was placed had been called the Bab Jairun, after a palace built upon columns by the Greeks. Now it came to be known as Bab as-Sâ'ât, the Gate of the Clock, and for a few years filled the night with its soft orbs, and the day with its tinkles.

In 1400 the Mongols set up mangonels in the courtyard to throw rocks at the citadel, and fire damaged the porticoes. Minor fires gnawed at the original work, until in 1893 the whole prayer-hall collapsed in a conflagration which Moslems claimed as their retribution from God for allowing Christians to work on the mosque, and which Christians blamed on the carelessness of Moslem renovators.

As I approached the great wall and pushed at the bronze

repoussé doors, it seemed absurd to hope that tragedies and restorations had not effaced every sign of early work. From the Gate of the Post in the west, I stared through a vestibule of porphyry pillars into four hundred feet of stone-paved emptiness. On three sides the supine paleness of the floor was chastened by honey-coloured colonnades, fifty feet high from the pavement to their eaves, On the fourth stretched the prayer-sanctuary. I was enclosed by a circus of unfamiliar textures and tones: green and gold mosaic among the arches; the peach, grey and fawn veins of the porphyry; the cobalt and cream of poorly-worked Turkish faience. In a pillar by the porch was set a marble panel in grey and broken white, like the snow ridges of a mountain.

The western colonnade is perhaps the most beautiful in all Islam. Its upper arcade of demi-circular arches and colonettes is borne on a portico whose mosaics depict acanthus leaves curling from fluted vases or Cornucopiae. The blocks of the Roman outer wall are exposed, but chafed with holes where marble panels were once jointed in. Along its upper courses stretches a fragment of mosaic, measuring a hundred and twelve feet and reaching twenty-six feet up the wall. The colours, mellowed by twelve hundred years, are exquisite: a panorama in greens and blues on a field of gold which sometimes glitters fiercely from the Byzantine habit of inclining the tesserae in the plaster at an angle of thirty-five degrees; and banded top and bottom by rosettes and flower petals.

Perspective and proportion are abandoned for a child-like harmony. A river glides in deepening shades of blue beneath tall bridges, fingered by waterfalls. Superb trees rise from its banks. Towers and rotundas and houses with curved roofs spiral into the sky on filaments of green or a wisp of columns; and lamps of mother-of-pearl glint in Doric galleries.

This unpeopled scene is the nearest the Syrians came to portraying living beings in their mosques, but it is a sylphine picture. The river, the orchards and the houses are follies from a halcyon time. People interpret them variously, for the fantasies are built of detailed substance: here and there a narrow dome, or the cockleshell sanctuary of a Byzantine church, or the pent roofs and window colonettes of the pre-Islamic houses. Scholars have discerned Chinese temples here, Ptolemaic pavilions, Byzantine mansions and motifs from Pompeiian frescoes. Some say the scene was influenced by patterns from the Palace of Constantine on the Bosphorous. Yet the Damascenes believe it represents the Barada valley, and point to familiar trees. It is, perhaps, a return to the landscape of innocence, the lost paradise; for even after its facets have been explained, its essence is indecipherable, like notes for musical instruments no longer known.

On the east wall the mosaic momentarily breaks out again, but it has vanished from the long north portico. I walked along it through an arcade of shadows, by broken bands of Kufic script. Its pillars are lightly moulded. The shallowness of their carving and the tone of the plaster obscurely evoke the reliefs of ancient Egypt. Inscriptions proclaim a forgotten Seljuk sultan: '. . . the most great king of kings, the sovereign of the Arabs and Persians, majesty of the religion of God . . . defender of the worshippers of God, buttress of the caliph of God. . . .'

Behind a window lies the tomb of a nephew of Saladin, whose installation in the mosque so angered the Damascenes that they were only frightened into silence when one of their leaders was hanged from its bars. Beyond, I reached the eastern arcade, and looked back into the courtyard at the octagonal fountain, lying midway (runs the tale) between Istanbul and Mecca. In the west an elegant pavilion, raised on stunted Corinthian columns, used to house the state treasury. Now it is filled with pigeons, for the Christian talismans which guarded the mosque from birds and insects were burnt in the fire of 1069.

The towers of the Great Mosque were the first minarets in Islam. From them the earliest muezzins shouted into the dawn. But now the call to prayer is pre-recorded from the songs of professional muezzins in Mecca or Cairo, and loudspeakers hang unashamed from half the city mosques. In the south-east of the Great Mosque shines the Tower of Jesus, crowned with the sudden grace of a pencil minaret. On its summit, say pious Moslems, Christ will alight at the Last Day, dispense judgement to the city and condemn its Jews and Christians to hell.*

In the west is an Egyptian minaret, filigreed in stone, patterned with basalt and ringed with lights at dusk; and from the north wall rises the Minaret of the Bride, the oldest of them all, from whose pinnacle a beacon was relayed to Cairo when Mongol armies arrived on the Euphrates. Sometimes, at midday, you may hear a lilting chorus from its balustrades: lovely, archaic sounds. You look up and see old men, frosted in beards, who chant and lean out over the railing like courtiers in a Persian miniature.

* An older tradition links Christ's descent to a 'White Minaret' near the Roman Charki Gate.

Work on the mosque never ceases. Mosaicists are covering the transept wall with designs reconstructed from the eighth-century remnants in the west portico. The art of subtle dyes, which the ancients knew, has been lost, and the inspiration of the first artists—their grace and rhythm—is irrecoverable. But their patterns are being meticulously reproduced in colours almost as dazzling as the old: the revel of cobalt and cadmium, and manganese in tones of amethyst and ebon.

I asked how long it would be before the whole mosque was covered as before. Nobody knew. 'Perhaps a hundred years. But our grandchildren, or their children—they will see it.'

The prayer-hall stretches along the south wall of the court-yard. The double arcade of columns which strides through its gloom accentuates its length, and it is filled with the mutter-chant of prayers, like water running through a cave. A triple row of chandeliers gives it an outlandish, Viennese luxury. It is already full of paradox: the sickly blue of the roof; the intricately inlaid *mihrab*; exquisite window arabesques and marble pulpit; loudspeakers; transept ceilings in the old, rich paint; the swing of grandfatherly pendulums.

In the east stand a marble font and two short pillars, remnants from the Christian church. Their sides are dappled by sea-fossils and the flattened ghost of shells, millennia old, which the Syrians cite as proof of the Great Flood. Near by stands a domed tomb. Men's fingers polish and caress it, and women linger there and kiss its grille. Moslems claim that it is the tomb of St John the Baptist, and that his head lies in a silver coffer in the crypt. Herod, they say, sent the head of the Baptist to Damascus so that Roman officers could bear witness to the execution. Mediaeval chroniclers record that when the Church of St John was demolished, a cave was discovered beneath it. Walid was called, and entered the mosque at midnight with candle-bearers. In the cave he found three interlocking shrines, which enclosed a casket, and in the casket lay the head of a man 'still covered with skin and hair, without the least change'.*

Christians frequently told me that the tomb had no connection with the Baptist, but contained the body of St John Damascene. 'A head keep its flesh? *Yegallek Allah!* Any rational man

* Damascenes still occasionally swear by the head of *Yahya* (John). Aleppo, Venice and several other towns are rival keepers of the Baptist's head, but there is little chance that any of the claims are true. Probably the head was buried in Herod's dungeon-fortress of Machaerus in the Moab hills.

knows that it's the Damascene lying there. The Moslems tried to remove the body, but they could not.'

It was dark when I left the prayer-hall. Lamps were glowing round the courtyard and along the gates. The place does not appear to be dedicated to any god, but to age itself, and silence. It wears the patchwork styles of Islam like a loose cloak. Back to back with the *mihrab* is preserved an ancient triple entrance, mewed up in the wall. Over the lintel of its middle gate are still carved in Greek the words: 'Thy kingdom, O Christ, is an everlasting kingdom, and thy dominion endureth throughout all generations.'

*   *   *

The glory of Damascus ran to her head like the forbidden wine. Her dominions were larger than the Roman Empire had ever been. Arab arms penetrated to the banks of the Indus and the marches of China, and Afghanistan was overrun by a force so magnificently accoutred that men called it the 'army of peacocks'. Northward into Russia, Moslem armies probed beyond the Jaxartes, burnt Zoroastrian fire-temples and broke up the Buddhist idols of Samarkand. And in 715, in the courtyard of the Great Mosque, Walid received homage from four hundred of the captive Visigothic royalty of Spain, their crowns still fixed in their flaxen hair, who laid at his feet the gem-encrusted altar of Toledo Cathedral.

Excursions against Byzantium occurred twice yearly. For a few months raiding-parties foraged among the uplands of Asia Minor, then descended into the Syrian desert before the passes of the Taurus were throttled by snow. In 668 the Arabs besieged Constantinople herself, occupied the Cyzicus peninsula for seven years and filled the Sea of Marmara with grappling warships. Constantinople was saved by Greek fire, whose inventor, Callinicus, had defected to Byzantium from Damascus.* The fire seemed almost supernatural; it could be shot from

---

* It may be that Greek fire was known in Damascus long after its secret was considered lost. In 1190, while the Crusaders were besieging Acre, they used three enormous wooden towers which the Saracen naphtha-throwers were unable to destroy (the towers were faced with raw hides, soaked in wine and vinegar). A 'common soldier of Damascus' volunteered to demolish them, and asked for certain materials—what they were remains unknown— which he boiled in naphtha. These were lit in cauldrons and flung against the towers, which exploded in flames and burnt to the earth.

a fortress wall or the prow of a galley and would even burn along the surface of the sea. Theophanes recorded that of eighteen hundred Arab ships only five returned safely to Syria.

In Damascus, an Arab influx dominated the old population. Arab blood was a condition of aristocracy. It became a fetish. It was rumoured that only an Arab woman could conceive after the age of fifty, only a Koreishite woman after sixty. And it was important that the caliph be a pure Arab. Yezid III was the first caliph born of a foreign mother, and there were murmurs and insults even though she came of the royal house of Persia. Conversion to Islam was discouraged. Converts had to become clients, *mawali*, to an Arabian tribe, but they were never regarded as equals, for their inferiority did not run in their beliefs but in their veins. 'Three things only stop prayer,' ran a saying, 'The passing by of an ass, a dog, or a client.' They occupied, with the Christians and Jews, the clerical and professional jobs which were the pith of government, and they soon formed dissatisfied strata of society throughout the empire.

Christians and Jews paid special taxes and were barred from military service, but generally they were tolerated, and preserved their own systems of justice since Moslem law, inseparable from sacred belief, was not equipped to judge them. Omar II was the only Ommayad to force humiliating conditions on the Christians, whom he ordered to relinquish public office, wear distinctive clothes, and ride without saddles.

The slave market was the most extravagant of its day. The caliph received slaves as tribute and passed them on to his favourite emirs, who might own as many as a thousand each. But a girl who had borne her master a child could not be sold or given away, and her sons would be counted free subjects. Slowly this undermined the ascendancy of Arab blood, for in half a century the city was filled with men whose fathers were Koreishites of revered lineage, but whose mothers were Turkish tribeswomen, Circassian princesses or Greek fishwives.

Yet Damascus became an Arab city very quickly. In the time of 'Abd-al-Malik the first stable Islamic mint was founded. The *denarius aurens* became the Arabic dinar, drachmas were turned into dirhem and Koranic texts effaced the urbane visages of Byzantine emperors. More significantly, Arabic superseded Greek as the language of government. Rich in a vocabulary suited to sharp observation, the tongue betrays the people: its syntax simple, catering poorly for abstract thought, and supplying only two tenses for the delineation of time.

The city's outer aspect began to change too. Muawiya built only the royal palace—a building of green marbles and painted ceilings, now vanished. But by the end of Walid's reign, Graeco-Syrian architects had transformed Damascus. Yezid of the Wines cut a new canal for the Barada so that it irrigated his private lands and enriched the southern orchards, and soon the river system was developed until all through the city the sounds of water never died.

In his palace the caliph sat through audiences which grew more pompous as his grip on the empire slackened. Cross-legged, among gold cushions, he pondered the claims of suppliants, while his paternal relatives on his right, and his maternal relatives on his left, muttered and confabulated and grouped themselves in attitudes of graceful ennui. Around them stood lawyers and secretaries, guild-masters, poets and a plethora of minor officials. At the private audiences—the *majlis khas*—the relatives were permitted to sit on small chairs around the caliph, who would take the opportunity to dress in radiant brocades.

Eunuchs and elaborately-organized harems were almost unknown. They were learnt from the courts of Byzantium and Persia, and the Ommayads only adopted them fully a few years before their caliphate fell. Arab ladies were not yet regarded as ornaments for the eyes of their husbands alone. In public they walked veiled, for this was the custom before the time of Mahomet, but in their houses they entertained guests with dignity. The wife of the formidable 'Abd-al-Malik gently ruled him. One Ommayad princess owned her own stables and took part in horse-racing. Another, the daughter of Muawiya, was courted by a poet in public verse. Muawiya, with tolerant common sense, told the poet that he would negotiate his marriage to any woman in Mecca. The match was made and the lyrics ceased; but the romance caught the fancy of the Damascenes and there is still a grave which is pointed out as that of the princess.

The caliphs loved best the arts which the Arabs had brought with them from the Hejaz. Ignoring the puritan ministry of Mahomet, they summoned up the spirits of an older Arabia, the disgraced muses of poetry and singing, the gods of love and wine. In building, painting, astronomy, medicine, philosophy, they learnt from their subject races, and the Damascus caliphate, when it fell, passed on to Baghdad the germs of new culture. Here on the Tigris, amid the pomps and prostrations of a Persia-orientated court, the works of the Greeks were studied, developed and embalmed in Arabic compilations which survived throughout the Near East and Andalucia against the second dawn of Europe.

In the reign of Walid, Damascus touched her meridian. The city was as beautiful as the poets described her. For a moment the feuding tribes were held in a perfect balance, and the paradise which Adam had sold for an apple was resurrected with the riches of half the world.

8. The Poet Dies

Oh Damascus the verdant, mayest
thou be spared from perdition, what
has clothed thy boughs in blackest
dye?
  She replied, 'I have forsaken my
beloved people—and for grief have I
put on this mourning attire.'

Muhyi al-din al-Qalanisi

THE EMPIRE OF the Ommayads, from its birth to its destruction, was never as strong as it seemed. There was no hope that in a few generations their crimes would be forgotten. The Arabs are poorly equipped for forgiving, and the enemies of Ommaya, even now, are bitter and sometimes fanatical, though the dynasty has been dead twelve hundred years.

The sect of Shia, the followers of Ali, typify this centuries-long stasis of thought, and in parts of Iraq men talk as if the blood of Kerbela were still wet on the ground. Shia shrines exist even in Damascus, and are pervaded by the mystique of a lost cause.

Eastward through the orchards, where the olives give way to starveling walnut trees, a green dome hangs over a courtyard and a mausoleum. It is believed that it covers the body of 'Our Lady of Zeinab', daughter of Ali and granddaughter of Mahomet. Inside, the shrine is spacious and full of light. The floors are paved in marble and porphyry, covered in a wine-red film of Persian carpets.

I saw many people ambulating round the grave, and was told that they were Shia. I had only imagined the Shia armoured and fanatic among the hill-forts of Persia; but these were suave businessmen in black suits, and sloe-eyed peasant girls kissing the bars of the sepulchre.

The sarcophagus rests behind a fence of silver bars—an intricate and beautiful casket, inlaid with ivory and subtly-toned marble. Over it is set a gold crown, with an inscription which says simply: 'Welcome to Zeinab.' Above it flies a Persian dome of peacock blue and gold, for the building is the work of

Iranians, who are ardent Shia. Birds and animals, which Syrians rarely portray, have stolen into the motifs of carpets, and the strangeness of the place is completed by gilded clocks and chandeliers, conjuring some Parisian salon, unaccountably filled with Bedouin.

The Shia congregate wherever a member of Mahomet's family is thought to be buried. One of their holiest shrines lies behind the east portico of the Great Ommayad Mosque itself. A painted wooden cage encloses the coffin of the son of Husain, and for a single day after the battle of Kerbela, the head of his father was laid in a recess now bordered with silver and marble. In a room beyond, two caskets stand behind bars. One, covered by a radiance of blue silk, contains a strand of Mahomet's hair. The other, draped in green, keeps the head of the beloved Husain.*

In the cemetery of the Bab Saghir the Shia pray at many tombs. The most frequented is a double-domed mausoleum, where I saw several Iraqis pressing their faces against the glass doors. I waited until they had gone, but I found the building locked. A woman appeared, wearing a purple-flowered dress, and behind her sauntered a train of tiny, nonchalant girls, all in purple-flowered dresses. The woman dangled a fistful of keys. After she had unlocked the doors, she stood outside the tomb to see if anyone was watching. Then she beckoned me inside and down into a marble-paved crypt. 'This is the grave of a great-granddaughter of Mahomet, Husain's daughter,' she said. On top of the coffin were plastic pots, artificial flowers, and money left by pilgrims. The walnut-wood sarcophagus was carved with angular and dignified Kufic letters interwoven with flowers and stems, and an inscription on the western panel read: 'This is the tomb of Sukeina, daughter of al-Husain. . . .' But the inscription is probably false, for the coffin and the tradition date from mediaeval times. The spirited Sukeina, celebrated for her many marriages and for the beauty of her hair, died in Medinah and was buried there.

These cherished tombs are all enigmas. Near by, under a silver dome, I saw a fine stone sarcophagus which may enclose the body of another descendant of Mahomet. Some of the Shia believe it to be the grave of Fatima, the daughter of Mahomet and wife of Ali—a strange, melancholy woman. But a script, like a jungle of superb musical notes, reads: 'This is the tomb of

* This may be legend. Arab historians say that the head was buried at Kerbela, which is now an awesome Shia shrine.

Fatima, daughter of Ahmed, daughter of al-Husain, that God be satisfied with her!'

The Saghir graveyard is full of the monuments of Companions of the Prophet and of martyrs hanged by the Turks. It has been a burial-ground since the time of the first caliphs. For fifty acres the fields blanch with marble leaves and flowers. The clay mounds are humped very high and set close together, the tombstones tall and tapering. Only the squat huts of family mausoleums and the graves of wealthy men, meshed in wrought iron, variegate the whiteness; and all day, black-clothed women chatter over the mounds, lisp the Koran and reshuffle the myrtle boughs.

As I left the tomb of Fatima at dusk, they were straggling home with empty picnic-bags, and a beggar stumbled after me on crutches, brushing down the branches from the headstones. '*Backsheesh!*'

I stopped by a green dome, which pushed up against the twilight over a tomb of limestone and basalt. Inside, under a canopied coffin, rests Bilal the Abyssinian, Mahomet's muezzin, the first man to call the faithful to prayer.

Even now, as if in salutation, voices welled up along the edge of dusk: first a long-drawn, musical sigh from the mosque of al-Mouradiye, and a muffled answer from the al-Jarrah. Then, in an underbreath of melody, the gossamer-voices chimed in from all over the city, rising in splinters of sad sound, falling tenuously away.

> Allah akbar
> ashhad an la ilah illa -llah. . . .

Every sunset the phrases are bandied between the minarets of the city; the tenor near the Palace of Justice is buttressed by a deep-toned, passionless exhortation from the Mameluke tower by the Street Called Straight; elaborate cries issue from the loud-speaker of the Tingiz, and all the pre-recorded voices of Mecca and Cairo and Jerusalem fill the air with grace-notes and roulades.

It seemed to me, standing by the tomb of the first muezzin, as if the singing had started from here. But the cries, which sound so frail, never die. Soon they would follow the death of the sun up the villages of the Barada valley.

> God is great
> There is no God but God. . . .

Ashrafiyeh, Huseiniyeh and Fijeh would take up the call, and from a hamlet in the hills above Bessima the voice of a Caruso among muezzins threads down the valley on a legato of silver.

Northward, the harmonies steal into Anti-Lebanon, infiltrate the foothills of Antioch and force the Cilician Gates. From pink-roofed mosques the cry is thrown among the wooded steeples of the Taurus, disseminates through Anatolia and bursts over the minarets and chestnut trees of Istanbul. For a moment it is lost in the clamour of Bosphorous fishermen, and fades away where the Golden Horn dies a muddy death at Eyüp. Then, turning back in the red steps of the sun, it vaults the Iron Curtain and mingles with goat-bells in Bulgaria, insinuates itself among the mosques of southern Yugoslavia, until it overlaps the night.

Westward the voices move towards the Pillars of Hercules, hover round Mecca and Medinah like the playing of flutes, and purl over the rice-fields of the Nile. Already men bow to prayer on caïques in the Arabian Sea, and the last *suras* are being intoned through the mosques of East Africa. From Libya to Tunis the message springs into the crenellated villages of Berber tribes-men, and scales in redundant echoes the peaks of the High Atlas. Westward again, from the tiled towers of Rabat and Marra-kech, Moorish voices peter out against the deaf waves of the Atlantic. . . .

'*Backsheesh!*' The beggar had caught up with me at last. But in my mind the cries had already reached Brazil, where a faith-ful member of some Syrian community was groping for his prayer-mat with a Portuguese oath. Black Moslems were turn-ing their blunt faces to the east, and the call was flitting from Indonesian isle to isle, taken up by a hybrid mosque in Singapore, thrown from the bunion cupolas of Lahore to the domes of Isfahan. . . .

'*Backsheesh! Backsheesh!*' I handed him a larger coin than I had intended. 'O how generous art thou, God!'

It was almost night.

*   *   *

The Shia were the first to undermine Ommayad supremacy, and their accounts of the dynasty still cloud its true character. From the moment the house of Ommaya fell, historians grabbed for their quills in vengeful joy. Ommayad eccentricities were accen-tuated into monstrosities, and countless anecdotes choked their history.

Yet there is something pleasing in the way those tolerant, sybaritic rulers took their royal road to destruction, banked round by the fanaticism of the Shia, the bitterness of vendetta-haunted tribes, the hatred of the orthodox and the rebellion of half their empire. The judgement of modern historians has swung a little in their favour, not only recognising them as clement and broad-minded men, but also, in the main, as intelligent rulers.

It is said that the tone of each reign could be gauged by every-day conversation in the streets of the capital. In Walid's time men spoke of building projects, in Omar's of religion, in Suleiman's of women and good living. Suleiman succeeded to his brother Walid, and his caliphate was a happy time for Damascus. From scattered sketches he emerges as an eloquent, handsome, courteous man, a glutton, and such a lover of silks that he asked to be buried in them. He reigned only two and a half years, dying of indigestion after consuming seventy pomegranates, a lamb, six fowls and many pounds of currants.

Omar, his cousin, succeeded him. He sits in the Ommayad pantheon like a misplaced seraph—pious, ascetic and rather bigoted. A fragile, beautiful man, he bore on his forehead the mark of a horse's hoof, and it had been long predicted that such a ruler would govern the world with justice and peace. He was horrified even at the luxury of the Great Mosque, melted down the six hundred golden lamp-chains for public use and asked his wife to surrender her jewellery and bridal gifts to the treasury.

His clothes were so patched that new petitioners at his court would often mistake one of his followers for the caliph. 'I have forty dinars and two dresses,' he remarked to the poet Jarir, as he refused him an exorbitant pension, 'one of which I wear while the other is being washed. I will share them with you, though, Allah knows, I have more need of them than you.' Jarir declined the offer. 'Had you not done so,' replied Omar, 'I confess that you would have inconvenienced me greatly.'

Historians say that he was poisoned at the instigation of his less seraphic relatives. He died at the age of thirty-nine, and not even the Shia have found ill to say of him. 'Give your bribe money to the treasury,' he said to the slave who had poisoned him, 'and go away where nobody can see you.' As he was laid in his grave, runs a tradition, a paper blew down on him, inscribed by a beautiful hand, and conferred on him immunity from hell.

Yezid II, a son of 'Abd-al-Malik, succeeded to an empire

fragmenting into war again. He was a handsome, portly man, like his brother Suleiman, engrossed in courtly pleasures. The songs of Arabia so intoxicated him that he would leap into the air during a recital and dance until he swooned away out of sheer ecstasy and crashed into the arms of his attendants. His love for his slave-girl Habbaba exceeded all else. He had bought her in Mecca for four thousand pieces of gold. Suleiman, who was then caliph, had been annoyed and returned the girl to her merchant, but when Yezid ascended the throne his wife enquired of him: 'Is there yet any one thing in the world, my love, left thee to desire?'

Yezid replied: 'Habbaba.'

His wife brought the girl from Egypt, adorned her as a bride, and hid her behind a curtain. She repeated her question to Yezid, and on receiving the expected answer, drew back the curtain and departed.

For months Yezid closed himself away with Habbaba, refusing to allow in her presence anything offensive to her. Then, in a garden in Palestine, he playfully threw a pomegranate seed into her mouth. She choked and immediately died. For three days Yezid clung to her, kissing her lips, 'until she began to stink when he ordered her to be buried. . . .' One of his brothers represented him at the funeral, afraid that the people would take offence if they saw the state of the caliph over the death of a slave. But Yezid had Habbaba disinterred, and himself died of grief a few days later at Arbela. Attendants carried his body back to Damascus, and buried him between the Little Gate and the Jabiya.

Yezid's brother Hisham reigned for nineteen years. He was intelligent and just, but his provinces were chronically rebellious and the Ommayads were increasingly regarded as the usurpers and slayers of the family of the Prophet. During his reign the sect of Abbassids set up a rival line of caliphs stemming from Abbas, an uncle of the Prophet, gained the support of the Shia and honeycombed the eastern empire of the Ommayads with their secret societies.

When Hisham died of quinsy in 743, Walid II, his nephew and heir,* had already vanished into the desert with a court of his own. 'Leave unto me the slim Salma,' he wrote to his uncle, 'wine and the female singers and the cup: this is all that I desire,

* Hisham's son and original heir was killed in a hunting accident, to which his father commented stoically: 'I brought him up for the caliphate and he pursues a fox!'

As long as I pass my days in the sandy valley of Alij
   in the embrace of Salma, I need no more.
Take your throne, may God never protect it!
I give not a farthing for it.'

On hearing of Hisham's death he lapsed into indecent jubilation, rode to Damascus to be invested, then disappeared into the
sands again. In his desert palace he sat enthroned like a mimesis
of the intemperate traits in his family. Such visitors as reached
him would glimpse an indolent shape in robes of saffron and
green, lolling behind a gauze curtain. The veil would only be
ripped aside if some singer had especially pleased him. Then the
ruler of half the world would hurl himself into a swimming-tank
of wine, sucking in the juice like an elephant, or empty twenty
stoops of it until it coursed down his perfumed robes like blood.

He was cultivated and artistic in a way which none of his
ancestors had approached: an acclaimed poet, steeped in letters,
and a fine musician. But his irreligion ran riot. He sent a
drunken concubine to lead the faithful in prayer, dressed in his
clothes; he hung up a Koran for target practice and shot it to
pieces with arrows, and he planned a debauch on the roof of the
holy Kaabah itself. The Damascenes rose against him for his
heresy, for 'doing the forbidden things publicly'; and after a
year's reign he was slain while hunting in the Palmyrene desert,
meeting his end with valour.

Of Yezid III, the cousin who came after him, little is known
except that he was pious and that the half-year of his reign was
filled with battles. His brother Ibrahim followed him, but in
three months he had been overthrown by Merwan, an illegiti-
mate grandson of 'Abd-al-Malik and son of a Kurdish slave-
girl.

Merwan reigned four years before the black banners of the
Abbassids streamed over Khorasan. Then every city in the
eastern empire erupted in arms, and the Shia rose to vengeance.
The Yemenites in Syria, whose swords had once kept the caliphs
on their thrones, were disaffected, and rebelled. All through
Persia and Iraq the Ommayad garrisons were slaughtered. Their
armies broke behind them without the loosing of an arrow.

Merwan faced his enemies at last on the battlefield of Zâb,
east of the Tigris. The Abbassids, clothed from head to foot in
black in symbolic mourning for Husain, their horses and
camels draped in black cloth, moved forward in silence. An instant before battle, a flock of ravens flew over the Syrians and

settled on the banners of the Abbassids: an ill omen. But the battle was long and ferocious, and only when they saw the riderless horse of Merwan, which had escaped its groom, did the Syrians break.

Now only Damascus stood firm, but on 26th April 750, the fourteenth day of Ramadhan, she was stormed by a force of eighty thousand. Months later, Merwan was surrounded while taking refuge in a Coptic church, and died groaning 'Now is our dynasty passed!'

The hunt for the surviving Ommayads was eager and relentless. In Basra their bodies were cast to the dogs. They were massacred in the holy cities, which bore them no love. In Palestine eighty of them were slaughtered at a feast of amnesty, after which the Abbassids spread a carpet over their bodies and resumed their meal. Almost alone, a grandson of Hisham escaped. For five years he fled across North Africa to Spain, where he founded the glorious kingdom of Cordoba and perpetuated there the government and arts of Syria.

Even the tombs of the caliphs, except for that of Omar, were broken open and emptied, but their bodies had already decomposed. Only the corpse of Hisham remained strangely well-preserved; it was lashed with whips, burnt and thrown to the wind.

In the life-span of a man, Damascus had risen from a provincial centre of commerce to the capital of the world's greatest empire, and fallen again to her former state. It is recorded that the Abbassids did as they pleased with her. The walls were demolished stone by stone and the marble and golden palaces wrecked. The Great Mosque became a stable for war-horses.

I have wondered if some soldiers ever dug under the paving of the royal palace. Perhaps, in the Arabs' everlasting lust for hidden treasure, they uncovered the mother-of-pearl wardrobe of the wife of Walid I. And there, in a chrysalis of bones and rotting cloth, lay the Ommayads' legacy to the Abbassids: a dead poet.

*   *   *

I was told that the grave of Muawiya survived in Damascus. Why the Abbassids should have spared it, nobody knows. Perhaps it was due to the manner of his burial, for he asked to be interred in a robe which Mahomet had given to him, and that the pared finger-nails of the Prophet be ground down and sprinkled on his eyes and mouth.

Somewhere near the Street Called Straight, I lost my sense of direction in a coil of lanes. At the end of a blind alley I reached a gaunt, domed monument of rough-faced stone. This is the official tomb of Muawiya. It is almost gutted, and rubble is piled to its windows. Through the grille I saw a hump of baked clay, like the grave of any peasant.

Yet this grave could scarcely be authentic, for the Arab historians insist that Muawiya was buried in the Bab Saghir graveyard. The guardians of this cemetery, who know all the tombs as if they were their children, point to a clay hut in the burial-grounds as the true sepulchre. Inside it, three shrubs in paint-pots adorn a limestone sarcophagus; the rest of the hovel is monopolised by the bed of the caretaker, who is convinced that he sleeps by the side of the greatest of the caliphs.

Yezid of the Wines was also believed to have lain in the Bab Saghir, and Shia from Persia and Iraq made a pious habit of casting rocks at his grave. The sepulchre splintered and broke. It came to be marked only by their heaps of stones. A few years ago, men searching among the rubble found nothing at all; the tomb and the body had been pulverised out of being. Now nobody even remembers the place where it lay.

*　　*　　*

Sometimes I think that the Ommayads must have perpetuated their spirit in Damascus with a certain hauteur, a love of good things, a pearly skin of decadence. The people of Aleppo, her rival and sister-city in the north, accuse the Damascenes of laziness. 'The Aleppans speak more like men, the Damascenes like women' runs a saying, but the Damascenes attribute this to the *gaucherie* of the Aleppans, and say that they are bourgeois and have no sense of style.

The difference is ostensibly one of manner, and it is a wonderful thing, in the silence of a Damascus alley, to watch two portly men of substance approach each other like freighters on a canal.

'*Salâm 'alêkum.*' The words are the essence of the timber and clay walls about them. 'Peace be on you.'

'And on you be peace.' Deft, iconic smiles.

'May your day be ever prosperous.'

'May your day be prosperous and blessed.'

The grace of the Damascenes is still spoken of, their love of fine clothes and food, their passion for music. It is probably absurd to ascribe this spirit to the pleasure-loving eighth-century caliphs, yet if they returned to the East tomorrow, I believe that Damascus would be the city of their choice still.

Some cities oust or smother their past. Damascus lives in hers. Her marble courtyards stir the mind to strange fancies, for once, in the curious hush near the tomb of Saladin, I glimpsed the end of a joyous procession: Yezid of the Wines had passed by in his silken hunting dress, cheetah at pommel, hawk on wrist; and behind him, picking out the fleas from under its divine garments, rode the infernal monkey. . . .

* * *

'In Syria we don't like England,' said the barber, deftly whisking a few stray hairs away with his razor. 'But of course English *people* are different. We like them. All the same, you will have to be careful. . . .' I had asked him if he knew of anybody I might stay with in Damascus.

'There is one person,' he said, and I saw in the mirror that his face had stretched into a grin. 'A man called Bahena. A very good man. I will ask him if he will have you. If he will not, then Damascus is only fit for dung-beetles. *Kull en-nas hum ikhwan.*'

So I stayed in Damascus with the Bahena family. We lived in a rough-walled flat on the Street Called Straight, overshadowed by a Turkish mansion with wooden pilasters and shutters. It stood in the middle of the Christian quarter and I would often wake up to the sound of bells, and look out over hundreds of roof-railings to the cupola of the Greek Orthodox church.

Elias Bahena was a cabinet-maker, and one of the largest Syrians I ever saw. His head dissolved into a bull neck and steeply sloping shoulders, and he carried his gigantic hands carefully, like mallets. Once a week, he would squeeze into the shower-room and then stride about in his underclothes, his stomach and massive hips tapering to the shrunken calves peculiar to the Arabs.

His wife, Umm-Toni, 'Mother-of-Toni', was 'like a chicken' beside him. Toni was her eldest son, and although she hated him, Arabic custom expects a woman to be known as the mother of her first boy. Umm-Toni was good-looking, with a long, smiling face and dark-brown hair. Every evening this hair was combed by Rahda, her ten-year-old daughter, who would perch on cushions while Umm-Toni, seated in a chair, muttered and grimaced at each tug of the comb. Then, sprayed with Lebanese perfumes, she would loll on the family divan in attitudes of Circean languor, and await the return of Elias.

There were six children and Rahda dominated them all. She was less like a little girl than an enormous smile, set up on spindly legs. The grin started diffidently at one corner of her mouth, puckered her cheeks and eyes in giggling wreaths and finally confounded her whole face in an explosion of merriment. Her hilarity pervaded the three-roomed flat, and was only silenced when her grandparents shuffled in during the evening and everybody sat in the hall and drank sweet coffee. Umm-Toni's mother was heavily-built and dignified. Her father scarcely ever spoke, only appeared to listen for something with a wonderful pair of bat-ears.

Other relatives would enter the house with pieces of news which sounded to me like murders or revolutions. Like the Bedouin, the poorer Syrians shout instead of talk. After several minutes I would understand a sentence and would realise that only a bargain was being discussed, or the price of tangerines. Umm-Toni's eyebrows would shoot up and down during these holocausts, her eyes screw into worried dots, her mouth drop and breathe out: 'Eh! . . . Wullah! . . . Leha! . . . Ihoo! . . .' until her feet were drumming the ground with excitement and the dénouement bring a long-drawn 'Wullaaa. . . .'

By midnight the relatives had gone home, and the Bahenas crawled into two beds, the children arranging themselves into a jig-saw among the blankets. But sometimes in the night I would hear one of them whimpering after a bad dream; or perhaps Rahda had turned over in her sleep and put a foot into Senah's mouth, or Thérèse had fallen out onto the tiling.

One evening Elias spread out his arms in a gesture of plenty. 'We will have a bigger house soon, God willing. We will have a huge room to eat in, and a sitting-room, and a courtyard where the children can run. Everybody will have a room to himself!' Crouched, as we were, like trolls over the stove, it sounded like some biblical promise.

'I do good work,' he went on, bending and flexing his arms. 'I am going to sell this place. I have been saving money for years now. All the time economy, economy! But really, you know'—and here he looked sad—'I should have stayed in Lebanon. I worked on the railroad there for the French. Good money. Then one day a French overseer came. 'Do this . . . do that.' He touches me. I won't have a Frenchman touch me. So I hit him. Boom! Boom!' His fist cleft the air like a mattock.

'Heavens. Did he live?'

'Yes. Of course he lived. After a while he got up and reported me. So I came to Damascus. Then the English arrived during the war and I was a carpenter for them out at Katana. Good men, they were, really good. Do you know Corporal Smith? Of course he may not be a corporal now. That was twenty-three years ago. What about Sergeant Coates? Probably he is finished now. And anyway I don't know what they thought of us. By God, we stole from those soldiers! *Wullah!* Everything! Boots, socks, biscuits, revolvers! But I spent most of the time asleep. After that I stayed here as a cabinet-maker. No money! So you see I should not have hit that Frenchman. I was young. And now. . . . All the time economy! Look at the children! They are like cats! Do you know how much I would have earned in Lebanon? Yes, really . . . every *week*. . . .'

His voice and thoughts drifted away. He was looking back along the years, which always makes the Arabs sad, who have an old sigh: 'I sowed an "if" in the valley of "it has been", and there grew up an "I would it were".'

There would soon be another child in the house, for Umm-Toni was pregnant, and sometimes became very pale, the lines runnelling down from her eyes like patterns of water. She talked and thought only about the children, of which I had become one. My room was the brightest of the three and was always filled with saucers of eggplants, honeyballs and sugared beetroot. Every evening, once an hour, she would carry in a tiny cup of coffee and spill it with an 'A-ooh', wiping her tray and ejecting the children who came in after her.

Whenever I went out into the Street Called Straight I would meet somebody I knew. Razouk lived near by. His brother had gone to the Aleppo recruiting centre and had signed on for five years, although he hated the army. 'He has no choice.' Razouk shrugged it off. 'What can he do? He never made good marks in high school so he cannot do anything at university. And there are no jobs for anyone here. They treat you like a pig in the army, but he will at least be clothed and make some money. And he will be an officer.' He caressed his shoulders, conjuring star-studded tabs and the drip of epaulettes. 'Otherwise it is better to leave the country!'

Razouk often seemed to despise his own love for Damascus.

He had once taken a boat from Beirut to Naples, and the vision of a life in Europe was never far from his mind. 'Some day I will leave here,' he said. 'Nobody here has any sense. People can't think about anything except eat, sleep, go to work. When I came back from Italy I started to tell my friends about the places I had seen—Naples and Rome. When I had finished I looked round and they had all changed towards me. They thought me a traitor or something . . . their faces were red.'

Many people in Damascus talked about leaving, but usually in the tones of a day-dream. Some of them wanted to know how things were in England. 'Is there work for a tanner there? Can you get me a work-permit? . . . Of course I have seven children. . . . God be praised, *ten* English pounds a week. . . .'

I was having lunch with Razouk one day when somebody battered on the front door. Razouk ran into the courtyard and for a while I heard mutters and the shuffle of feet over the marble. He came back exultant. 'Good news! Four of my friends are leaving for Europe. They will go to Paris for ever.'

I asked if they had finished their national service. 'No,' he answered, 'they are still at university.'

'Don't they have to have a stamp on their passports to leave?'

'Yes,' he said. He was beginning to look sour.

Would the authorities give them stamps? I had thought students could not leave until the summer vacation.

'They won't get stamps.' He returned sullenly to his meal. 'They make empty talk.'

Empty talk, here more than elsewhere, is the cure for bitterness and boredom.

9. The Beloved of God

Verily, of the faithful hath God bought their
persons and their substance on condition of Paradise for these in return: on the path of God shall
they fight and slay and be slain: . . .

Koran ix. 112

I LOST MY way continually in Damascus. My maps and
diagrams, which unfolded in disordered sheets, attracted every
passer-by. Helpers would form into factions, debating the best
way to reach a place. Dissidents would say that the place had
vanished, or never existed; and soon the alley would be dense
with people and gesticulating hands. Eventually the arguments
would grow academic and I would escape down side-lanes
(Damascus is superb for escaping), until cries for *backsheesh*,
dodging after me, lost themselves in labyrinthine lanes.

At such times I began to think unkindly of the Damascenes,
drawing on the desert for an explanation of their ways, because
their ancestors were nomads. They have lost the desert tough-
ness, but have retained something of its intolerance, its
fatalism and crude esteem of power. Privacy, which a tribal life
never knows, is meaningless to them. Silence, which the desert
men counteract by a hurricane of words from dawn to night, is
still feared as the brother of boredom.

Sooner or later an Arab would ask me to drink coffee with
him, for they are the friendliest race in the world. The coffee
parties develop into parliaments for every topic, and for politics
in particular. An invincible anarchy reigns. I would watch myself
sloughing a few skins of Nordic constraint and in the end, cured
of irritation, would wander home along the Street Called
Straight, drunk on talk and coffee. Damascus responds quickly
to the mood. '*Salâm* Damascus! Everything they say about you
is true! Bride of the desert! Gateway to God!'

At other times, anger was more gently appeased. Once,
escaping a curious crowd near the Great Mosque, I reached a
pair of doors, studded with iron stars. I recognised the classical
pediment of the Hospital of Nureddine above my head, and
entered a desolate courtyard. It was placid and sunless. Its pale
stones and window grilles were simple and pleasing: geometri-

cal patterns caught up with sculptured flowers. At a distance the paucity of their carving concealed itself. Above the porch, a stalactite ceiling rose steeply, and an inscription over the inner gateway read: 'All the good which you would bring to pass, you will find near God. . . . When a man dies, his achievement is destroyed, save three things: a work from which others may draw profit, a pious son who prays for him and a charitable foundation which endures. . . .'

This was such a foundation, built as a hospital for the poor with the ransom for a crusading prince. On its completion in 1154, it was the most advanced medical institution in the world, constructed on the cruciform pattern of Persia and Iraq. Now it is a government commercial school, whose students pile their bicycles in the marble *iwan*, scraping away its vine-leaf carvings. Two Christian altars, seized during the Crusades, are imprisoned in marquetry, and hundreds of pencils have flickered names across the marble, including the faded plea: 'Come and take Ali London.'

By 1154 more than four and a half centuries had passed since the Ommayads raised their Great Mosque. Not a building remains of those centuries. The Abbassids ground Damascus underheel, and the Damascenes, tormented by the memory of their past, murdered their governors. They vested their hopes in the *sofyani*, the pretender to the house of Ommaya, and from time to time the white banners fluttered from the city walls again. But the battle was long since lost and they were crushed out. Once only an Abbassid caliph made Damascus his capital, to avoid the tyranny of his mercenaries in Baghdad. A sick man, he was driven out within thirty-eight days by the change of climate and the fleas.

The city crowded a lifetime's sufferings into every year: revolts, earthquakes, sieges, fires, plagues. At one time her population of three hundred thousand dwindled to three thousand. Dynasties in Egypt and Seljuk Turkish princelings fought over and misgoverned her and tribal feuds flared up with such implacability that when a Yemenite stole a water-melon from a Qaysite, half Syria was convulsed in blood for two years.

Then came the Crusades. Damascus recovered under Tughtakin, her energetic Turkish ruler, whose Burid dynasty lasted until 1154. In this year a Jewish woman on the ramparts threw down a rope to the soldiers of Nureddine, emir of Aleppo, and they wrenched open the Charki Gate to his insurgents.

Nureddine crystallised an empire from Cilicia to Galilee, and the confusion and pettiness of the early struggles ended. Damascus put on new dress. Her people awoke to the sounds of building; mosques and *madrasas*—religious schools for poor students—rose up on ashlars of tawny stone and set men's minds in the mould of orthodox Islam. Damascene architecture renounced its stale imitation of classical motifs and cast off the thrall of early Seljuk influence. Iraqi honeycombed cupolas rose from the city roofs, and the halls of mosques were adorned with stucco friezes. Again the eyes of all Islam focused on Damascus. Theologians, lawyers, doctors and historians crowded her academies. She was the bulwark against Christendom and against a miasma of Moslem heresy; a training ground for mind and body. Warriors coursed their horses in the polo fields of the Green Amphitheatre west of the walls, and mercenary soldiers skirmished in the Hippodrome of Flints.

Nureddine renovated the city walls, reconstructed towers and built public baths such as the el-Bzouriye, which is still crowded in the sweat of summer. He pierced the citadel with the Iron Gate, which described five sharply-angled turns before reaching the courtyard inside—a speciality of Arab castles—and devised the Secret Gate, now vanished, by which the ruler could leave the fortress along a slim bridge over the moat. In the southern walls he reshaped the Roman Little Gate and built the striped Bab-al-Faraj, the Gate of Deliverance, in the north. And on the site of the ancient Portal of the Moon, he raised the most handsome of the entries to Damascus; because the river and dense orchards rendered it immune from attack, men called it Bab as-Salâm, the Gate of Peace. Mules and carts from the old city still travel under these iron gateways, which Flecker turned to pure fantasy:

> Four great gates has the city of Damascus
> And four Grand Wardens, on their spears reclining,
> All day long stand like tall stone men
> And sleep on the towers when the moon is shining.

Nureddine is revered even now. At the hour of prayer, slippers shuffle and whisper through his Madrasa Nouriye, and near by, under the rusty light of a corbelled ceiling, his remains are nursed in a big sarcophagus, scantly carved. Over it, the stone has been simply inscribed: 'This is the tomb of the martyr Nur-al-Din ibn Zangi, may God have mercy on him.' Men drink water from tin cups chained to the fountain in front of the tomb, then gaze at the sarcophagus and murmur a prayer of thanks.

The annals of these early years are filled with the emirs of Damascus prancing out under their battlements, surrounded by savage Dailamites from the mountains of the Caspian Sea. Sometimes Frankish barons, bound on the backs of camels, were bullied to their execution through the curses of the populace; and once, after the battle of Hattin, the king of Jerusalem, Guy of Lusignan, was paraded to the citadel, and the Holy Cross of the Crusaders dragged through the city dust.

By chance, the diary of a Damascene official during the early Crusades has survived. It describes, in 1113, the attack of Baldwin I's Crusaders, who had already apportioned the prospective booty and houses among themselves, and resold them to the bourgeoisie. It was the first of many attacks. If Damascus fell, the artery between Egypt and the Euphrates would be fatally cut, and the Moslem empire slashed in two. But the army marched into November rains, and the cavalry foundered in the mud.

In 1119 'some who came from Jerusalem told of the discovery of the tombs of the prophets al-Khalīl [Abraham] and his two sons Isaac and Jacob. . . . They related that they were as if alive, no part of their bodies having decayed, and no bones rotted, and that suspended over them in the cave were lamps of gold and silver'.*

The Crusaders again attacked Damascus in 1129. '. . . they halted at the Wooden Bridge . . . nothing was to be seen of them save their assembling, their perambulation round their camp, and the glitter of their helmets and weapons.' A few days later their supply-train for the siege was annihilated, and the Damascenes sallied out against their camp. 'A strong body of horsemen went forward to open the attack upon them, thinking as they saw the multitude of fires and the smoke rising in the air, that they were still occupying the camp. . . . But when they approached it, they found that the Franks had retired at the close of that night. . . . They had burned their baggage, their train, their equipment and their weapons, since they had no animals left on which to load them. . . . Then the people felt secure and went out to their farms. . . .'

* This cave—which is still claimed as the biblical cave of Machpelah, where Abraham and his family were buried—is to be found at Hebron, near Bethlehem. It has not been entered since the Crusaders sealed it up eight centuries ago.

In 1139 the Damascenes made an alliance with the Crusaders and stormed the Turkish fortress of Baniyas with the help of Christian knights. But the alliance was short. Nine years later the Crusaders gathered their whole strength under Louis VII and the Hohenstaufen emperor Conrad, and marched against Damascus. They were stubbornly resisted. At night, skirmishers from the city lay in ambush along the roads and brought back the heads of slain knights to claim rewards for them. The invaders grew disheartened and retreated southward. 'In the remains of their camps, moreover, and along their highroads there were found such uncountable quantities of burial pits of their slain and of their magnificent horses, that there were stenches from their corpses that almost overcame the birds in the air.'

The Archbishop of Tyre, who marched with this army, miserably reported that the orchards were dense and interlaced with walls, and that arrows and stones were showered down on the knights from towers in the trees. 'Along the wall inside lurked men armed with lances who, themselves unseen, could look out through small peep-holes carefully arranged in the walls and stab the passer-by from the side.'

The Crusaders never seriously threatened Damascus again. A lighter but subtler instrument of destruction was the Assassins, a fanatical offshoot of the Shia, who set themselves against Christians and orthodox Moslems alike. They enforced their will, or took their revenge, by the murder of prominent men, and lodged themselves in inaccessible castles among the mountains of Persia and Lebanon. Their leader, whom the Crusaders knew as the Old Man of the Mountain, employed agents, or *fedais*, who may have been drugged on hashish (hence the name 'assassin'). They would insinuate themselves into the service of their victim, and plan his murder with delicacy and cunning. They attempted the life of Louis IX in the heart of France, and attacked one of the Great Khans in the depths of Mongolia. Conrad of Montferrat and the second Count Raymond of Tripoli died by their hand, and Edward I of England, while a young prince on crusade, was only saved by his wife, Eleanor of Castile, who sucked the poison from his wound.

In 1113, the diary records, Mawdūd, the vizier of the ruler of Damascus, was singled out by the Assassins. As he entered the Great Mosque, surrounded by a bodyguard holding naked swords and daggers, 'a man leapt out from among the crowd, without exciting the attention of anyone, and approaching the emīr Mawdūd as though to call down a blessing upon him, and beg an alms of him, seized the belt of his riding cloak with a swift motion, and smote him twice with his poniard below the navel. . . .'

In 1129 the sultan of Damascus planned the extermination of the Assassins in the city. By now their power was so swollen that they flaunted their identity, and their leader was the sultan's own vizier. On 4th September 1129, the vizier as usual joined the council of emirs in the Rose Pavilion at the palace in the citadel; but as he rose to withdraw, the sultan signalled to a man who killed him with a sword. Immediately the Damascenes hunted out every member of the sect and butchered several hundred of them, blackening the battlements with crucified bodies. Afterwards the instigators of the purge awaited the Assassins' revenge every hour. They walked about the city in a thicket of guards, and took to wearing chain mail.

In 1131 the Assassins insinuated two of their initiates into the Khorasani bodyguard of the sultan and attacked him as he was returning from his bath. He 'threw himself from his horse, and escaped with his life, while the men-at-arms mustered in increasing numbers against the two assassins and hacked them to pieces with swords'. But the sultan died of his wounds, and for another century and a half the ghoulish fraternity of Assassins went about its business unchecked.

A curious footnote to the time has been left by a Moslem warrior, who writes that the ruler of Damascus kept a lion in a court adjoining his palace. To entertain guests one night he drove a sheep into the courtyard so 'that we may see how the lion annihilates it'. No sooner had the sheep seen the lion than it ran and butted it. The lion fled round and round the courtyard fountain, with the sheep chasing behind.

On Nureddine's death in 1174, and after an interim of uncertainty, he was succeeded by the suzerain of Egypt, whose empire soon stretched from Nubia to Byzantium. A man of ambition and discernment, with the warrior qualities and frugal tastes of his Kurdish ancestors, he was ideally suited for propagating the holy war against Christendom. His name was Saladin, which the Arabs, more musically, pronounce Salah-ed-Din.

A few buildings contemporary with his reign have survived, mostly mausoleums. They are handsome even in ruin. Well-hewn stones support eight- or sixteen-sided drums, elegantly domed in plastered brick. But neglect has turned them into symbols of mortality: the sepulchre of a prince of Baalbek a nest for sparrows; the tomb of his son, heaped with tins and the entrails of cars. Huge, ophthalmic cats stalk in and out of the dome of Sultan Hassan, which once shielded the rain from the graves of the family of Saladin, and down a secret passageway beside it, an unknown woman lies in the gutted tomb of Sitt ech-Cham, under a mound of bottles. Yet two sepulchres have preserved their exquisite plaster mouldings almost intact: the wan-stoned cupola of al-Moqaddam which houses an emir of Aleppo, and the Madrasa Chamiya, built by a sister of Saladin, where the graves of three more of his family lie like sleeping armadillos in an enormous room.

Saladin's most famous brother, el-Adil, whom the Crusaders knew as Sephardim, is buried in the Madrasa Adiliya. He had become a friend of Richard Coeur de Lion, who conceived a peculiar plan for ending the Holy War: he would give his sister in marriage to el-Adil, and Jerusalem and Acre would be their dowry, forming an independent kingdom. Negotiations were long, complicated and insincere, and after Saladin's death, it was el-Adil who maintained the precarious Moslem unity.

The façade of el-Adil's tomb is plain and massive. In its courtyard stand lemon and orange trees and shrubs of bloated citrons. A fountain is sloughed into a dark pool. The library of the Arab Academy has intruded on the tomb-chamber of the warrior-king, and his coffin is sunk in the centre of the room, surrounded by the *Encyclopaedia Britannica* and Larousse's *Gastronomique*.

The citadel which he rebuilt—now a state prison—has been inviolable for thirty years. Covered markets suffocate its ramparts on almost every side, but here and there the angle-towers, remote and awesome, break free and display the formidable machicolations which first passed to Europe from Syria. The Chevalier d'Arvieux, in the seventeenth century, entered the citadel disguised as a Turk, and saw there 'an enormous dome, supported by four pillars which were so huge that I believe they would carry the dome of St Peter's in Rome'. Now only the northern walls are accessible, their towers dignified above the fetid river. A gateway permits a glimpse into the castle courtyard, cluttered with police and lorries. The audience halls, baths and gardens have all disappeared, together with the buildings of the early Turkish princes—the Cupola of Roses and the Palace of Joy.

*   *   *

I could imagine the streets to be much as they were in Crusading times. Timbers break through the plaster walls and overlay the sun. Light is splintered and corrupted. Old hinge-grooves have wounded the stone. Even a century ago, doors within the gates used to grate shut after the last call to prayer. The nights held their breath until dawn, tattooed with the whistling of the watchmen and the muffled '*Iftah ya Haris!*' of late-comers under the sector gateways. 'Open, O watchman!' The old man would grumble in the gate recess and the silence split apart with rattling chains.

Fear of each other caused people to live behind many gates in tortuous alleyways, and they clung to the Byzantine preference for concealing houses behind blank walls. The Roman city decomposed into self-sufficient districts. The Christian sector was immured in the north-east and the Jews sealed themselves up in the south-east. Shops and markets were propped against the arcaded streets, and the forum was invaded by stone-built emporia for jewellery and precious fabrics. So the mediaeval city locked itself in a chaos which the centuries only confirmed.

Because of this, one can never forget the space and silence beyond the north gate of the Great Mosque. The view is enclosed by a spinney of pines, their branches warty with cones. On one side, a knot of overhanging houses harbours a ruined arch; on another falls the cataract of a eucalyptus tree. Beyond the pines a courtyard wall encloses jasmine and orange trees, and above it erupts the dome of the tomb of Saladin, grooved like a cantaloup melon.

A caretaker squats in the sun-filled porch, reading the Koran. The garden is simple but luxuriant. A fountain lisps in a nervous spray—a style peculiar to Damascus. Vines slither down from a trellis to its pool, and rose-coloured leaves stir along the paving.

The caretaker saw me and shook his keys outside a doorway braided in bougainvillaea. Inside, the sepulchre is fittingly austere. Its walls are ribbed in basalt and limestone, and clothed with tiles in the colours of the sea. A faience inscription gives thanks to Saladin for liberating Jerusalem from the 'blemish of the unbelievers'. The floor is lightly carpeted. But Saladin lies in an ornate and ugly sarcophagus presented by Kaiser Wilhelm II. The emperor was courting the favour of the Sublime Porte at the time, and made an ostentatious visit to the grave, on which he laid a wreath of artificial flowers. A golden lamp still dangles over the coffin, engraved with the monograms of Wilhelm and one of the last Ottoman sultans, Abdul Hamid II. But on a close examination of Wilhelm's bouquet, the Damascenes were furious to find, hidden among its fronds, a tiny Maltese cross.

The original sarcophagus lies by the side of the modern one. Funerary turbans are wound in extravagant coils at the head of both. The carving on the old walnut wood coffin is artistic and delicate, but the lid has rotted away, together with two of the side panels, on which was inscribed the epitaph: 'O God receive this soul, and open to him the doors of paradise, that last conquest for which he hoped.'

Tradition has quickly filled this empty coffin. Men said that Saladin's secretary was entombed here, and the caretaker has promoted him to a Grand Vizier.

Legends thicken around the name of Saladin, but his true quality remains unobscured. Even Dante, who thrust Mahomet into the ninth malbowge of Nether Hell,* granted his general—
e solo, in parte vidi 'l Saladino—an honourable place in limbo. Saladin's associates accused him of unpolitic kindness, and at his most severe (as after the battle of Hattin) he followed a strict sense of justice.

A stream of stories flowed through my mind: of Saladin's leaving a suit of fine raiment in the public baths in place of the tattered clothes of one of the bathers . . . of how, after the capture of Jerusalem, he broke down in tears at the sight of the bereaved Crusader women . . . of his sending a horse to the dismounted Richard Coeur de Lion in the pith of the Battle of Jaffa . . . and even of the story from *The Talisman*, in which Richard and Saladin display their swordsmanship—one by clumping an iron block in two, the other, with a flicker of his scimitar, severing a falling veil.

Saladin died on 4th March 1193, at the age of fifty-six, a few months after concluding a peace treaty with the Crusaders for three years, three months and three days, giving only his handshake as surety. One of his friends declared that he had died so poor 'we were obliged to borrow money to purchase everything necessary for the funeral, even down to the things that cost him but a halfpenny. . . .'

As he lay dying, it is said that he summoned his standard-bearer and told him: 'You who have carried my banner in the wars will now carry the banner of my death. Let it be a vile rag

* This was ungrateful of Dante, who almost certainly took the whole layout of his Inferno from Moslem writers.

set upon a lance. . . .' And on his orders the standard-bearer cried out as the simple procession wended through the streets, 'Lo, at his death, the king of the East could take nothing with him save this cloth only.'

The dynasty which Saladin founded—the Ayyoubid—was short and glorious. In times of half-peace, traffic with the Christian kingdom of Jerusalem sailed in and out of Acre, and Egyptian caravans came up through Tiberias to Damascus. Camel-trains slobbered and roared in the caravanserais. The warehouses were pungent with camphor and aloes, the incense of Hadramut, and Tibetan musk, the halls cluttered with silks and porcelain from China, spices, precious stones, ivory, brazil-wood, indigo and Arabian dates. Venetian merchants scattered the fabled Damascus blades all over Europe to flash in the hands of Norman barons and Plantagenet kings; and the city armourers adorned their work with the subtle gold or silver inlay still called 'damascene'.* Her glass-makers were the most accomplished in the world and damasks provoked the flattery of constant imitation in Europe, the weavers excelling in silks which shone on both sides with lustrous and intricate patterns.

Refugees from the Crusader sack of Jerusalem built the new suburb of Salihiye on the slopes of Mount Kassioun and the Ayyoubids regaled it with religious buildings, and even erected a few in the dense city. In an alleyway near the Gate of Peace still stands the Madrasa Badraiya, now a quiet mosque, but once the house of the last of Saladin's great lords, who embellished it with sculptures from the Crusader pillage of Constantinople.

In a lane to the south is an Ayyoubid religious school, the Qilijiya. The mausoleum of its founder is bolted. Even the script above the gateway has been perjured by a house partition; but on the lintels of the windows are carved the verses of the founder which explain the Moslem's love for turning his tomb into a place of charity:

> This, which is our home and resting-place, is a true
> house, though all else should perish,
> Build, then, if you can, a house where men may bear
> you in a while,

* Damascening did not originate in Damascus, but reached its highest development there. It seems that the art of making 'Damascus blades' was preserved in Khorasan by the captive Damascene armourers whom Tamerlane transplanted there in 1400. The craft thrived in Khorasan as late as the nineteenth century, long after it had deteriorated in Syria.

And practise good that it may join you there, as friend
  unites with friend.

Suburbs beyond the walls contain the graves of a few of
Saladin's successors: a prince of Circesium, a governor of
Salkhad. And at the prayer-hour, venerable men murmur and
bow in the porticoes of the Ayyoubid Tawba Mosque, their
features like a pantheon of master-passions. After they have
prayed, they sit on the straw matting and doze in a serenity of
sunlight. There is no visible evidence that there was ever a
building here before this one; but they call the mosque Jami'
at-Tawba—Mosque of the Return of God; because it replaced
a brothel.

In those days the return of God seemed more than a fancy.
The heavy horses of the Crusaders no longer trampled through
the orchards. The merchants were rich and the craftsmen re-
spected, and when the nobles died, they turned their wealth to
piety in the mosques and schools of the Kassioun Mountain. To
the Damascenes it must have seemed that their punishments
were over, as if the ground had at last absorbed the blood of
Abel.

10. Under the Slave-Kings

. . . the destiny of Damascus is full of
violence and rebellion, such is the influence of its star, which is in the sign of the
Lion, and when it is in the ascendant, the
people of Damascus revolt against their
governors.

Istakhri

A BROWN MOUNTAIN rimmed with white mosques and
schools, a refuge of piety and peace; such was the Kassioun
mountain after the Jerusalem refugees had built Salihiye against
its side. Under Saladin's dynasty, the Ayyoubid, men came to
think of it as holy and eternal, and the bones of many hundred
prophets speckled the land between the city wall and its lower
slopes.

Today Salihiye is linked to the walled city by the boulevards
of the modern one. Often a haze blurs its houses into the mountain rocks, so that the black doorways and windows resemble
clean-cut caves. Its southern outskirts are very quiet, the houses
and apartments shuttered. Lines of plane trees slope up the
streets, and myrtle saplings drowse over the Barada. Beyond
the canal of Yezid, the modern houses fall away and the main
street of Salihiye traverses the mountainside.

I remember many broken cupolas with cockleshell window-
lets, and the façades of anonymous tombs. Golden-stoned walls
clasped each side of the road. Above them rose a stunted minaret
the colour of evening sunlight, and opposite stood the mausoleum
of a thirteenth-century vizier, decorated inside by an Andalucian
sculptor, like some dark room of the Alhambra.

A few yards beyond I came to a mosque with cracked walls
where a dome had once shielded the grave of a princess of Mosul.
In a near-by street stood an Ayyoubid mosque, whose timbered
ceiling poured down a *mélange* of fans and chandeliers. A pair of
grey-flecked Crusader columns flanked the *mihrab*, and a grandfather clock had decided on an eternal ten minutes to three.
Every religious building in Damascus is filled with European
clocks, but the Moslems have thwarted them by refusing to wind
them up or by twiddling their hands round into fanciful hours.

The clock in the Ayyoubid mosque had been still for years, and the prayer-hall was empty, but a mausoleum stood at the end of the court. Its white plaque declared: 'Tomb of the Lady Ismat, wife of the Sultan Nureddine the Martyr.' I grated open the door.

'Come on in,' said a voice.

A man in a fez was sitting in the gloom. I was bewildered to see that the room was full of chairs and tables, and that he had installed his medicine-chest against the wall. He pointed out the stained-glass windows, and told me which of the plaster mouldings were new and which old. After a while I asked what had happened to the wife of Nureddine, now that he was living in her tomb.

'She is under our feet,' he said, stamping. 'The dome fell in some years ago and smashed the sarcophagus. It is all sealed up under the floor now and they have built a new dome, praised be God. I am caretaker here. My house is next door, but there is not room for all my furniture there. So God sent me this place. . . .'

On the far side of the road lay an exposed grave. It belonged to Mitqal, an officer of Saladin, and its casket was banded with inscriptions: 'May God have pity on one who implores His mercy in favour of Saladin, conqueror of Jerusalem. I was in his service . . . the day of Hattin, and at the capture of Saint Jean d'Acre and Ascalon. . . .' And on its west side, the broken words: 'Whosoever . . . this tomb, alters, modifies or diminishes it, or effaces one of these inscriptions, or tries to steal a part of it, or executes a work which reduces it, or tries to . . . this tomb, either in words, or in acts, may God . . ., may God hound him, may God exterminate him, may God bring him to justice on the day when neither riches nor family protect a man if he comes not to God with a pure heart, and thereafter may he be cursed of God and angels and all men.' But it is the wind and the sun which scratch at the grave of Saladin's general. Men ignore it.

The streets were full of fruit-sellers with boxes of tomatoes and aubergines and water-melons ribbed like Turks' turbans. Boys from restaurants were carrying plates of soup and peppers to mysterious customers in the lanes, and children were playing brick-bat against a canteen which was once a food-dole for the poor, built by the Ottoman sultan Suleiman.

Opposite, through a handsome doorway, spread the empty, whitewashed courtyard of the derelict Qaymari hospital. In mediaeval times it had been filled with doctors and nurses, a chemist and an occulist. A patriarchal fig-tree now reached out over the courtyard pool, its branches shedding big leaves into the water. Four tall arches flanked the court. Under one glowed plasterwork rosettes like pale suns, and beneath them ran a band of script, worked round with flowers.

'Beautiful,' I said to an old man, who had appeared at my elbow. 'Do you know anything about them?'

'How should I? They were done long ago. You could never do such work now. Djinns' work. They did such things'.

I stared at him, thinking that perhaps he was laughing at me; but his face was serious and rather sad. His mouth was swathed in a keffieh, so that only the smudge of his moustache quivered when he spoke.

I told him I thought the djinns had emigrated to the mountains long ago; but he only peered at me, as if puzzled by my ignorance, and stubbornly muttered 'Djinns' again, this time to himself. He sat down on a bench facing the fig-tree, pulled his keffieh over his forehead and fell asleep. I looked at his bundled figure in its crumpled jacket and *cheroual*. It was the first time I had heard a Damascene express his belief in djinns.

His ancestors had told tales of crabs as huge as hills; of a serpent which drops from the clouds when they pour rain, and devours everything in its path until it dies; of valleys of diamonds and mountains of precious stones, and of the demon voices in a djinns' market in Kashmir. If he dreamt of a line of camels, might he believe, as his fathers had, that angels were descending to inspire his children? If he woke with a bleeding nose, he could think himself freed from the witch who tries to part Syrians from their mothers.

I remembered a village schoolteacher telling me that if a man is murdered his head flits away in the form of an owl—he cupped his hands round his mouth: '*Ihteres!* Woooh-ooh-ohoooh!' In past times, if a man's death were unavenged, the owl would shriek out 'Give me to drink!' And if somebody sees what he imagines to be a dog at dusk, it may be 'a certain small animal that has no good in it', which makes a special point of lifting its leg in the direction of Mecca.

Djinns picked their curved teeth in rooftops at daytime and flapped out at midnight in horrid shapes. Afrits fell in love with women who wore anklets and followed them wherever they went. Frogs had wonderful properties: they would stop the boiling of cooking-pots, draw confessions from sleeping people, delay the growth of hair and fill women with a madness for love. To spit three times down a frog's mouth was an infallible contraceptive, and if you sat in bat's gravy you would be healed of paralysis.

But the old man was still sleeping when I left the Qaymari, and I never discovered what more he knew. Next door, glowed the rose-coloured courtyard of the Mohiy ad-Din Mosque. From a grove of pillars in the prayer-room I looked out over vines and roof-tops and saw Damascus: a view which had touched even the heart of Tamerlane. Down the courtyard stairway, the tints of the stone deepened, until they reached a sanctuary decorated in Turkish faience, higher than a man's reach. In the centre of the room stood the sepulchre of Ibn el-Arabi, the most famous mystic in Islam, surrounded by a silver and brass grille. By his side lay a heavily inscribed sarcophagus from Tunis, the grave of the Algerian warrior Abd el-Kader.

Two men were never coupled more strangely in one tomb. On one side rests the soldier who resisted the French in Algeria for seventeen years and found honourable exile in Damascus; on the other lies the prophet who taught the divinity of all exist-ence, and declared that he had learnt the secrets of alchemy, treading a delicate course between heresy and sainthood:

> My heart is capable of every form
> A cloister for the monk, a fane for idols,
> A pasture for gazelles . . .
> Love is the faith I hold: wherever turn
> His camels, still the one true faith is mine.

El-Arabi had a dangerous breadth of outlook in a society blinkered by tradition. His position became so difficult when he wrote a volume of erotic verse to a lady of Mecca, that he had to append footnotes, imbuing the poems with a purely mystical meaning. Now the family and friends of the heretic-saint are buried near him in the mausoleum, and the grille of his tomb has been smoothed fine by the kisses of women.

The grave of Abd el-Kader, the hero of Algeria's struggle against France, is remembered but not worshipped. Standing in the quietness of the Mohiy ad-Din, I could not think of his wars, only of his incongruous imprisonment on the Loire, and of his release by Louis Napoleon; of the emperor and the emir squatting down to eat cous-cous on the floor of the Château d'Amboise; of Abd el-Kader kneeling to afternoon prayer in the vestibule of St Cloud, and of his accidentally seeing the standards of his warriors among the captive banners hanging in the Hôtel des Invalides—'Those times are past. I wish to forget them. Let us always endeavour to live in the present.'

It was growing late. The sun had lost its heat and lay across the lanes in flaccid streaks. Every afternoon Damascus seemed to be caught too early in this ambush of light, and to trifle with it a long time before darkness. It was the hour when men start to walk about in pyjamas and sandals.

I reached the outskirts of the old town—a dribble of *madrasas* among the flats—and saw the Omariya school, the oldest building on the mountain, its ruined arches festooned with washing; and the big, white courtyard of the Mozaffari Mosque, with ancient columns and a prayer-hall rich in carved wood, where people stared at me and kissed their Korans. I passed the Madrasa Sâhibiya, charged with the treble roar of school-children, and the lanes slanted to a mosque whose walls were stippled in shrubbery—the last building of Saladin's city. Beyond it, only modern houses trampled downhill along the neck of the orchards.

The Kassioun Mountain had grown tawny as a camel in the dusk, its arteries darker. I leant against the wall of a house, and looked down into the plain between the hill and the main city, where autumn poplars stood among a tangle of orchards which looked as if they would never bear fruit again. Inside the house a woman was singing a popular song:

My eyes, pour out your tears now all you will,
Tears are not saved. . . .

The clop of horses' hoofs over the cobbles filled the lane with their sound, and died away.

I am an unlit star which falls through the long night,
A cloud without rain. . . .

Below, flights of pigeons flickered white in a snare of sun-light, like scraps of paper tossed through the trees. And twilight came rolling in from the desert.

*　　*　　*

Early in the thirteenth century a Turkish slave-boy was sold in the Damascus market for eight hundred pieces of silver. Because of a blemish in one of his eyes, he was returned to his trader and was eventually bought by the sultan of Cairo, who gave him the name Baybars. He grew into a colossal, dark-skinned man with a boorish voice and manner, and he was soon enrolled in the sultan's bodyguard, for the Cairene sultanate of the time ruled by the blades of a slave army.

The slaves were mostly captured Circassians and Turks, and were known as Mamelukes (from *memelik*, 'possessed', a word generally applied to a pale-faced slave). Twelve thousand of them had been bought from Genghiz Khan by the sultan of Egypt and trained into a matchless fighting corps, and they were replenished with slaves bought in the markets of Moslem Russia.

In 1249 the sultana, Shajar-al-Durr, 'the Tree of Pearls', murdered the sultan and crowned herself 'Queen of the Moslems, Sovereign of Cairo and Damascus'. But she had not ruled for three months before the caliph in Baghdad, who had once brought her into his harem as a slave, wrote to the Egyptian emirs: 'If ye have no men to rule you, let us know and we will send you one.' The mortified nobles chose the army commander for their sovereign, and Shajar immediately married him. Several years later she discovered that he was considering taking another wife, and murdered him as he was taking his bath. But she did not rule again, for slave women pounded her to death with wooden shoes.

The slaves now became kings, and the first of the Turkish Mamelukes snatched up the vacant throne which was to be theirs for close on three centuries. A military brotherhood in a foreign land, the dynasty is unique in history, and its misrule extended over all Egypt and Syria.

Syria was almost immediately threatened by the Mongols, who had eliminated the effete Abbassid caliphate. In a single week they gutted Baghdad, butchered a million people and destroyed Mesopotamia's timeless irrigation systems, turning her to marsh and desert. The caliph was tied up in a sack and bruised to death beneath the hoofs of Mongol cavalry. Under the command of Hulagu, a grandson of Genghiz Khan, they moved up the Euphrates and poured into north Syria. Aleppo was stormed and fifty thousand of her inhabitants slaughtered.

Then the Mongols turned on Damascus. In March, 1260, they pierced the walls with the aid of a force of Crusaders.* The

* Many of the Mongols were nominal Christians, and the Crusaders saw them as potential allies against Islam.

garrison retreated southwards, leaving them to tear down the citadel, burn the palace and capture the last of the Ayyoubid princes. But by now the Mameluke sultan Qutuz had gathered an army, which met the Mongols at Goliath Springs near Nazareth. It was one of the decisive battles of the world. The Mongols, had they won, might have spread into Africa, perhaps reached Europe. But they were routed in a magnificent cavalry charge; and so jubilant were the Mamelukes that they pursued them all the way to the Euphrates, leaving Qutuz to play polo with the head of the Mongol general.

One man dwarfed the sultan. His single good eye had sought out a weakness in the Mongol battle, and he had led the slave vanguard to their ferocious victory. Baybars was now a shrewd general, ambitious and truculent. In return for his services, he asked Qutuz for the governorship of Aleppo, but it was refused him; as the royal party was returning to Egypt, an accomplice took the sultan's hands to beg a favour, and while he held him, Baybars came behind and passed a dagger through the sultan's neck. For seventeen years after, Baybars ruled Egypt and Syria.

Buildings and charitable endowments enriched his reign. He dug canals, organised harbours and refortified the Damascus walls and citadel. He linked his two capitals by a road which enabled him to play polo in Cairo on a Saturday and lead prayers in the Ommayad Mosque the next Friday; and he built the dazzling Kasr al-Ablak—a black and ochre palace on the banks of the Barada.

Castle by castle, he chewed away half the Crusader kingdom. He even breached the outer walls of the Krak des Chevaliers, the monster fortress of the Knights Hospitallers, which lies like a grounded battleship among the hills west of Homs. Nureddine fought outside its walls and was routed. Saladin saw its towers from afar and marched away in despair. But Baybars smuggled into it a command to surrender, forged with the seal and signature of the Count of Tripoli—and the castle passed into his hands.

Forty years after being sold in Damascus as a slave, Baybars was buried there as a king. He had mistakenly drunk a cup of poison which he had set out for one of his emirs.* His tomb had once been the house of Saladin's family, but Baybars' son bought it for a great sum and turned it into a funerary college for his father.

* Other accounts say that Baybars died of drinking too much *kumiz*, a Mongol drink of mare's milk.

It was opened for me by a guardian with a gigantic key. A tall dome shed a bowl of whiteness into the room, which was encircled by shelves, filled with the manuscripts of the National Library. Under glass cases glistened illuminated manuscripts, exquisite, like insects' work.

'Sultan Baybars,' said the man, pointing over a book-shelf. He rests under a pale grave in the centre of the room. A band of fine mosaic gleams dully round the walls. Below it shine marble panels, heavy with black and dark blood colours, which recall the brute in Baybars, the man who poisoned his enemies and who butchered two thousand of the captives from Safad in violation of his oath.

I stepped out gladly into the sunlight of the courtyard, studded with shrubs planted in painted tins. The beetling gate and well-jointed stones of the tomb represent the rearguard of stability in Damascus. After Baybars, the Mamelukes of Cairo distrusted and misruled her. Their independent commanders in the citadel scrutinised the movements of their seneschals in the city, and the murder of a sultan in Cairo often sparked the rebellion of a governor in Damascus.

A diary which survived the period gives a glimpse of bustle and unease, of armies rushing through Damascus to assault the wilting Crusaders, and of the relentless replacement of the city governors.

'. . . On Sunday we received the joyous news of the capture of Tyre, which the Franks had abandoned. The only people left there were less than fifty old men and women, for all the men had left to help the inhabitants of Acre.

'. . . the restoration of the citadel was begun, and the building of the palace and of huge battlements which the sultan had inaugurated at ās-Suja 'i. Men were sent to search for marble all through Syria, and the great columns of the Romans were torn from their places even in Damascus.

'1290. Capture of Qal 'at ar-Rūm. . . . Rejoicing in Damascus. For seven days the fanfares resound in the citadel, and the candles and the houses of the emirs have been lit up during the night. . . . Fabrics were spread under the feet of the sultan's horse . . . he made his entry preceded by Armenian prisoners and the Armenian governor of ar-Rūm.

'Prayers for rain at Damascus, without result. . . . A certain number of Maghrebins and others reached the Cave of Blood on Kassioun, and remained there four nights and days to recite the Koran, weep and invoke God and humble themselves before him: their prayers were so earnest that God answered them and sent rain.

'Announcement of a Mongol raid. . . .

'December 1292. Terrible wind, cold and rain; the people are dying, turbans are blown away and the wind bowls over any camel standing up . . . at Damascus charcoal is sold at a dirhem a *ratl*, meat at four dirhems. Many people die. . . .'

In 1298 the Mongols mustered beyond the Euphrates again, but their forces were hit by lightning and scattered with awesome carnage. Yet the next year an army of a hundred thousand debouched into Syria and defeated the Mamelukes whom they outnumbered three to one.

According to a scholar of the time, there was complete panic. 'People from the army passed Damascus overburdened with shame and pain. . . . Later it was even said that the whole army was crushed, and we spent a night God knows what sort it was. . . . Thereupon Arjawāsh [governor of the citadel] ordered the moats of the city to be inundated with water. . . . At that time there came men from the army and officers whose horses were exhausted and whose equipment was lost: they tore their clothes and threw away their shields. . . .' Two hundred convicts burnt their prison and escaped through the Jabiya Gate, and people began to flee in the direction of Egypt.

But when Gazan, the Mongol leader, arrived in Damascus, he claimed that he came to put an end to Mameluke oppression. The Damascenes received him in two minds. The civil governor honoured him as a king and sent up prayers for the Great Khan in the Ommayad Mosque. The commander of the citadel showered arrows on him. The Mongols then plundered the city, sacked the newly-built Salihiye district, and shot stones at the citadel. Gazan posted a warning: 'Whoever appeals to me for the sake of Damascus shall die!' and a hundred thousand Damascenes were slaughtered before he marched back into the desert.

For the next two centuries the Mameluke rule of Damascus was disrupted by wars. Typically, the Damascenes flourished, accommodating themselves to the whims of their conquerors. They developed their old flair for producing luxury goods and armour, and forged Damascus blades, which were so highly polished that if a man wished to correct the angle of his turban he would hold up his sword as a mirror.

The few Europeans who penetrated the city were dazed by her merchandise. Every kind of costly fabric shone in the bazaars, copper and brass damascened in silver, inlaid furniture, ivory, delicate glassware and the perennial stones and spices of India. The trades of the Mameluke workmen still exist today: mat-makers and water-sellers, vendors of henna, sweetmeats, flowers and fruit, potters and weavers and tanners, sellers of sorbet and Lebanese snow*—who all lived on the rim of starvation in one of the wealthiest cities of the world.

Damascus outgrew her walls on almost every side, and new villages nudged each other along the meadows of the Barada. Religion prospered with commerce. Salihiye alone owned seventy-one mosques by the end of the Mameluke era. The city was crowded by the nazirs and imams and khatibs of the mosques, and throngs of theological students. Charitable endowments might pay for the corsage of a bride, a pilgrimage to Mecca, or replace a broken porcelain dish.

Merchants saluted one another in the streets with fabulous solemnity, inclining deeply from the waist, hands clasped behind backs, and prostrating themselves alternately on the pavements so that their turbans rolled off their heads. Silks and red shoes became fashionable among their wives. By the sixteenth century the Mamelukes violated the women without fear. According to one traveller, they used to defile them in the taverns, and then attempt to look under their veils, but the women 'say thus unto them, Is it not enough for you, that you have abused our bodies as pleaseth you, but that you will also discover our faces?'

The Damascenes delighted in pageantry, and the parvenu Mamelukes took pains to satisfy them. The citizens loved to watch the sultans riding out from the citadel to the Great Mosque, clouded in the incense sounds of cymbals and drums, shaded under a silken parasol and preceded by banners.

In times of war the townsmen would line the roads to watch the slave-warriors caracole by: brutal horsemen armed with graceful scimitars, and clutching elaborately-painted lances and javelins. They were cased in cuirasses of mail, and wore greaves and spiked helmets which dripped laceries of chain onto their shoulders. They carried small, round shields of painted hide or embossed and studded metal, and some of them held broad-swords so heavy that the strongest man tired after a few strokes with them.

The yearly pilgrimage returned from Mecca in a tide of ten thousand camels, which would surge into the city for three days and nights. An old and revered Koran passed through the Gate

* Snow was even carried from Damascus to Cairo on relays of camels by men skilled in preserving it.

of God in a camel-born litter, behind drums and trumpets and a posse of crossbowmen. Then came horses and camels swathed in cloth of gold, and pilgrims who had journeyed out of the longest reaches of Islam, from Barbary to Sind: purple-bearded Persians, flat-faced men out of Bokhara and Samarkand, Turcomans shaggy in sheepskins, naked madmen banging tom-toms and calabashes. They brought back wares traded with foreigners in Arabia, and the townsmen rode out to barter with them as well as to greet them, until the roads were jammed with a Damascene blend of piety and profiteering.

The Mamelukes insensibly abandoned the building styles of earlier years. Mosques and schools no longer rose up in the sober harmony of well-jointed stones. Corbelling and lacework and many-coloured inlays began to clutter the new façades and minarets. By the fifteenth century the suburban streets were lined with these architectural prostitutes. The Meidan quarter, which stretches southward along the pilgrimage road, is still depressing. The encrusted resting-places of Mameluke emirs, shorn of their decoration, show a miserable paucity of construction. From the coarse-faced as-Sibaiya school, with its bloated minaret and immured Crusader altars, the street is a tale of artistic woe and decay all the way to Kadem.

There are many Mameluke works in the main city. A few are happy and modest, but most are aggressively decadent or imitative: the foursquare mass of the Madrasa Jaqmaqiya near the tomb of Saladin; the lone minaret of el Qal'i among bazaars; the *mihrab* and minaret of the Hisham Mosque; and the stalactite gate of the school of Tingiz, like a ferocious set of teeth.

Several buildings, including a secretive bath—the Bath of Roses—were built by the early Mamelukes west of the walls. Two of them, in particular, moved mediaeval poets to hyperbole: 'I came to the grand mosque of Tingiz and found it there in isolation, surrounded only by parterres.

' "Are you all alone here?"

'It replied: "Because of the beauty gathered here in me, I have been set apart from others." '

But the Tingiz Mosque has recently been rebuilt like a government department, and the faithful must climb three flights of cold marble stairs to a modern prayer-room.

The Yelbogha Mosque—'If anyone say "It has an equal in the world," he speaks lightly'—has decayed through neglect. It stands on the site of the old horse-market, and one of its gates bears the inscribed rules for the sale of horses. Like the Mosque of the Return of God, it was built on the pattern of the Great Mosque, with a long, colonnaded courtyard which has been infiltrated by houses. In its prayer-hall one of the most exquisite friezes of script in Syria breaks from a covering of plaster, and dances in pale sinews along the sanctuary wall.

*   *   *

Damascus grew half-immune to plagues, assassinations and petty revolts. Only extreme calamities harrowed the roots of her adaptability. Such a time came at the end of the fourteenth century, when the Mameluke cavalry rode out of the city against the governor of Aleppo. 'Nothing was seen of them but their eyeballs, as though they were lions, handsome men with fine armour,' wrote a contemporary. After they had left, the Damascenes sealed up their gates against the Aleppans and stoned the Mameluke sultan out of their streets. The sultan gathered a mob of bandits and Bedouin, and with the viceroy of Aleppo he attacked the city. According to an eyewitness, several quarters were immolated in flames, 'so that men said that Damascus would never be as prosperous as it had been. . . . From the smells of the burning and the slain it became a corpse. . . .' The next day a furious, indecisive battle was fought around the Kaysan Gate, and one of the city wall-towers collapsed during the night; but when the sultan appeared in the morning to admire the breach, he found that the citizens had rebuilt the tower by candlelight. Another day's carnage persuaded him to leave Damascus in peace.

Soon afterwards Ibn al-Hanăs, who had tried to cut off the city's waters, was captured in the Baalbek citadel. His end is a revolting comment on the pitilessness of an angry people. He and his chiefs 'were crucified below Qubbat Sayyār and the populace went out to take delight in watching them . . . the crucified ones arrived with Ibn al-Hanăs in the forefront, crucified on a camel, with the head of his little son tied around his neck. . . .'

*   *   *

Nemesis came out of the east. Tamerlane only captured Damascus by treachery, for his warriors were repulsed at the walls.

For three days and nights the city burned. Thirty thousand men, women and children were bolted into the Great Mosque, and convulsed in flames. Every surviving male over five years old was carried away to Samarkand, and Damascus lay among her orchards like the carcass of a mountain, peopled by tiny children.

11. The Unspeakable Turk

. . . and whenever Allah wishes ill
to his servants He appoints their fool-
ish ones as governors and their ignorant ones as judges. . . .
Shaddâd ibn 'Amr ibn Aûs

A borrowed fur does not warm, and
if it warm, it does not last.
Syrian proverb

'TAMERLANE WAS NO good!' shouted Elias. 'By God, if I had caught Tamerlane! Boom! Boom!' His enormous hands pounded the air. 'If people want to annoy us in Damascus, you know what they call us? They call us sons of Tamerlane!' His laughter detonated round the room. Umm-Toni's eyebrows were shooting up and down. Tamerlane had suddenly become an almost domestic concern. 'And you know why they call us sons of Tamerlane? Because this was the only place in Syria where he ordered his soldiers to take the women. God help them! It goes to show that our women were always most beautiful!'

It was Christmas day and I had casually remarked that the Mongols, who had terrified Damascus for two centuries, had once declared themselves Christians. Elias, in a proper defence of Christianity, had declared Tamerlane, at least, to have been a Moslem; and not only a Moslem but a Shia, who had destroyed Damascus out of wrath at the memory of the Ommayads, dead six hundred years.

Christmas day was otherwise peaceful. I had woken to the chiming of bells, and to Umm-Toni, who scurried into my room clutching a tiny cup of coffee, spilling it with an 'A-ooh'. Outside, the sunlight was already harsh on clamouring church domes and silent minarets.

The Bahenas had been to the Greek Catholic church at midnight, and they were tired. They sat under a small Christmas tree, which winked lights, and sheltered figurines of the Nativity. Nobody gave presents. There were too many of them, and no money. Only Rahda had a tin of milk, and watched herself in the mirror as she drank it, laughing most of it into splodges about her cheeks.

I had bought her a bracelet and a mouth-organ, and for the younger children some inexpensive clockwork toys made in China and Japan. Soon the hall was filled with cranking and burring and incredulous laughter: a monkey with a bell, a begging rabbit, a bear which raised its hat and twiddled on its back paws.

Elias sat in his underclothes on the divan, like a dinosaur. He kept beaming down at the mechanical chaos gambolling about the floor. 'Really', he said, quietly, 'really . . . I don't know what . . . I will tell you . . . By God, what I mean is. . . .' He hit his head in exasperation. Then, all in one breath 'you in Europe must be very-very-very-good!' The children were spoilt for any other Christmas, he said. Would I give him some envelopes with my address, so that every Christmas he could write and remind me of how I had spoilt them? Twenty envelopes would be enough. After that he would be dead.

The morning was very quiet, because Elias left for Beirut with two children to see Toni, his eldest son, who was at theological school there. Umm-Toni would not go, since she disliked her son, but she was always unhappy when Elias was away, and before he left she dabbed behind his ears most of the scent which I had given her for Christmas.

Relatives flowed in and out of the house all afternoon. The two smaller children slept in exhausted humps under the blankets, Umm-Toni was preparing something 'very rare' for dinner, and Rahda sat in the kitchen playing her Christmas mouth-organ. The ring-bracelet was too small for her hands, which were plumper than I had thought, but at last she wrenched it over her palm and onto her wrist. I do not think she will ever squeeze it off again, but she did not care. She kept dangling her hand in front of the mirror and simpering to her image in a parody of seduction. She was beginning to think herself beautiful. After a while Umm-Toni made her scrub the passageway floor.

The evening was the quietest I remember in the house, because Rahda went away to see her grandmother. Even on Christmas day the women and children do not eat until the men have finished their meal, so I sat alone over the stove in the hall, having dinner, while Umm-Toni grew sentimental and pulled out a box of photographs. 'This is Thérèse when she was two . . . here's Senah with funny hair. . . .' A relative had taken photographs each Easter: the children on their way to church, clutching gigantic candles and sprays of white flowers. As the snapshots became older, the children grew small and wide-eyed and vanished one by one. Umm-Toni's face cleared of its dints and lines, and Elias' belly dwindled into trimness. At the bottom of the pile she found the unctuously-tinted picture of a young woman. I would never have recognised her as Umm-Toni. Youth had filled out the hollows of her cheekbones, which gave her face its peculiarly aristocratic beauty, and had smoothed them into the formless velour which the Arabs admire.

'Ah-ooo,' she moaned, and smiled at the photograph so sadly that I thought she would cry. 'I was only seventeen. And so beautiful.' She looked at it and clicked her tongue and swayed her head from side to side. 'Now look at me!' She drew a hand down from her eyes to her chin, as if the flesh on her face had fallen into folds. 'Everything gone. Six children. And soon . . .' She pointed to her stomach. 'And there was another between Toni and Rahda, but she died. Dear God, that will be eight!'

She stood up suddenly. 'Now to work-work-work!' she said, as if the words could evict the past, and she heaved out a length of printed cotton which she had bought for Christmas. It was decorated with sour-faced dancing girls and would shortly be made into clothes for the children. The piece of cloth from the previous year was a simple check in blue and brown; it had made two dresses for Rahda and Thérèse, which they wore day and night, shirts for the boys and a skirt for Senah. Even the baby kicked his legs in blue and brown pantaloons. Next year's motif would be dancing-girls.

I went to an International Service at the Protestant church near the Gate of St Thomas. A handful of Germans and English had arrived punctually, and were sitting in their pews. For the first twenty minutes the Syrian Protestants scrambled into the church, hauling their babies over many pairs of outraged Teutonic feet. Worship oscillated among the four languages of the congregation. A German lesson and Armenian prayers were succeeded by an address in English. Then came the emphatic tones of Arabic, closest to those of Christ. In spite of our languages, we were united in our hymns, and anyone standing outside would have heard, in a strangely compounded tongue, 'Silent Night' and 'O Come All Ye Faithful'.

*　　*　　*

There is a romantic notion that after Tamerlane's sack Damascus lay waste for half a century. Damascus has never lain waste for more than half a year. The Mamelukes restored her, but did so like men uncertain of their time, as if they wished to grave their memory on a disintegrating world. They engendered a bluster of mosques and tombs, like those of Meidan, tricked out with incrustations. Commerce quickened into life again, but Venice, in a fresh stage of expansion, had destroyed Damascus' ascendancy. The art of making fine blades was lost to her for ever, and the spice trade was being garnered at its source by Portuguese sailors, who had discovered the seaway round Africa to the East.

Syria herself had changed. Her population was less than half that of Roman years. The superb forests which once darkened her hills had been hacked down by Byzantine builders and their successors. The rains had ignored the bare slopes and the soil had eroded. Men gave up their vineyards in despair. The ground seemed to be cursed. By Ottoman times a bundle of firewood was exchanged for its equivalent weight in meat. Travellers are still astonished by ruins standing alone in the desert: white-stoned churches, temples and whole towns; winepresses in a sea of stones; broken friezes of fruit and vines in the fallow sand.

It was already a woebegone land through which the Ottoman army of Selim I marched from the north in 1516. Since the disintegration of the Mongols, the Ottoman power had been elbowing its way through Asia Minor and Persia. Now it turned on Syria, and in contempt of the huge citadel of Aleppo, Selim sent a lame soldier armed only with a club, to whom the fortress was immediately surrendered.

The Mamelukes encountered Selim on the battlefield of Marj Dabiq. They still believed that great warriors could overcome all things. But the disciplined Turkish Janissaries—soldiers whom the Ottomans had captured as children and reared in the Islamic faith—were skilled in the use of firearms, and cannon mounted on wagons. Some of the Syrian contingents deserted the Mameluke army. The rest fought frenziedly against a foe who could strike men down before they had drawn their swords or shouted on their god. At the height of battle, the Mameluke sultan fell dead of apoplexy, and the day was lost.

For the next four centuries Syria belonged to the Turks. The Damascenes accepted Selim's governor merely as another foreign master. And they were glad to be rid of the Mamelukes. Selim himself arrived later and camped with an army of a hundred and thirty thousand near the Pass of Abraham; but soon after, he marched away to subdue Egypt, passing out of the city at night through the Jabiya Gate, by the light of torches.

He died four years later, and Damascus declared herself independent; but the Janissaries obliterated her army and destroyed a third of the city. Afterwards, with the rest of the Ottoman Empire, she was ruled without thought to her people. Her governors, like those of the late Mamelukes, were responsible only for prising taxes out of the citizens. Any signs of ability in a pasha were regarded with deep suspicion from Constantinople, and he would be removed from office at the merest whim. In the first hundred and eighty-four years under the Turks, the city saw a hundred and thirty-three different governors. But misrule was familiar to the Damascenes. Their grandfathers could remember no golden time.

*   *   *

A mile west of the Bahena's house, where the Street Called Straight ran parallel to the Great Mosque, loomed entrance-ways whose gates were anchored apart and bandaged in iron. Usually they led into the piebald light of broken ceilings and empty courtyards, yet most of them are still what they have always been—warehouses or wholesale centres, the *khans* of the Turks.

They were built to receive the caravans of the early Ottoman Empire, which came west from the Euphrates in trains of fifteen hundred beasts. When the drivers clouted the camels between their ears, they would stumble to their knees on the paved courtyards. Sacks of rhubarb and indigo were unloaded and locked in strongrooms as carefully as boxes of Bahrein pearls or European firearms. At night the merchants wrapped themselves in blankets and curled up along the galleries, sleeping above the heat of their camels. By midday the storekeepers were squatting in the *khan* colonnades, sucking their water-pipes and apparently oblivious of business. But the afternoons were shouted and whispered away in bargaining, while Janissaries, protectors of the caravans, strutted about in high boots and tall hats, plumed in feathers which dripped to their heels.

Damascus brass and ironwork, saddles and confectionery sold in all the markets of the empire. Chinese and Indian silk, which entered the city in bales of formless thread, left her in intricately worked brocades. The silver and copper trades still thrived. But already Far Eastern commerce was taking the longer but cheaper route around the Cape. By the eighteenth century printed cottons, pseudo-Cashmeres and the bright, simple woollens of England were vying in the bazaars with Italian velvet and the muslins and chintzes of India. Clothes arrived from Constantinople too, many of them second-hand, and the garments of people who had died of disease were spreading plague everywhere.

As the Ottoman Empire decayed, the *khans* saw less and less extravagant merchandise. Coffee and tobacco became the main luxuries from the East and wiry Agail Bedouin replaced the Janissaries. The opening of the Suez Canal ended the importance of the desert routes. Today not a single trading camel pads across the wilderness. Only a few lorries and buses use the Baghdad road. The *khans* have become markets of silence. They deal in local fabrics and sheepskins and have fragmented into dingy shops. If their roofs crash in, nobody will build them up again.

The Khan of Asaad Pasha is too huge for any wares which can be stacked there now. Black and white masonry, inset with balustrades and iron-grilled windows, reaches high to the pendentives, and flowers into a multitude of Persian cupolas, whose plasterwork has stripped away. Three of them have been shaken down by earthquake. The centre one, which reminded Lamartine of the dome of St Peter's, has also vanished, and a pool beneath it echoes its circle of sky. The imposts of the other domes are ringed with windows whose honeycomb tracery has been half preserved. In winter a group of porters, puny as church mice, crouches over a fire by the pool. In summer a rare tourist gazes up perplexed at the interplay of arches, and goes away.

Near by, in the Street Called Straight, a passageway of shops merges into the Khan es Zeyt, the old caravanserai of oil, now a warehouse for cotton and raw silks. Twenty small domes circle the porticoes of its open courtyard, and its pool has become a flower-bed, from which a vine wriggles to either end of the courtyard, flings itself over the railings, and kisses the balcony stone.

In the Zafrangiyah Khan a few simple elements conspire in a

chance harmony. It is shouldered by the robust fragments of classical columns, and preserves the painted ceiling of its arcades. An infant eucalyptus tree will one day drench the small court-yard in a fountain of green. The khan of Suleiman Pasha is piled with oil-drums. Even el-Harir, the old silk market, has lost its necklace of cupolas, and in the seven-domed Khan of the Customs the brocade merchants are rarely patronised.

The Ottoman Turks seem always to have built for pleasure. If so, the Tekkiyeh of Suleiman, where Whirling Dervishes danced every Friday and wove silk betweenwhiles, must have especially pleased them. Suleiman the Magnificent, most pow-erful of sultans, commanded its construction as a convent for the dervishes. Sinan, the magician of Turkish architecture, designed it in Constantinople, and it was built by Christian converts in six years on the site of the Black and Ochre Palace of Baybars.

The Damascenes had seen nothing like it. The nursery of Ottoman architecture had been Anatolia; it had passed into a dignified maturity at Bursa and grown magnificent in Constan-tinople. Now the *fait accompli* was placed like an opal on the banks of the Barada: a prayer-room with two pencil minarets, standing in a courtyard of slender-columned arcades. Almost a hundred small cupolas bubble above the porticoes, interspersed with pointed chimneys above the cells of the dervishes. Each doorway bears Damascene faience tiling over its entrance: a botanist's paradise of rare plants in sky colours. In the centre of the black and carmine courtyard a fountain breaks into a great square pool with unnatural violence. Cypresses and pine trees share the flower-beds with red and white roses. For a dwelling of mystics it is sensuous and earthbound. Nature here is not an enemy, but a loved one; not a place to be abandoned, but a realm with which to be united: the 'celestial grove' of the pantheistic Sufis.

Now the army has turned the northern colonnade into an arms museum and installed anti-aircraft guns and fighter planes in the gardens; but the mosque overpowers them by sheer femininity.

I walked through its northern gate into the avenue of a ruined market, which catered to the Meccan pilgrims camping in the plains to the west. Beside it lies the courtyard of a hostel for scholars called the Madrasa Selimiya. It has been locked and abandoned for several years, but a piece of wood had fallen away from the foot of the door, and through it I could see into the courtyard. A few feet inside the entrance sprawled a dump for iron bedsteads, where a dropsical cat lounged on its back. Beyond, the courtyard was muffled in weeds. Yet the cupolas swelled up from the arcades like ripe fruit, and a Persian dome appeared to have settled on the prayer-room from the sky.

Most of the Turkish buildings partake of the city's life. If you press open the door of the Sinaniye religious school, expecting to hear the murmur of the Koran, you will be greeted by the chatter and thump of two cobblers who have made it their home. The Kichani bath has been converted into a circle of shops, filled with bright, cheap jewellery and scarves. Its tilework is dim and smirched, but its pretty dome and painted piers join in the baroque fantasy with a good grace.

Half-fanciful paintings decorate the cupola of the Khayyatin bath, with the portrait of a Heath Robinson train (probably the Beirut railway) trundling into Constantinople; but the bath is now a laundry, an inferno of steam where enormous iron rollers press out piles of dehydrated linen.

In the Sinan Pasha, an Ottoman mosque with a green-tiled minaret, I watched the midday prayer. Ironmongers and carpenters rolled up their sleeves at the fountain and entered the prayer-room still dripping with the water of their ablutions. The hall is rich with Ottoman symmetry. Side-arcades uphold small galleries; sculptured pendentives rise to a voluptuous dome. The eye is not tempted upwards, but beleaguered by darkness wherever it looks. Praying men stand in dense lines facing a blank wall in the direction of Mecca. Time and again the mosque fills with the susurration 'God is Most Great', as the imam leads a new prayer. Foreheads touch the ground, and bare feet show pink on the mulberry carpets, while the tarboushes and keffiehs of prostrate heads almost rub the hennaed toes of the worshippers in front.

These happy mosques, children of Santa Sophia, followed the Ottomans round their empire. They, and all mosques before them, bespeak a people whose lives are preordained and whose religious duties are fixed. They have no need of the heights and distances of European churches, which awaken the imagination. The Arab imagination (contrary to popular belief) is poor, and the existence of God is accepted without thought. They reverence and praise but rarely ask anything of Him. Submission is second nature.

Everywhere the mosques die and are not always reborn. In the wastes of Cairo and the shrines of Anatolia, in Tunis and

Pakistan, Syria and Samarkand, the domes fracture and the tiles are stripped away. Abbeys and churches sometimes transcend decay. Mosques, perhaps because they knew no aspiration, are depressing in ruin. The mystics of Islam never loved them, but went to other places; to convents which were palaces of flowing water, and to séances of music like the waves of the sea.

Mysticism, in a faith so literal as Islam, developed warily, under the angry eye of the doctors of law. The Moslem mystic, the Sufi, passed from a study of Islamic principle into the way of communion with God. Through thought and learning, fast and vigil, the dervish grew to the state of *hal*, of association with the Almighty, and from thence to *maqam*, the perfect union, in which man was lost in God, himself became God.

One of the newest mosques in Damascus carries on its minaret a dervish fez in place of the Ottoman crescent moon. When I knocked at its gates, an old man in a woollen cap came to the railing and told me that the mosque was closed. I asked him if it had stood on the site of the Turkish convent for the Mevlevi, the Whirling Dervishes, who had originally been quartered in the Tekkiyeh of Suleiman. He nodded his head, but replied that the sect was not what it had been; anyway, what was it to me?

I said that I had seen his order in southern Turkey.

'Yes? In Konya? The Mevlevi?' A minute later we were sitting in his room, surrounded by photographs of dancing dervishes and pontifical Sufis in chimney-stack fezzes and spectacular beards. On the walls hung a pair of *niyes*, Mevlevi flutes, whose sound is called 'the Voice of Angels'. The picture of a lugubrious white-headed seer represented Celal-ed-Din Rumi, the thirteenth-century Persian who founded the dervish order. He had come to Damascus as a young man in a troubled spirit, but had returned to Turkey and remained there.

'This is me,' said the old man, pointing to a heap of photographs. He was a sheikh of dervishes. The pictures showed him glancing down with histrionic condescension at men who were kissing his hand. I looked from the illustrious, bearded Sufi of the photograph to the half-shaven man on the divan. 'I have twelve children,' he was saying. 'My children, you understand?' He moved his palm close to the ground as if following a toddling child, and pointed to photographs round the walls of the room; serious-faced boys spiralled there in white heavy-hemmed robes.

'Are all your children dervishes?' I asked in astonishment.

'Six of them are girls,' he answered. 'You understand? Girls.'

He described a superb pair of breasts. 'The girls are not initiate. But six of them are boys. You understand? Boys,' he went on relentlessly, 'you know.' Here, a prodigious penis.

I wondered if the sect still whirled in Damascus. The old man's children must by now have produced a new dervish generation. In Turkey the order has been outlawed and must perform its rites in secret. Only once a year, on the anniversary of their founder's death, they are permitted to dance publicly. But they have spiralled along the rim of heresy ever since their foundation, searching, in the intoxication of dance and music, for union with a pantheistic god.

'Is your sect strong here?' I prodded.

'It is not like it was. Once we were honoured. Now we are tolerated. And recently some people have been making trouble for us.'

'So you still dance?'

He hesitated momentarily. Suddenly he said: 'Come on Friday night. I will wait for you here. I will explain to the others that you know of our brotherhood from Konya. Come alone.'

I arrived after the last call to prayer. Men were still kneeling in the mosque, or splashing their arms and ankles in the fountain. The door of the sheikh's room half opened and a rod of light fell across the courtyard.

He beckoned me in. I sat on a divan with a group of quiet men. Soon the room began to fill up with dervishes, carrying their robes in white sacks under their arms. Some were businessmen, their stomachs pressed snugly against waistcoats of English cloth; but most of them looked like peasants, half shaven, with diffident faces. As each man entered the room he bent and kissed the sheikh's hand. One of them was his brother, the *Samazehn-Bashi*, who trained the dancers. Several men brought their sons, ten or twelve years old. We were each given a glass of tea and a dry cake. One of the dervishes held the Mevlevi drum and *daff* tambourine near the oil stove, until the skins stretched tight.

'The boys are learning to be Mevlevi,' said the sheikh. 'Already they can dance.' The men were changing into white, ankle-length robes, tied at the waist with cords and sashes in geometrical designs. Out of the bucket-shaped tins they pulled the peculiar tall *kulah* fezzes and placed them on their heads over white skull-caps. Then they struggled into long-sleeved jackets of white cotton, and draped themselves in black cloaks which enveloped them like chrysalids.

There was a very big man amongst them, an Algerian with a searchless face, always smiling. 'He is our imam,' said a dervish. 'He leads us on the good path. He keeps our mind and spirit.'

The sheikh only wore a cloak over his clothes, and his *kulah* was fringed with a green sash. 'You will enter the mosque with my son here,' he said to me, 'holding your shoes like an Arab. Don't speak to anybody.' He stood up slowly, flicking back his sleeves over his wrists. The dervishes hugged themselves in their cloaks, stepped out of the door and dissolved into the blackness.

The praying had already started when I entered, and more than a hundred people stood in the mosque in brilliant light. The prayers lengthened into intricate measures and calls, twined in flute-sounds. I moved along a wall and leant near the door behind a double-rank of old men in ruby-red tarboushes. Some women dithered in the entrance. One of them twisted her veil across her mouth, disclosing a forehead and nose which ran together in a straight line like coin-portraits of Cleopatra and Zenobia.

The people began to bow rhythmically. The tambours and flutes keened. The dervishes kissed the sheikh's hand and discarded their cloaks. The people chanted in breathless rhythm 'la All*ah*! illa 'llah! la All*ah*! illa 'llah!' until their bending and straightening became fierce and distorted. The dervishes stepped into the rectangle of men, their white robes chaste and feminine under the artificial light. They began to whirl, slowly at first, with their arms closed across their chests, their faces secret and peaceful. 'La All*ah*! illa 'llah! la All*ah*!' The sounds grew hoarse and beseeching. The dancers' dresses began to flare round them along the carpets as they twirled. Their hands spread away from their chests until they only touched the sides of their ribs in archaic gestures. Then, one by one, they outstretched their arms as if miming a flower unfolding its petals.

The dance imitates the revolving of the spheres. The left palm of the dervish faces upward, the right downward, for with one he will accept God's blessing, and with the other pass it on to earth. His head is bent to one side, his soul diffused into the world, his body an empty casket.

Three times the music stopped, the dancers drifted away, the chanting fell silent. Prayers and flutes held the mood of the dance on wisps of sound. The sheikh watched the dervishes intently, with his back to the *mihrab*, and his brother, the

Samazehn-Bashi, walked among them as they danced and studied their feet and faces.

At last they moved forward in their black cloaks, revolving very slowly, their hands grasping their robes in the foetal position. The boys turned with them, faces still as seraphs'. The people bent and unbent violently now and a rabid-faced sheikh invoked them with a supplicating motion of his fingers. The chant of 'la All*ah*!' had changed to groans, which burst out in heady, animal rhythms. The men's feet were almost kicked from the ground by the energy of their motions. Their heads jerked like marionettes. The music rose and fell around them— the panting of tambours, the disembodied ecstasy of the Voice of Angels—impalpable sounds which drugged the senses and overran the brain.

Some of the people had become frantic. Half-articulated cries escaped them. Their bodies heaved from side to side. Sweat spread from their foreheads to their cheeks, and glittered at their chins. The ranks broke up, coats fell to the ground and men jostled and butted each other sightlessly.

The sheikh's son took my arm. 'It is nearly finished. We must go now. Quickly.' We wedged our way through the women and rammed our feet into our shoes at the door. But a man reached us. He was angry.

'What did you think of that?' he rasped at me. 'It is barbaric. You understand it is not of Islam. It is not of Mahomet. You understand that?'

But we were pressed apart by a crowd of veiled women and sweating men, and I walked under the lip of the mosque stair to the sheikh's room. The dervishes were all concerned about the man. He had tried to make trouble for them before. I looked round at their puckered brows and wondered how long the order could go on, before they might be forced to whirl in secret and fill only private houses with the Voice of Angels. We all left together, the dervishes kissing the sheikh's hand again before the night effaced them.

Dogs disputed a mutton bone in the Street Called Straight. The night was warm and almost empty. Two Druse women moved along the paving, their full-length brocades glistening fantastically in the lamp-light. I had never seen Druse women walking about at night before, but the evening had lost its senses long ago. Mevlevi music spiralled in my head. I remembered the man's question: 'What did you think of that?' But I had no ready answer. I only knew that whenever I had looked at the sheikh I had felt obscurely confused. His robes, his fez and his heavy-rimmed glasses had invested him with a sorcerer's majesty. Yet every time I glanced at him through the maze of transported dancers, an earlier voice kept interrupting the ceremony: 'You know . . . Girls . . . You understand? Boys. . . .'

12. The White Death

Damascus is waxed feeble and turn-
eth herself to flee. . . . How is the
city of praise not left, the city of my
joy!

Jeremiah xlix. 24-25

A red death is a death in war. A
black death is the fruit of treachery.
But a white death is a death in the bed,
which is to be despised.

Arabic Tradition

A TURBULENT CITY seems to be ennobled by times of
danger. In peace her emotions fester ignominiously; in war
they are justified and expended. The long lull of the Ottoman
years was more humiliating for Damascus than the catastrophes
of earlier times. Her rebellions appear petty or pointless, and
only brought her a succession of callous governors from
Constantinople.

Overland traffic veered to Alexandretta through Aleppo,
which opened her gates to Venetians and Genoese, then to
French and English trading companies. But Damascus was the
holy city of Syria, the gateway to Mecca and the resting-place of
many of Mahomet's companions. European merchants were not
permitted to settle in her precincts. Her own Christians and
Jews were compelled to walk in her gutters and wear special
clothes. Western travellers had to change into Turkish costume,
dismount at the walls and enter through quiet gates.

Her unease festered under a cult of inactivity. On the banks of
the Barada the tinkle of coffee-cups barely disturbed the quiet of
the cafés, where a whispered word could begin the fall of a pasha
or the death of an emir. The city houses, bordering dirt-filled
streets, threw up crumbling and anonymous façades. But from
their doors emerged merchants plumed and robed like Brazilian
birds, or Ottoman civil servants who rode robust and beautiful
horses. The Janissaries, grown incompetent by the end of the
eighteenth century, stuck their sashes with pistols and curvili-
near daggers, and trailed elegant swords through the dust.
Men's beards were short and carefully-barbered—a perfect

beard, they say, may be concealed in the clenched hand—and their heads, after the Ottoman fashion, were shaved, except for a defiant top-notch by which the angel of salvation might pull them up to heaven on the Last Day.

A woman went incognito beneath the all-enveloping *izzar*. Her yellow boots, as she walked splay-footed in baggy trousers, enhanced her appearance of a monstrous duck. Beneath the cloak, perhaps, a gold-edged veil fell below her eyes, or she wore the flower-painted shroud which may still be seen in Arabia and old Jerusalem. Sometimes Nubian slave-women, distinguishable only by the whites of their eyes, walked behind their mistresses, or they were followed by little slave-girls in flowered silk pantaloons and velvet jackets, a transparent veil billowing behind them.

The governor of Damascus kept great state. He moved in the midst of a Moorish or Kurdish bodyguard and was attended by a host of pompously-titled attendants, puffed out by gigantic turbans sprayed with jewels and egret feathers. In a year or two he would be promoted through a covert bribe, or recalled to the capital to face some trumped-up charge and execution. Even in Damascus, the citadel precincts were forbidden to him. Here officers responsible only to Constantinople dawdled on the battlements, or gazed from the watchtowers from under turbans like coils of whipped cream.

In late Ottoman times the pasha might vanish from the city for three months every year, collecting taxes from his provinces. He would be followed by a small army, and there were bitter battles in towns and mountain villages before the tribute was exacted. Only a few of the pashas ruled with any efficiency or conscience; but they had to contend with rooted lethargy and corruption. Abd-Allah, *Arabian Nights* fashion, wandered the streets in disguise doing justice; Asaad Pasha al-Azem saved the city from famine; Midhat Pasha undertook building and street-planning reforms.

The Damascenes regard Asaad Pasha as the shrewdest of their governors. He curbed the wealthy merchants, who kept bazaar prices high by creating artificial scarcities, and he temporarily dealt with local dissensions and stemmed the Druses, who were constantly in revolt. 'I have fleeced the rams,' he once remarked, 'and not skinned the lambs and kids.'

He remained governor of Damascus for fourteen years—an extraordinary feat—and the palace which he built in 1749, and which is named after him, still stands. Its construction disrupted the city. For months he used every mason and carpenter, and water which should have welled up in mosque pools and private courtyards was irrigating the pasha's new gardens. Ox-carts of classical pillars arrived from the Roman ruins of Deraa and Bosra, and the Baniyas river was diverted from its course so that ancient paving could be recovered from its bed.

The entrance is imposing still, and leads through a broad passageway of tiered masonry in orange, white and black. Engraved table-tops line the walls like armorial shields. The design of the palace is classically Syrian, its rooms ranged round two courtyards. The larger, the *Haremlik*, housed the pasha and his family. The smaller *Selamlik* was used for the reception of friends; but in 1925, during the revolt against the French, the wooden pavilion over the palace gateway was burnt down, and the flames spread to the *Selamlik*, where the intricate decorations and furniture smoked up uncontrolled for three days.

I felt more like an intruder than a guest here. There was no sound, as if many doors had been closed quietly behind. The courtyard seemed to remember its wounds. Citron leaves floated across the surface of its pool, and goldfish drifted there, like the flotsam of a sunset. The rooms had been rebuilt in the simplicity of their first years; for the fire cleansed away the baroque trivialities of 1830, the false tapestries and glamorously inlaid woods. Now the *iwan* where the guests sipped coffee has been peopled by the waxwork figures of the Museum of Folk Art and Tradition.

I walked through a bent passageway into the vestibule of the *Haremlik*, and heard the wind in its courtyard. The great round brasses were clanging against the corridor walls, lanterns clinked distractedly in its arcades, and fountain water scoured along the paving among whorls of leaves.

A storm in this garden seems like a madness in nature. The courtyard encloses peace as if it had found it here and walled it round. Even as I watched, the rampaging clouds began to break into static lumps. The striped masonry of the buildings around the garden accentuates its spaciousness. Near its entrance falls a star-shaped fountain. Beyond it, among exhausted citron trees, a pencil of water leads to a rectangular pond, on whose edge crouches a small, white lion, a soft toy in stone. And at the back of the courtyard is a marble dais, where the pasha could sit on summer nights in a snare of jasmine.

The arcades and windows are filled with lanterns: glass bowl lamps, octagonal wall lamps and enamelled lamps with green and yellow candle-holders projecting beneath them, like stiffened octopuses. The marquetry and inlay of the arcades and walls is subtle and restrained, and the paving-stones blend from black and white to saffron and dusky pink.

The sun slants through the garden in straw-coloured rivers. The only sounds are water and the causerie of leaves—heirs to the tinkle and whisper of the harem. Few but the family and servants of the pasha ever saw it: an enclosed garden of the kind the Arabs cherish. Its spiritual ancestors are the gardens of ancient Rome, and the sober courts which Roman men of letters bequeathed to mediaeval Tuscany: gardens for the service of the soul as well as the intoxication of the senses.

The whole *Haremlik* has scarcely changed since Ottoman times. The long robes and monstrous turban of the pasha could loom up at any moment among the trees. Another breeze may bring the self-important forms of eunuchs and wardrobe-keepers, or Circassian odalisques, lissom as flowers.

The rooms of the palace are not linked to one another, but open onto the courtyard in a fashion which was probably Roman. At the entrance to each chamber is a marble-paved threshold in which a fountain is set like a huge snowflake. On one side, or on both, a room is raised a foot above ground level, its walls lined with silk-covered divans where the pasha's family used to loll among Ming porcelain and Damascus glass and a thousand objects made in Europe to flatter and degrade oriental taste. On fierce summer days only a dream of sunlight would reach them through the draped windows. In winter the tall rooms chilled the most obese pasha, and the concubines curled complaining round their fires as the heat spiralled away through enchanting conical chimneys.

Waxwork figures pervade the whole palace with their discomfiting presence. In one room stands a bride in a royal blue robe embroidered with golden flowers, her head bound in a long veil by a white garland, and her hands dyed with henna in a pattern like snakes' skin. In another room rests the *mahmal*, the green and gold canopy which accompanied pilgrims to Mecca, and there are a few rare examples of Damascus swords, forged before the time of Tamerlane. Their steel was probably imported from Hyderabad and kneaded to iron in such firm layers that it took on a curious watered appearance, which was called 'the ladder by which God's servants reached His Heaven'. The blades were so sharp that they could slice a leaf as it fell through the air, or sever an armoured knight from his crest to his spur.

But lying in the vitrine of the dark palace, they look almost fragile: thin, brightly-polished and damascened in gold. After Tamerlane destroyed Damascus, the Mediterranean never again knew such instruments of death and beauty.

Seven years after the completion of his palace, Asaad Pasha was removed from office. He left Damascus bitterly, opening the gates of the prisons before he went, and the city erupted in chaos. The Janissaries and the Druses fought one another in the streets, along with the Moorish infantry, the Kurdish cavalry, the new governor's forces, the Baghdadis, the Turcoman dālis, the Mawsilis and the levies of the Ashrāf. At the same time the Mecca pilgrimage was attacked by Bedouin and without help the whole caravan was plundered and engulfed in the desert, where twenty thousand people died of exposure, or fell under the scimitars of the nomads.

Asaad Pasha was accused, probably unjustly, of inciting the Bedouin. In 1758 he was strangled by an agent of the Sublime Porte in the public baths at Ankara. The sultan's men ransacked the palace at Damascus for concealed treasure, dredging the fountains and ripping out pavements and panelling. Yet the building remained in the hands of the pasha's family, and at the time of the French occupation sixty-four of his descendants were sharing its precincts.

*   *   *

Asaad's palace is reflected, on a small scale, by every old house in the city. Outside, the walls give an appearance of poverty, which betrayed nothing to Ottoman extortioners; each door opens into a dark passageway, which turns sharply to lock out curious stares. The courtyard beyond comes as a sensuous shock with its idle fountain crowded by plants in pots, the extravagance of marble and the smell of fruit trees. In summer the vines climb up the walls and fall from wire trellises in dribblings of green. In autumn jasmine and bougainvillaea, oleander and verbena overlay the windows, and pots are filled with the damask rose—more wizened, but more fragrant, than its scion in Europe.

The fountains are sometimes inlaid with porphyry, even mother-of-pearl. The marble paving, patterned with vulcanite or sandstone, may cover the sides of the walls for several feet, and in houses which have completely preserved the Damascene style, thick bands, usually brightly painted, run round the sides of the court. The windows are latticed or barred, and steep staircases lead up to the bedrooms.

The nineteenth century brought a pseudo-baroque orgy against which the Damascenes knew no resistance. The comparative restraint of Arabic decoration was overrun. Even the fountain-pools were embellished with neurotic cascades. I once spent an afternoon in the Bêt Moujalled, the prime *maison baroque* of Damascus. It is owned by one of the city's rich ex-landowners, who told me, without bitterness, that the socialist government had stripped him of most of his estates.* It was the will of God. And he still had the house, which his ancestors had decorated in the style of Istanbul. Copses of columns supported mirror-backed niches encrusted in coloured marbles, and crowned with ormolu arches and swags of vines. Wall paintings displayed the domes and cypress trees of Istanbul, and Ottoman galleys floated through the flaking plaster. Even the courtyard was filled with the gambolling of a rococo arcade.

It would be mean to resent a style like the Istanbul baroque if its fancies had not smothered the framework of beauty. But the essence of the Damascene house is simplicity. Its luxuries are water and shade, and its decorations find harmony and discipline in a love of the intricate. The Beit es Sibai, with its consummately-inlaid doors and the muted colours of its ceilings, is typical of this devotion to detail—too reserved in its total effect to detract from the fountain-courtyard, where the vines, even in winter, are garlanded strangely from tree to tree.

The Dahdah palace in the old Jewish quarter is another fine example of Damascus decorative work. It is owned by a well-known merchant, and the dark, graceful woman who comes to its door is his American wife. The walls of its *iwan*—the recessed hall on the south side of the courtyard—are inlaid with coloured stucco after a fashion peculiar to the city, and its rooms are full of ancient coins and Hittite figurines, as plump and mimetic as plasticene animals.

These houses, like thousands of smaller ones, preserve their simple luxuries. On summer evenings a north breeze blows into the *iwan*, where the host and his family sit on divans to receive their friends.

* This was the left-wing Baathist government of General Ameen Hafiz, which was overthrown a month later in February, 1966.

'*Qahwa dayiman,*' murmurs the guest as he fingers his tiny coffee-cup. 'May coffee be found for ever in your house.'

The ritual is immemorial. Narghilyes are lit up with practised care, for in the house in which no pipe is offered, they say there is no compassion. The courtyard walls extinguish the noises outside, and those within—the song of a bird or the bubbling of a fountain—become the distillation of all evening sounds.

But domestic life has changed for ever. Only fifty years ago a man might take four wives and many slave-girls. Now he has only one wife. 'Of course,' someone will murmur, 'I know a certain merchant in Keimariye Street . . .' and the voice trails away into a discreet whisper; but there are no more harems in Damascus.

The concubines were generally foreign peasant girls sold by impoverished parents. Immured in the harems, they must soon have forgotten their childhood. For they were beautiful in silk pelisses of lilac and rose colour, split-sided and open at the bosom, their trains gathered up behind them to the waist. Underneath bloomed wide trousers, a gold-threaded bodice, and a gauze chemise. Golden coins clinked in their hair, and jewelled pendants at their ears. Their fezzes were ornamented with pearls and brilliants, and a Damascus scarf, twined in roses and orange-blossom, fell over the left shoulder.

The most favoured concubines were the smouldery-eyed Georgians and the porcelain beauties of Circassia. They preserved their beauty well. They lay idle in perfumed baths, nibbled sweetmeats and grew jealous of one another. The wives themselves could not always leave the household when they pleased. Some, even today, are immolated behind their lattices; and on the few occasions when they go out, they sit apart from their husbands, who rarely stoop to speak with them in public.

In Ottoman times disobedient wives were so cruelly beaten that their crying pealed through the streets. (An American visitor, kept awake by screams and blows from a near-by house, was horrified to see the woman's funeral cortège leave it the next day.) It is still insulting for a friend to mention a Moslem's womenfolk. An informal remark can be construed as an aspersion on a girl's character. I once mistakenly asked Mustafa how Refaiyeh was, and the retort blazed back: 'Refaiyeh is a good woman! She works in my father's house!'

Many travellers were distracted by the Damascene women, who in Ottoman times were esteemed the most beautiful in the Levant. The Jewesses, who took employment as singers and dancers, were especially praised. Only the sophisticated D'Arvieux, ambassador of Louis XIV, looked at the peasant girls and 'thought 'em all-over ugly'. The Reverend Vere Monro, in his 1833 travelogue, devoted a sentence or two to St Paul, but wrote pages about the less spiritual beauties of Damascus. A Spanish monk guided him round Christian houses where he surprised decolleté slave-girls throwing water over each other or sleeping on divans. Their hair, he remarks, 'fell down their backs to the waist, concealing their marble shoulders in its hyacinthine flow: their eyes, large and languishingly blue, something richer than the turquoise, something brighter than the jewel of Giamschid, lighted up complexions clear as aether, and the vermeil blossoms of the pomegranate would lose in comparison with the blushes that bloomed on their cheeks. . . . But,' the reverend padre adds ruefully, 'I cannot like their painted toe-nails.' Later he asked after their husbands and the monk replied that he had ordered them to be absent. 'I do not mention this fact to draw any undue censure on the good friar individually,' he hastens to say, 'but to give some idea of the authority that is usurped, from which evil consequences *might* ensue.'

Eventually however, the padre left Damascus 'in disappointment not unmingled with feelings of regret', and he reproached the city in Latin from the comfortable loftiness of the neighbouring mountains. It was a place 'ad libidines abominandas dedita' and little better than Sodom and Gomorrah.

Damascus, in reality, has for centuries been an honest and morally conservative city. Brothels are few and even eighty years ago an unveiled woman was assumed to be a prostitute, and would be executed without trial. Spies were employed to watch lonely streets for clandestine meetings. A Frenchman who came to the city in 1818 recounts how a girl raised her veil and revealed her face to him, upon which a passing Albanian blew out her brains and strolled on.

However lovely the women may have been, the veils increase their allure. The lives they were forced to lead allowed them few accomplishments. Beneath their cloaks their minds were vacant or petty, and their voluptuous mouths were frequently chewing gum—an old Eastern habit—or muttering obscene language. Their husbands made them the receptacle of bigotry and ignorance and they, in turn, would have been horrified by a hint of change.

*   *   *

Change came only once, and fleetingly, in four centuries of Ottoman rule, when Ibrahim Pasha, the son of Mehemet Ali of Egypt, took Damascus from the Turks in 1832. The Janissaries, by now no more than a gang of robbers, had marched out against him with a great deal of 'boast and vapour', carelessly arrayed and ridiculously armed. No sooner had they glimpsed the Egyptian army than they turned about and marched back into the city, to the hoots and laughter of the Damascenes, who crowded the walls to watch them.

During the ten years of enlightened, French-influenced Egyptian rule, men were not allowed to carry arms in the city, and Christians and Jews were placed on an equal footing with Moslems. For the first time, foreigners could enter Damascus in European dress. New building schemes were undertaken. But the Damascenes resented the changes. Angered by military conscription, they expelled Ibrahim Pasha, and fell again under Ottoman rule.

Their xenophobia was not merely an inheritance from the Crusades. Cut off from the civilising influence of the Mediterranean by the barrier of Lebanon, Damascus has always been insular and bigoted. Nature left her no defence against infiltration from the desert in the east; she is still the bridge where warriors and tribesmen become merchants and artisans, and desert emotion permeates her. The Damascenes twice revolted simply at the prospect of a British vice-consul arriving from Beirut to take up the appointment long ago granted him by Constantinople. They revolted at a scheme for cleaning the city streets, because it was a European innovation, stormed the progressive governor in his citadel and threw his head over the walls of the Franciscan convent with a label tied to it: 'Here's your friend.'

They have a long history of massacres. In the reign of Nero they slaughtered ten thousand of the city Jews in a single day, after keeping the plans hidden from their wives, who were mostly addicted to Judaism. But to talk of 'the battle' or 'the massacre' in Damascus now, can only mean the Moslem risings of 1860.

The Druses in the Lebanon, fomented by Constantinople, had been conducting annihilations of Maronite Christian villages ever since Ibrahim Pasha had been expelled. In 1860 the agitation spread to Moslems in Damascus, and they invaded the Christian quarter. The killing lasted three days. The Christians, if they had fought, might have saved themselves (the

Greek consul sat at his window with a bottle of *raki* and shot every Moslem who approached his door; eventually the heap of bodies warned men to keep away) but most of the Christians hid. They were flushed out by fires or suffocated in chimneys and wells. Several hundred were burnt in the Church of St Mary, and those who tried to escape were pushed back into the flames. Fires ravaged all the principal churches. It is said that several hundred women were driven naked through the streets and sold to the Bedouin for a few shillings each.

The Turkish chief-of-police and his men joined in the killing, luring Christians out with promises of safety, then shooting them down. Only Abd-el-Kader and his Algerians roamed the quarter in an effort to prevent bloodshed. Soon his courtyard was packed with Christians, including European consuls and merchants, and he escorted hundreds of others to the citadel, where they were granted grudging protection by the pasha. But by the end of the third day two thousand five hundred men in the Christian sector had been murdered.

Europe was horrified and angered; the French landed troops in Lebanon. The Sultan, to pacify the Great Powers, sent his foreign minister to mete out justice in Damascus. The governor, the chief-of-police, several Turkish captains and a hundred and fifty others were quickly executed, and for weeks the bodies dangled from gibbets along the city streets. Damascus, as a holy city, had been exempt from conscription, but now more than twenty thousand of her young men were forcibly enrolled and marched in wooden stocks over the mountains to Beirut. Christian Lebanon was declared a separately administered state, or *mutesafariyat*, within the Ottoman Empire. And Europe was pacified.

13. A Parcel of Giddy Boys

Travelling! Young men travelling! I
cannot, my dear, but think it a very
nonsensical thing! . . . To see a parcel
of giddy boys . . . hunting after—what?—
Nothing; or at best but ruins of ruins.

Letters of Harriet Byron to Lucy Selby.
From Richardson's *Sir Charles Grandison*

EARLY GIDDINESS WAS conditioned by religion, by the
wish—almost talismanic—to tread on holy ground. Only pilgrims
ventured from Europe to brave the East, and out of the Dark
Ages to Damascus came men so short of words that one cannot
guess their feelings.

At the head of this procession, whose age and restraint have
lent it a half-legendary stature, rides the Gallic bishop Arculf in
A.D. 670. Nothing is known of him, and of Damascus he simply
records: 'The king of the Saracens [Muawiya] has seized the
government, and reigns in that city, and a large church has been
built there in honour of John the Baptist. There has also been
built in that same city a church of unbelieving Saracens which
they frequent.'

Scarcely fifty years later came St Willibald, 'perfect in charity
and gentleness', whose family tree is adorned with saints and
with the kings and queens of Wessex. He is recorded, with
biblical simplicity, as having arrived with his party at 'Damascus, where St Ananias rests', seen the church of St Paul's
conversion, 'And there they prayed, and walked on to Galilee'.

To the mediaeval Arabs travelling was easier. Not only were
they members of the world's greatest empire, but the custom of
hospitality opened men's doors to them wherever they wandered.
Highly-developed powers of observation made many of them
fascinating travellers. Mukaddasi, a native of Jerusalem in the
tenth century, journeyed on foot for twenty years, living the
lives of those among whom he moved and joining bizarre
religious sects. Even in those days of Damascus' decline, he reported superb baths and fountains, but 'the climate is scorching and the inhabitants are turbulent; fruit here is insipid and

meat hard; also the houses are small and the streets sombre. Finally, the bread there is bad, and a livelihood hard to make.'

But Damascus had long since been consecrated by the tombs of men who had stood close to the Prophet, and by the time of her recovery in the twelfth century the praises of poets hyperbolised her meanest stream and orchard. She has become the Bride of the Earth and Mother of Cities, the Star of the Wind, *al-Fayha*—the Verdant, the Diamond of the Desert; her winds are wine and her soil is perfume, her gardens encircle her as the halo round the moon, and contain her as if she were the calyx of a flower; she is the mole of beauty on the cheek of nature, and the angels have spread protecting wings above her. Perhaps only after knowing the long harshness of the surrounding deserts could a poet bless a city as such an elysium:

> I found it such as the tongues of men have described it—
> Containing all that hearts desire or eyes delight in;
> . . . And I there continued breaking open the seals of my
> desires. . . .

The Andalucian Ibn Jubayr, the prince of Arabic travellers, came to Damascus in the time of Saladin. 'She is the Paradise of the Orient,' he wrote, 'the place where dawned her gracious and radiant beauty, the seal of the lands of Islam where we have sought hospitality, and the bride of the cities we have observed. She is garnished with the flowers of sweet-scented herbs, and bedecked in the brocaded vestments of gardens. In the place of beauty she holds a sure position, and on her nuptial chair she is most richly adorned. . . .' He made an exhaustive tour of her holy places and gives a detailed account of the Great Mosque in the days before Tamerlane wrecked it; and he advised men to live in Damascus to study religion in seclusion 'before a wife and children cling to you and you gnash your teeth in regret . . .'. The manners of the Damascenes, he observed, were florid and ridiculous. They walked with their hands clasped sagely behind their backs, prostrated themselves in greeting like women, and sometimes took leave of one another by the curious habit of shaking hands. He left the city as the soldiers of Saladin returned leading Crusader prisoners from the capture of Nablus; and he remarked in fascination how the professional armies of Europe and Islam fought all through Palestine, while their merchants traded with each other as if nothing was happening.

Ibn Batutta, a Berber of Tangier, journeyed almost continuously for thirty years. He covered more than seventy-five

thousand miles from the mountains of China, and Java, to
Timbuctoo and Anatolia, marrying and divorcing with lackadai-
sical frequency. Of all the cities of his travels, only Shiraz could
rival Damascus, to which he returned after twenty-one years'
absence. Eager to see the son who had been borne to him of a
Damascene woman while he was in India, he entered the city at
the height of the Black Death in 1348, only to discover that the
boy had been dead for twelve years.

Jews travelled through the empire with less dignity but almost
as much freedom as Moslems. Benjamin of Tudela, a rabbi from
Navarre and the most celebrated of Jewish travellers, arrived in
1160 and relates that in the Great Mosque 'there is a wall of
Glasse built by the workmanship of the Magicians, distinguished
with holes equall in number with the dayes of the Sun . . .' and
he glimpsed inside the courtyard an enormous bone, which was
believed to be the rib of a giant. But most mediaeval Jews seemed
to pass through Damascus nervously, confining themselves to
descriptions of the local synagogues.

The most frequently-read travel writer of the fourteenth and
fifteenth centuries was the author of the *Voiage of Sir John
Maundevile*. There is an irresistible matter-of-factness in his
descriptions of dog-headed tribes and valleys full of devils, of
snails so large that you may sit inside their shells, of men who
live on snakes and hiss instead of speaking, and of people whose
lower lips arc so gigantic that they use them as sunshades.

The author must have considered Damascus too well-known
to romance over safely (except for a tale that St Paul and St
Luke practised there as physicians), but the convent of Seidnaya
is remote enough for eccentricities. Its black wooden icon turns
to flesh unless kindly treated, and there is a river near by which
only flows on Saturdays.

The last record of Damascus before Tamerlane's sack came
from three Tuscan pilgrims in 1384. Frescobaldi, a Florentine
noble, had been given orders to spy out the country for a new
Crusade, but declared 'I am no expert in these matters' and was
happier savouring the Damascene game birds, which were
excellent 'especially francolin and partridges'. Gucci, who had a
plebeian eye for detail, wrote about the weather and the prices
of things, but remarked that the walled quarter of Damascus
alone was three times larger than Florence. He gave a description of the food-vendors carrying small tables on their heads,
with fire-grills and meat and a bowl 'and they live not so cleanly'.
Each man, he remarks, has several wives 'and they never keep

them together, but each one alone in her own house; and at night each man goes where it likes most . . .'.

Sigoli, the third of the Tuscans, was impressed by the city's double wall and moated citadel, the rose gardens and the merchandise, 'such rich and noble and delicate works of every kind that if you had money in the bone of your leg, without fail you would break it to buy of these things . . .'.

But 'in Damascus they first offended us with words', wails Gucci, 'and the worst blasphemies in their power; then they pulled the cowls off our heads; then in the crowd they would put their foot between our legs to trip us; and then those on horseback would ride the horse on us and make it bite and kick us. Then from the windows or from the ground they threw water on us; and they spat in our faces, and threw dust in our eyes, and threw stones at us, hit us with canes, with their fists, and slapped us: . . .' So the persecuted but admiring Tuscans rode away from the city, leaving two of their servants dead of plague.

For fifty years after, no traveller describes Damascus. Tamerlane came and went, and after a long silence Europe received an eyewitness account of his sack. Johann Schiltberger, a Bavarian mercenary, was captured from the Hungarian army by the Turks at Nicopolis, then seized by the Mongols from the Turks and pressed into the army. He remembers how thirty thousand people burnt or suffocated to death in the Great Mosque, and bluntly mentions that it took the Mongols three days to build three towers with their charred heads: the only type of constructive work which Tamerlane undertook in Syria.

After more than twenty years' captivity he escaped to Europe and garbled his tale to a scribe. He recounts that he was seized by the Mongols at the Battle of Ankara in 1402, and describes the battle accurately; but he also asserts that he captured Damascus with the Mongols—which would have been in 1400, when he was still a prisoner of the Turks. The rustic simplicity of Schiltberger's approach, which has endeared him to authorities, begins to pall and one suspects that he deserted the Hungarian army before ever it glimpsed a Turk.

Bertrandon de la Brocquière, who arrived thirty-two years later, was a thorough-going realist, a knight and a counsellor to the Duke of Burgundy. He rode to Damascus over the Lebanese mountains, through nights of cold and dew, and burning days, and as he entered the city—the final straw—somebody knocked off his beaver hat: 'I mention this circumstance to show that the inhabitants of Damascus are a wicked race.' He estimated that a hundred thousand people lived in the city, and remarked on its colony of Italian and French traders.* And he met the famous merchant Jacques Cœur, whose financial genius as paymaster general to Charles VII had enabled the French to expel the English from their soil and end the Hundred Years War.

Of Tamerlane's sack he remarked: 'Vestiges of this disaster now remain; and toward the gate of St Paul there is a whole quarter that has never been rebuilt.' But he thought the city second only to Cairo in the Moslem empire. Seven hundred thousand people, he was assured, left Damascus every year on the Great Pilgrimage, and if the number was deficient, God sent his angels to make it up. He watched three thousand camels returning from Mecca, with two young men who had gouged out their eyes after seeing the tomb of Mahomet, so that they might retain that vision unsullied for ever.

In 1499 came Arnold Von Harff, a German knight from Cologne, who declared that he had climbed the Mountains of the Moon and discovered the source of the Nile. He was a delightful traveller. Germany was still very mediaeval and only a dull man would merely recount what he saw; it was only good manners to introduce a few wyverns and a basilisk to gratify the public.

His book is a guide for pilgrims, sets down the number of miles or days' journey between interesting points, and gives a useful list of pardons and indulgences. 'Item. from Cana in Galilee to Damascus, 2 days' journey . . . Item. we went first into a little chapel in which St Paul was baptised. Here is absolution for seven years with seven quarantines.' A quick walk around Damascus can collect twenty-one years' absolution in an afternoon—all sanctioned in the *libri indulgentiarum*. Von Harff supplements his text with woodcarvings, which include the Three Wise Kings in good Saxon hose, a pair of lugubrious aquatic goats termed 'sea monsters', and many beasts of heraldic improbability, which are labelled 'crocodile', 'ostrich', 'the Doge of Venice', etc. There is also a sketch of himself—a leprechaun figure covered in rosary-beads, looking very smug and much as one imagined him, returning to Cologne as a Knight of the Holy Sepulchre, loaded with indulgences.

*   *   *

* The first consulate in Damascus was Venetian, and was operating as early as 1331.

By now the mediaeval outlook was waning, at least in Europe, and the soldiers of fortune and unwashed pilgrims faded behind men of more cunning stamp. Venetian and Genoese merchants scurried about the Levant with dinars quilted into their doublets. Portuguese dispatch-bearers strayed south on their way to the Persian Gulf, and a courier from Queen Elizabeth passed through on a mission to Ivan the Terrible.

Their glimpses of Damascus are swift and often eccentric. William Biddulph came with a party of English merchants whose way was blocked at the village of Daraya by five hundred Christians with a Greek patriarch and Armenian bishop, kneeling in the road at the place of St Paul's conversion. Ludovico di Varthema, a Bolognese gentleman of the High Renaissance, remained in the city long enough to learn Arabic. He decided to profess Islam (it was the age of the Borgias) and enlisted in the Mameluke guard on the annual pilgrimage to Arabia, where he reported seeing unicorns in the Kaabah Mosque of Mecca.

In the year 1614 appeared William Lithgow, the first Scottish traveller. According to Lanark lore, he had been discovered with a certain Miss Lockhart by her four brothers, who sliced off his ears. So 'in the stripling age of mine adolescency', 'Lugless Will', as he was called, tramped through Europe and the Ottoman Empire. His journey grew less and less comfortable as he blundered down from Aleppo to Damascus. He rode in a party of thirteen hundred Armenians, soldiers and businessmen, with boar-skin water-bottles leaking, all choking from thirst, and 'amongst narrow and stony passages, thronging, we oft fell one over another in great heapes; in danger to be smothered; yea'. This peculiar procession reached Damascus, and lodged in a khan opened to travellers by the Ottoman sultan. The Turks, says 'Lugless', are disgusting. 'They never uncloath themselves, when they goe to rest, neither have they any bed-cloathes, save onely a coverlet above them: I have seene hundreds of them, after this manner, lye ranked like durtie swine in a beastly stie, or loathsome jades in a filthy stable.' But Damascus herself was 'the most beautiful place in all Asia', resembling, he decided, Antwerp. And the Turks, he declared, had fenced round a garden in the city where they kept the forbidden apple tree of Eden. 'Lugless' had returned to Europe before his real troubles began. Here the Spanish Inquisition pounced on him, and his unjust tortures resulted in his exhibiting his 'martyred anatomy' to the court of King James at Theobalds.

Pietro della Valle, who reached Damascus the same year, was an Italian nobleman, intelligent, observant and dazzlingly romantic. Jilted by a beautiful Roman, he made moodily for Constantinople, where a hundred and forty thousand people had died of plague before he set sail for Alexandria. For a while he explored mummy-pits in Upper Egypt, and was the first European to penetrate the pyramid of Chephren. Then he wandered northward, entering Damascus with his sick servant humped in a camel-pannier, and purchased some valuable Hebrew manuscripts from Samaritans living in the city outskirts. Later he fell in love with a beautiful Christian called Maani, but on the Persian Gulf she contracted fever while many months pregnant. She bore him a still-born, perfectly proportioned son, six inches long, and after weeks of pain, she herself died. Thereafter, wherever Pietro travelled, her embalmed body followed behind him in a coffin, and was finally smuggled back to Italy in a bale of spun cotton and buried in the church of Ara Coeli in Rome.

In 1630 the buoyant figure of a Portuguese priest, Fray Sebastien Manrique, arrived in Damascus. For a few days he roamed the city freely, and in a style of writing which a Spanish critic calls 'castellano desastroso', he describes the Great Pilgrimage leaving for the 'hellish and abominable sanctuary of Mecca', adding that a few days after its departure eighteen thousand camels and many of the pilgrims were buried under a freak snowstorm. But soon a rumour was put about that he had entered the city with precious stones belonging to the Sultan of Constantinople, and for nine days he hid in a cellar by the light of a candle before escaping to Sidon. After a lifetime's travelling in perilous parts of the world, he was murdered in London and was floated in a wooden box down the Thames, where he surprised some fishermen one quiet dawn.

The most meticulous and observant seventeenth-century traveller to Damascus was Monsieur de Thévenot. For some reason the Damascenes were convinced that he was the brother of the King of France and immensely wealthy, and he was forced to lock himself away for several days, knowing that the Janissaries would attempt to confiscate his goods. But he managed to enter the citadel, and from the window of the little marble mosque of the Turkish pasha, gazed down into the Great Mosque, whose precincts were forbidden to Christians. Many of the customs which he noticed subsist in Damascus today, such as that of women visiting their husbands' tombs on Thursdays, pouring water through a hole at the top of the grave to soothe the dead, muttering confidences through it and asking for advice.

He visited the so-called House of Judas, which shielded the tomb of Ananias, the pillar on the banks of the Barada where God fashioned the First Man, and noticed a gigantic stone, carved with the legend that when it was covered with water, Damascus would be taken. And, like a true Frenchman, 'I finish my notes on Damascus with a warning that the wines are violent and treacherous, and that Smirnium Creticum grows on all the roofs and terraces.'

De Thévenot was followed by the Chevalier D'Arvieux, ambassador of the Sun King and master of five oriental languages. He too entered the citadel, and saw the remains of a cupola whose pillars, he said, could have carried the dome of St Peter's. And he concerned himself with the paradise legends. The Jews, he remarked, believe that Cain slew Abel at Beitima and not at the Moslem site. One or other must be wrong, but what is true is that 'the grapes there are quite excellent, very big and very sweet and not a single pip'.

Fifteen years later came Henry Maundrell, chaplain to the English merchants' factory at Aleppo, who left an accurate description of Damascus and the convent of Seidnaya 'possessed by twenty Greek monks and forty nuns, who seem to live promiscuously together, without order or separation'.

'The late Charles Thompson, Esq.' is more elusive. His account of his stay in Damascus is a guileful amalgamation of the sketches of Maundrell and de Thévenot, bulked out by a dissertation on the Garden of Eden. Charles Thompson, Esq. never went to the East, and nor did Aaron Hill, who dedicated his travel-book to Queen Anne. In an enthusiastic passage about a trip to Egypt, Hill even descended into the Great Pyramid, discovered an underground tunnel and re-emerged half a mile away in the head of the Sphinx. But no doubt Her Majesty was pleased.

*   *   *

The cavalcade of ambassadors begins to trail away, and the scuffling of the merchants is smothered by other sounds. The grandiloquence of the seventeenth century surrenders to the styleless travelogues of the eighteenth, and out of the new era rides Dr Pococke with his Vitruvius and his tape measure; Carsten Niebuhr, robust and sensible and Hanoverian, on a scientific trip for the King of Denmark; and Volney, who tramped from Anjou to Marseilles with a knapsack on his back and a musket on his shoulder, and spent eight months learning Arabic at a convent in Druse country.

The gentleman-traveller makes his shy debut. He winkles out obscure classical cities, measuring their columns and ruminating their identity. The dirty and incomprehensible 'Turks' are etched into his lithographs of Baalbek and Byblos to give the ruins romance or proportion, and are transmuted into gay, turbaned cavaliers or shepherds leaning against pillars in postures of Arcadian indolence.

Onto this dry landscape the nineteenth century rained a squall of romantics. Lady Hester Stanhope* entered the holy city of Damascus unveiled and on horseback, and badgered the astonished pasha to give her a house near his palace. The bazaars soon purled with rumours of an infidel queen, lovely and pale as the full moon. Crowds pressed round her doorway every morning to watch her emerge in Bedouin guise, strew coffee-beans in her path and admire her highly-arched feet.

The next spring she rode a hundred miles through the wilderness to Palmyra, with her English lover and a crowd of Bedouin chiefs. Beyond the Vale of Tombs the ancient city stood desolate, like the skeleton of some diluvian creature which had died in the desert, its bones apricot-pale and delicate as egg-shell. All along the Street of Columns, on consoles which had once held the busts of Romanised businessmen, garlanded girls froze into statuesque postures. As she passed, they sprang dancing to the ground, and from the Arch of Triumph the loveliest houri of all leant over her like a Tiepolo angel with a wreath of palms.

After the apotheosis of Lady Hester there was little left for a romantic to do; but Lamartine arrived some twenty years later with an extravagant Arab escort, twenty-six horses and bandboxes full of small, frequently-kissed dogs. For a few weeks he was a familiar sight in the Armenian quarter—the Byronic wildness of his looks clenched by middle-age into a strikingly

---

* Hester Stanhope was William Pitt's niece and had been his social hostess at Downing St., where she exercised majestic sway. Among those rumoured to have been in love with her were Canning and Sir John Moore, who died at Corunna with her name on his lips.

aesthetic face. His *Voyage en Orient* devotes several luxuriant pages to Damascus, where he bought a white stallion and a peach-coloured mare of a strain called 'chief of the hoof'.

By the mid-nineteenth century travelling in the East had become acceptable to Grand Tourists. Michaud, the historian of the Crusades, was permitted to wander through the city during a tax riot; the Laborde family, despite the Moslem hatred of pictures, returned to France with sketches of the Tomb of Sheikh Arslan and the city gates; and the handsome and cavalier Major Skinner courted a secluded Arab lady with a bunch of violets, until she emerged to greet him smelling of fish.

James Silk Buckingham (one of the founders of the Athenaeum) was even granted an audience by the pasha. He witnessed a type of glittering charade which characterised Ottoman official life. the pasha sat in pomp before an arc of officers, while a Jew—the wealthiest citizen of Damascus, who had enough influence to remove The pasha at will—grovelled at his feet dressed in infidel colours.* Among the officers was also a mad dervish dressed in rags, 'his naked limbs obtruding themselves most offensively, and his general appearance being indecent and disgusting'. He was placed in the seat of honour—for madness is a visitation from Allah—and served with perfumes and ice-cooled sherbet.

Ibrahim Pasha, Mehemet Ali's son and general, arrived in 1832, and in his train rode the first British consul to Damascus, to take up the position so long denied him. Previously the only havens for foreigners had been the Franciscan Terra Santa convent, occupied by illiterate Spanish friars, a Capuchin foundation which had dwindled to a solitary monk, and a pair of French Lazarists, who spent their nights repairing their monastery, since they could not afford to bribe the pasha for building permission.

The year 1835 brought Alexander Kinglake, dapper and elf-like on the hump of a Bedouin camel. He digresses on the Damascus orchards, weaves in a lavender-coloured passage on a deserted English garden, and describes a tipple with the monks of the Terra Santa, for 'Christianity permits and sanctions the drinking of wine; and of all the holy brethren in Palestine there are none who hold fast to this gladsome rite so strenuously as the monks of Damascus . . .'. Damascus was now safer than

* Before the arrival of the armies of Mehemet Ali, non-Moslems were forbidden to wear the sacred Islamic colours, which included green, red, yellow and white.

Oxford, he observes, and he walked on the pavements as freely as if in Pall Mall.*

Bigotry was only sleeping. George Robinson, who arrived at the same time, was wrenched from his horse for riding too near the holy walls, and his flowered turban torn off his head because it contained traces of the sacred green colour. He entered the city under a tempest of stones, clogged with mud and 'other impurities'; but he demanded redress of the pasha, and to the astonishment of the whole city, the principal culprit received two hundred bastinados on the soles of his feet.

Several notable visitors decorate the 1840's. Layard, soon to become famous as the excavator of Nineveh, dragged himself half-naked to the British consul's door, after twice being robbed on the Petra road. And a Viscount Castlereagh appeared, very consequential and English, and was outraged because the Damascenes thought that the kings of England were appointed by the Sultan.

*　　*　　*

For Europe, the Levant was still mysterious and richly coloured. Germany underwent a rage for orientalised poetry. France saw a rash of pseudo-Eastern fables, admired the rich tints of Delacroix and swooned at the Moorish insinuations of Saint-Saëns and Félicien David. England watched her Chinoiserie give place to Arabic fads, danced to the *Mamelukes Waltz*, read Byron and Fitzgerald, *The Thousand and One Nights* and *Veiled Prophet of Khorasan* with fascination and dreamy longing. Chateaubriand rushed to Jerusalem, swaddled in Bedouin robes; and Thackeray followed him—'What a figure we cut in the moonlight, and how they would have stared in the Strand!'

But Syrian travel was no longer purely a man's province: along the fractured Roman highways rode a parcel of giddy girls. Lady Hester ended her life in an eyrie in Lebanon, where she presided with a mace over her Syrian servants, who were not expected 'to smile, or scratch themselves, or appear to notice anything'. The enigmatic Lady Venus incarcerated herself in Mecca; and for years the Marquise de la Tour d'Auvergne sat

---

* Kinglake's Englishness was all-pervading. While looking at the river Jordan he had thought of the Thames at Eton, and when a Cairene magician offered to reincarnate any dead acquaintance, he had named Dr Keate, but the reincarnation fortunately failed.

decked with bangles in a tower on the Mount of Olives, awaiting the Last Judgement.

Across these decades of radiant insanity rides Harriet Martineau, sensible and graceless, and looking, as Jane Carlyle described her, 'the picture of rude, weather-beaten health'. Ear-trumpet cocked for political information, she passes through Damascus in an eddy of practical comments: the Manchester cottons which the Damascenes make their wives wear instead of those expensive silks are perfectly adequate. The food is inexcusably poor. If the Syrians can cultivate land, why can't the Irish? She found five snails making slimy tracks under her bed. . . .

The Lombard Princess Trivulce di Belgiojoso was more adaptable. She had held a salon in Paris and was famous for having embalmed a dead friend of hers in her cupboard, while his funeral—with a log in the coffin—was conducted with pomp. She raised a battalion of Milanese volunteers whom she led into battle against the Austrians, but after the Italian defeat in 1848 she was exiled, and wandered the Levant for three years.

She settled in a large house in Damascus, where she entertained her friends one night by hiring two famous danseuses, 'each weighing at least one hundred and twenty pounds, their flesh untightened either by corsets or whalebone'. Animated by brandy, they danced in the lamp-lit courtyard, and the princess watched uncomprehending as her audience of emirs, consuls and black slaves ogled and applauded. The dancers finally fell down in a wriggling, drunken heap, which 'was not the least repulsive part of the performance'.

The Arabs used to believe that Englishmen were possessed by evil spirits, which forced them to frequent ruins and plunge across deserts. There was no other explanation of Englishmen. Even the average Victorian traveller behaved obtusely, and Damascenes stared in perplexity at *Milady* feeling seasick in a mule-born litter, young women boxed into long, straight pelisses, and mulberry-faced gentlemen sweating into their cravats, all moving dizzily along under white calico parasols, with the thermometer at 105°.

Less conformist Englishmen only increased the image of a bedevilled nation. In 1855 William Holman Hunt rode up from Jerusalem—a figure for Arab wonder in his knickerbockers and strange headgear. He planned to illustrate a few of Tennyson's poems with views of Damascus, a city, he said, which had 'escaped the rage for improvements and remained richer in

Orientalisms than any other town'; but he had little time left
before embarking at Beirut, so he rode away with his shabby
umbrella, his twenty words of Arabic, and his sketch-book
unopened.

Four years later a second artist arrived: a shy, lonely, short-
sighted man in ill-fitting clothes. He liked to be called 'Edward
Lear, the landscape painter', and the fact that people paid little
attention to his paintings and fell in love with a few scraps of
nonsense verse he composed, frustrated him.

> His mind is concrete and fastidious
> His nose is remarkably big,
> His visage is more or less hideous,
> His beard it resembles a wig.

He sketched frenziedly: drawings in pencil and brown ink,
scribbled over with peculiar, often humorous notes; later he
would sometimes wash on weak colours, but most of his land-
scapes were pen-drawings. His scenes are closely-worked, but
seem uninhabited and remote—a world of detailed unreality
in which it would be no surprise to find a sieve-full of Jumblies
floating down the Barada river.

It is strange that the French, the world's *pantouflards*,
travelled so much in a country as pitiless as Syria. But they, more
than any, hoped for spiritual discovery in the East. From the
petty boredom of provincial France, Flaubert found himself in a
world blistered by poverty. Disenchanted long before he ever
travelled, he watched it with contempt and fascination: humanity,
immuable et inébranlable. The dung and ruin of Jerusalem em-
bittered him, and his craving for the outlandish was answered in
the Holy Sepulchre itself, which was monopolised by a full-
length portrait of Louis Philippe.

He reached Damascus after night-riding to avoid bandits.
There was no more pleasure for him in travel; perhaps he was
already gathering ideas for his sickly *Salammbô*, or dreamt of
being back with Louis Colet, riding through the Bois de
Boulogne. In Damascus he seemed to seek out the macabre. He
noticed a naked madman petitioned by barren women; and in
the Christian cemetery 'nous nous sommes penchés a l'em-
bouchure d'un de ces caveaux et nous avons vu dedans plusieurs
débris humains pêle-mêle. . . . Çà et là quelques têtes sans
corps, quelques thorax sans têtes, et, au milieu, jaune, blond
doré, serpentant dans la poussière grise, une longue chevelure
de femme.'

Ernest Renan, the French humanist, came to Damascus the year after. An unfrocked priest, he tramped through Syria hounded by thoughts of Christ. For several days he wandered the few miles of Jerusalem road near Damascus, trying to understand the vision of St Paul for his *The Apostles*. Maybe sunstroke—the heat of the desert followed by the cool of the orchards—caused Saul to faint. Then Renan, perhaps thinking of his own unease, decided that any outer cause must be unimportant, that the vision was in the guilty man's soul.

He felt no happiness here. 'Damas est triste et sombre', he wrote to Berthelot.

Amongst the lost giants came a babble of pedants and echoes, and a few enterprising missionaries, like J. L. Porter, who abandoned his flock from time to time to explore the ancient cities of northern Syria. But there was also a more eccentric strain—a few people who became possessed by the East. The Swiss explorer Burckhardt reached Damascus with a salt caravan in 1812, and for two years used her as a base for his travels. Here he planned his venture into Africa, growing so hardened to Arabic life that he resembled a Bedouin, and became the first European to enter Petra, Mecca and Medinah.

Forty years later Sir Richard Burton penetrated the Holy Cities dressed as an Indian Moslem and was the first white man to reach the lake regions of Central Africa. In 1868 he was appointed British consul in Damascus. He bought a house in the Kurdish quarter, and his wife Isabel, whom he nicknamed 'Zoo', embellished it with a number of animals, which devoured one another until there remained little more than a single fat leopard. Isabel Burton, a zealous Roman Catholic, prayed in her private chapel, while her husband, a demi-Moslem, joined in the cry of the muezzin on the minaret outside his window.

They were both in love with the East. He, a bawdy and rebellious giant, had a profound understanding and knowledge of the Arab world, and spent much of his time in Damascus working on his version of *The Thousand and One Nights*, pacing the bazaars in disguise to winkle out information or resolve some ethnic problem. The bizarre, the mystic and the sexual fascinated him. He spoke twenty-eight languages, of which one, said his detractors, was pornography. He fitted into no known category, and his crime in the consular service was to be just and impetuous; 'a black leopard', wrote Blunt, 'caged but unforgiving'.

Isabel Burton loved the East through him. She never grew to

understand it. One moment, veiled and bloomered, she might trundle through the bazaars, the next play the coiffured *grande dame*, riding-whip in hand; then she would drape herself in a travesty of Bedouin clothes, gird herself with pistols and daggers and gallop into the desert 'doing a great deal of good', as she termed it, to the local tribes.

On summer evenings an outlandish trio squatted on the consul's rooftop in the Kurdish quarter, and exchanged esoteric lore: Burton, whose wild features were of peculiar oriental cast; the emir Abd-el-Kader, now in his sixties; and Lady Ellenborough who had wedded an Arab sheikh after three scandalous European marriages. They would talk until long after the sun had drowned in the desert, echoed only by the jackals' threnody in the Kurdish graveyard and the groaning of the orchard waterwheels, like giants in pain. Lady Ellenborough divulged harem intimacies, and many of her comments must have found their way into the footnotes of Burton's classic *The Thousand and One Nights*. Her life had been a sequence of outrageous romances. Her husbands or lovers had included an English lord, a Bavarian baron, a Corfiote count, an Austrian prince, an Albanian brigand-general, Ludwig I of Bavaria, Otho I of Greece and Honoré de Balzac. Finally she had married a sheikh of Palmyra, led raiding parties riding a dromedary, milked the tribal camels and washed her husband's feet like a dutiful Bedouin wife, her eyes kohl-blackened, her chestnut hair, once the toast of Europe, falling in two long plaits to the ground.

One half of the year she spent in the desert under the black tents, the other in a house she had built on the Damascus outskirts and fitted with ormolu, Buhl furniture and armorial tapestries. She designed herself an English cottage garden, inset with rustic bridges and beds of sweet-Williams and Canterbury bells, but through it prowled Persian hounds, a pelican and a hundred cats.

Burton was removed from office in 1871. His tactlessness and integrity were fatal to him. But after he had gone, the Arab people, who loved him, filled the Great Mosque with the noise of an incredible public prayer: a plea to Allah for the return of the British consul.

*   *   *

During the last half of the nineteenth century the Levant became tourist ground. Thomas Cook was at work. Files of immaculate men and bonneted women—*Cookiyeh*, as the Arabs called them—could be seen tripping along the Street Called Straight.

One of the first American pleasure steamers to the Mediterranean, the *Quaker City*, puffed down to Lebanon from Turkey, where its tourists had barely been prevented from carrying away half the ruins of Ephesus on mules. Mark Twain, a newspaper correspondent posing as a sick Baptist minister, disembarked in a gust of irreverent chatter. The United States consul in Beirut was pestered for transport to Damascus—'We were desperate—would take horses, jackasses, camelopards, kangaroos—anything.' So, with a few others, Twain rode over the mountains carrying his Bible and woollen shirts and 'a towel and a cake of soap, to inspire respect in the Arabs'. Over the Lebanon they went, 'like a fleet in a storm', with tents 'high enough for a family of giraffes to live in', until they burst into the bazaars of Damascus, tumbling off their horses among scowling merchants and sheeted women—'The Damascenes are the ugliest, wickedest-looking villains we have seen.' Then he caught cholera. 'I had nothing to do but to listen to the pattering of the fountains and take medicine and throw it up again. It was a dangerous recreation, but it was pleasanter than travelling in Syria.'

For eight months in 1876, Charles Doughty studied Arabic with a Lebanese tutor in an upper room of the Santa Maria church. Every afternoon his lofty, red-bearded figure could be seen wandering along the Barada, looking more like a pagan god than a Christian man. His plans to accompany the Great Pilgrimage to the sacred boundary, from there to vanish into Arabia Deserta, were thwarted for months, and the consul 'had as much regard of me, would I take such dangerous ways, as of his old hat'. But Doughty, dressed as a poor Syrian, was accepted into the company of some Persian *hajjis*, and began his momentous voyage anonymously, with little more than a store of caravan biscuit.

The nineteenth century, drawing to a close, brought Wilfrid Scawen Blunt, who was planning a united Arabian kingdom, with Abd-el-Kader at its head. He loved Damascus, placing the view from Salihiye amongst the six most wonderful in the world, and he bought a house next door to Lady Ellenborough and for a while was to be seen striding through the horse-markets—a great grassy headland of a man, with a tiny, wistful wife.

With the twentieth century, narrow-gauge railway trains fretted into the baroque station with increasing numbers of

Cookiyeh. Blunt returned after more than twenty years' absence, and was pleased to find Damascus much the same: no innovations, by-laws, or 'other Christian tomfooleries'. And he viewed, with old fervour, a flight of many hundred storks carried before a south-west storm on their annual migration.*

For two decades Gertrude Bell rode in and out of Damascus, and the French mandate brought a new conflux of visitors: Foreign Legionnaires spreading alarm through the red-light district; John dos Passos sweaty from the desert; Hilaire Belloc full of aggressive fallacies; gentle Freya Stark, lying sick in a 'fundamentally clean' bed, too sensitive to refuse the lethal food offered by her Moslem hosts. Finally a French family arrived on a carpet-buying expedition. During a trip to the desert they were stripped of all their belongings by the Bedouin, except for their carpets, which the Arabs recognised as valueless imitations; and wrapped in these, the family returned to Damascus.

After 1914 travellers began to see Damascus in a different light. Tenement flats already overlooked the rivers of paradise. And the travellers, who had once searched for visions in the East, had changed too. Flecker and Barrès were perhaps the last romantics.

In January 1912 Flecker sat down in Beirut, after a Christmas spent in Damascus, and wrote his *Four Great Gates has the City of Damascus*. It is a flight of sounds and rhythms, for his gates are not truly those of the city, which are hoary and robust, but mythical portals whose watchmen shout messages into the sky:

> . . . thou shalt sell thy wares for thrice the Damascene
>   retailer's price,
> And buy a fat Armenian slave who smelleth odorous
>   and nice. . . .
> O spiritual pilgrim rise: the night has grown her single
>   horn:
> The voices of the souls unborn are half adream with
>   Paradise. . . .
> And God shall make thy soul a glass where eighteen
>   thousand aeons pass,
> And thou shalt see the gleaming worlds as men see
>   dew upon the grass.†

* Storks: a regular and wonderful sight in autumn—their distant ancestors, perhaps, were those Herodotus had noticed on the same unalterable skyway from Scythia to the Upper Nile.

† This last line is carved on Flecker's memorial tablet in Dean Close Chapel.

The letters of Flecker and his wife express blunter points. 'Unfortunately it rained during the three days of our stay there,' she remarks, 'consequently our impression of Damascus was not that of the Arabs, who call it the Garden of Eden.' and Flecker wrote: 'This town is interesting, but I wish we were in Chipping Candover all the same.'

In 1914 the French writer and nationalist Maurice Barrès stood on the slopes of Kassioun. He looked down enraptured on the orchards and camel-coloured hills. Damascus! 'The country of the imagination, a dwelling of poetry, a palace of the soul.' He loved her immediately. She pleased his mystic, romantic soul. He was, perhaps, her last visitor to talk about penetrating the heart of the East, about discovering a 'mystic spark'; the last who dared suggest that behind the black eyes of Damascene students glowed occult and complicated souls. 'Behind these secret walls,' he wrote, 'I want to know how love and death are understood.'

Now it is usual to rush south to Jerusalem, or west to Beirut, after a single, over-guided day in Damascus. The tourist-works are beautifully oiled. A deep-worn rut reaches from the Suq Hamidieh to the Great Mosque to the Azem Palace, with a visit to the Ananias Chapel and the gate from which St Paul could not possibly have been let down in a basket. And the trip ends at a tourist shop, probably owned by a relative of the dragoman, whose prices, he rightly declares, are *exceptional*.

Nobody leaves the city now with the bruises of Gucci, or the heartache of Isabel Burton, or even the absolutions of Arnold Von Harff.

14. The Minorities

Commandments there be which some minds reckon lightly,
Yet no man knoweth whom shall befall perdition.

Ma 'arri

FEW CITIES TESTIFY more poignantly than Damascus to
the persistence of religious barriers. A thousand years ago the
Jewish sector was to be found south-east of the Street Called
Straight, the Christian to the north-east. And it is the same
today.

The south-east quarter is still called Haret al Yahoud, the
sector of the Jews, but they occupy only a small part of it. Among
the minority peoples of Damascus there is no sadder community.
The Damascenes' instinctive hatred of them reaches back to the
time of David, and is now nurtured and artificially inflamed.
There was a time when they were the bankers of the Ottoman
pashas and when their rich men owned villages and built private
synagogues. Their families could trace their tenancy to the
time of Ben Haddad, who gave his promise to Ahab that 'thou
shalt make streets for thee in Damascus, as my father made in
Samaria', and it is possible that the Jewish sect of Essenes
originated here, later filtering down to the Dead Sea to 'make
straight in the desert the Prophecy of our God', and to write the
Dead Sea Scrolls.

If you ask where the Jews have gone now, the wry answer
comes quickly 'Palestine'. In 1947 fourteen thousand Jews lived
in Damascus. Now there are perhaps four thousand, who have
sprinkled themselves through the city in a minor diaspora. The
Christians have bitten into the old sector from the north, the
Moslems from the west and south.

Only two or three streets still belong to the Jews. They are
very quiet. The doors of sunken courtyards are edged open and
slammed shut to receive children from school. The walls are
pocked and misshapen. Nothing is ever repaired. A subdued
ripple of Arabic sometimes courts the silence from some window (Hebrew was abandoned centuries ago) and the noises
sound like prayers. The Rebecca who flaunted her flower-
plumed head-dress on the Sabbath is scarcely a memory.

The Jewish graveyards south-east of the battlements are as desolate as those in Jerusalem's Kedron valley; but the soil of Jordan has armed their tombs in thistles and sucked them down. Those of Damascus stand out in greying fields. The ground has not received an inch of their hard caskets.

I searched for the religious centre of the Damascene Jews not in Damascus, but in Djobar, two miles to the east. The village is surrounded by olive trees, which seem old almost from birth. Nothing stirs but the flicker of their leaves in a bated breath of wind, and a waltz of dust which follows the ploughs through the fields. In Djobar the Jews once had a synagogue where Elijah is claimed to have anointed Elisha, and Elisha to have anointed Hazael. When I arrived I discovered that most of its precinct had been turned into a school for Palestinian refugees.

'We took this ground from the synagogue years back,' one of the teachers said mischievously, 'we pay them something. But there are no Jews here, God be praised.'

The masters in the school gave me sweet tea and told me they hated England. 'You see the children out there? You know who they are? England gave their homeland to the Jews. You have heard of Lord Balfour?'

I said I had heard of no other Englishmen since entering Syria.

'Today is the anniversary of the Balfour Declaration. In a moment each of us will speak to the children about what has been done to them; how an Englishman gave Palestine to men who had never even been there. And how it will be taken back again.'

I asked them if they thought this a happy education. 'By God, we have reason to be unhappy,' they answered. More sweet tea. 'But we do not hate the English people. It is the government we fight.' This assurance precedes every political discussion; if the British premier came to Damascus, he would be told that only his policies were resented. The Damascenes cannot resist people.

'If you wish to see the synagogue-hall you may,' a man said. 'But God is not there.'

An Arab caretaker opened the door to me. Now the place was empty, but on festival days the Jews sit on divans round the walls, while the priests and elders perch on a dais in the centre of the hall. A big stone lay in the entrance. Its sides fell away in petrified ripples, and on it was inscribed: 'It is here that in the year 3043 of our era* the prophet Elichaa ben Chafat was anointed by Eliahou hanabi.'

The walls of the room were so muffled in carpets and tapestries that the building's age eluded me. The air was tortured by lamps and chandeliers. Outside I could hear the children of the Palestinian school assembling in the courtyard for Balfour day.

Skull caps covered a table. The caretaker donned one and sniggered to himself. I walked across the mosaic floor, noticed curtains printed with English hunting scenes and brushed against inscribed brass and silver plates which were hanging against the tapestries. A side-chapel lay at the back of the synagogue. No light reached it. The Jews say that in a small cave below, Elijah found refuge when Ahab sought his life, and that the ravens came and fed him here. Mediaeval travellers were the first to connect the tradition with Damascus, but a synagogue at 'Gobar' is mentioned even in the Talmud.

For a moment I stared into its darkness. Then the shout of a schoolmaster broke the silence, teaching the children to hate.

*   *   *

After the Islamic conquest, the Jews and Christians were pressed into those parts of Damascus which were furthest from the west winds and the fresh water of Lebanon. But where the Jewish quarter has shrunk, the Christians have expanded. Some sixty-five thousand Damascenes are Christians—a tenth of the total population—and almost half of these belong to the Greek Orthodox Church, whose trappings are Greek but whose priests and liturgy are Arab. Most of the rest adhere to the Greek Catholic Church; and other denominations—Syrian Catholics, Chaldeans, Protestants and Latins—have their churches scattered through the Bab Touma and Kassaa districts. There also exists a group of Maronites, whose liturgy is still read in Syriac. They were originally distinguished for having adopted the Monothelite creed of the emperor Heraclius, and since Byzantine times they have been numerous in Lebanon, where the First Crusaders, marching down the coast from Antioch, found them invaluable as guides and archers.

More free in their thought than the Moslems, more specula-

* This date is an enigma to me. According to standard Jewish dating (*anno mundi*) it would be 717 B.C., at least a hundred and fifty years later than Elijah.

tive and ambitious, the Christians exercise an influence out of proportion to their numbers. The sector begins far outside the walled city, where on one side sprawls the modern quarter of Kassaa and on the other the graveyards of Catholic and Orthodox, Maronite and Armenian, almost rub against one another. In a small Protestant cemetery, among the graves of English missionaries and the wives of consuls, I came upon the unpretentious tomb of Henry Thomas Buckle, author of the unfinished *History of Civilisation in England*, who died of fever in 1862 at the age of forty, after being bled by a Damascene leech.

In the grave beside him lies the Countess Harley Teleki, a beautiful divorcee who died of plague a few years after Buckle, while touring the Levant. When her desk was opened after her death, it was found to contain a letter written before she had begun her tour; she had been reading Buckle's *History of Civilisation in England*, and mentioned, whimsically, that if she should die in Damascus she would like to be buried by his side.

The Bab Touma district at the east end of the Street Called Straight is still the hub of the Christian sector. The lanes have forgotten their fears and opened to the sun. At the street's eastern extremity, behind the Roman gate, stands the church of Saint Sarkiss, which is the centre of the Armenian Orthodox faith in Damascus. Armenians have inhabited the city for centuries, but many settled after the First World War, when Turkish massacres drove them southward in such numbers that a million died on the road. The Damascenes regard their industriousness and acumen with a mixture of jealousy and admiration. 'It takes three Jews to cheat a Greek, three Greeks to cheat a Syrian, and three Syrians to cheat an Armenian.' But in twenty years the Armenian church's flock has dwindled from seventeen thousand to five thousand.

'Ever since the Russians invited people to return to Armenia, we have had fewer worshippers,' said the priest of Saint Sarkiss, while showing me round his modern church—the previous one was burnt down in the 1860 massacres—'Everyone is slowly drifting away. Our patriarchate is at Aleppo, and there are still eight thousand of us there; but the church looks very empty these days.'

Further along the street rises the Greek Orthodox patriarchate, transferred from Antioch. Portraits of past incumbents fill the huge rooms with a crossfire of olympian stares, and nuns, small and fur-wrapped as patriarchate mice, creep along its marble terraces. The long, red-tiled roof of the Cathedral of

St Maria spreads beyond—a portent of Italy. It is the greatest centre of Christian worship in Damascus. Tall columns divide it into three naves and its marble walls and floors are glacial white, haunted by the sadness which attended their construction, after the first church had been burnt to the ground with three hundred Christians, during the Moslem massacres.

The Syrian Patriarch sits in a small office attended by his priests, who grow more importantly-bearded as their years lengthen. 'We bear no hatred to the Moslems.' He looked at me with watery eyes. 'We are all at peace now. A hundred years is a long time. Who would wish to remember?'

The Moslems have not forgotten, but they like to blame the massacres on outsiders; on Ottoman bureaucrats, on the half-nomadic canaille of the oasis villages; on the mountain people; and above all on the Druses.

The Moslem parts of old Damascus, although they bear an aspect of conformity, are honeycombed with minority sects. Over many years four thousand Alawi wandered down from north-west Syria and settled in the city: hardy men, and brown-haired women distinctive for their deep violet headscarves, and their embroidered bodices drawn tight under the breasts. The Damascenes think them backward and ignorant. They live 'like the pig' and 'God does not listen to them'; and slanderous stories are told about their religion, which is an esoteric branch of the Shia, steeped in pagan and Christian influences—the Alawi mountains are patterned with their sacred groves and streams.

Several other sects have held fiercely to their rites: groups of Ismaili, a handful of devil-worshippers, and some hundreds of Shia, who still enact a passion-play on the anniversary of the death of Husain in their village near the tomb of Sitti Zeinab. The Ismaili, who seldom settle in Damascus, are the most extreme of the Shia sects, and are now fragmented. Some, the followers of the Ali Khan, live miserably in the deserts near Palmyra and Hamah. Others, descendant from the Assassins, still dwell in the mountains of northern Lebanon.

But of all Moslem Damascus, the Kurds are the most homo-geneous community. Saladin, himself a Kurd, settled them on the slopes of Mount Kassioun, and you may still climb through their quarter, the Akrad, east of Salihiye. The streets do not bunch nervously together like those of the Moslems, because the Kurds have gained a reputation as warriors. Apart from the unusual exuberance of the children, you could walk through the sector without noticing anything strange. Yet behind their doors some of the people speak their own dialect of Kurdish. Not long ago they used to offer up blood sacrifices each year on the dried-up bed of the Yezid Canal, to appease its djinns, and their sheikh would ride to the house of Abraham at Burzeh over the prostrate bodies of his people, who would stand up unscathed after his horse had galloped over them. The name of Saladin is scarcely ever mentioned among them, but in a cocoon of alleys in the Akrad lies the tomb of a holy man, who is revered as a relative of the sultan. The Kurds recount in wonder that his body has never wasted, and the tomb, in proof, has crumbled away to reveal one of his feet.

*　　*　　*

The Druses are the most beautiful people in Damascus. Even in the markets one might believe they were children of naiads. Their faces are those of the mountain people, broad and fair.

The notion of their Crusader ancestry is a haunting one. Their features are regular and aristocratic, their manner robust and open. I saw a flaxen-haired man who would have looked well in the streets of Hamburg, a woman with the fragility and straw-coloured tresses of a Dresden shepherdess. And their clothes have a mediaeval tinge. Women's dresses are girdled at the waist, and their circular caps are covered by gauzy white veils which glissade down their shoulders and backs. In the Druse Mountain, one suspects, their mothers may flaunt butterfly head-dresses and houppelandes, and hum the airs of Provence.

Sometimes their hair straggles free and long, sometimes it is bound in pigtails, knotted with ribbons and joined by gold chains at the ends. The older women's dresses are black or auburn. The younger look as if they have been fitted out from an ancient but expensive wardrobe. They love artificial brocades in outrageous colours, and during their first year of marriage, girls come to the city in crimson dresses.

The women are renownedly chaste. On the eve of her wedding-day a bride hands her husband a knife, and asks him to stab her should she not prove a virgin. And if she is unfaithful after marriage, her husband will certainly kill her.

Some sixteen thousand Druses live in the city, and the Christians speak little good of them. 'They don't know anything. . . . They have no book from God. . . .' Their religion is no longer enigmatic, but during the last century it was believed that they worshipped a golden calf.* (I knew a Circassian who lived in Druse country and told me that he had seen them praying in front of cows.) But the Druses become angry or evasive at the mention of it.

The faith is like a brotherhood, and for centuries, in the manner of mountain communities, it has been militant and exclusive. Only one in seven of the Druses is an *'uqqal*, an Intelligent One, who has access to their holy scripts and secret meetings, and a half-belief in predestination makes conversions pointless. Their God has passed through many incarnations, once as Christ, once as Ali, and lastly as the lunatic Egyptian caliph Hakim, 'the Caligula of the East', who will return to lead to victory the eternally-fixed number of his faithful, which includes the Chinese and British, who are reincarnated Druses.

It may be that the Druses are of Indo-European origin, mingled with the Persian and Mesopotamian tribes transplanted by the Ommayads. For, alas, the chronicles of the Crusaders report that they found them already formed into a distinct sect, living in the Lebanon around Baniyas. So the idea of early travellers that they were the descendants of the knights of **Godfrey de Bouillon** or of a certain **Comte de Dreux**, is untenable.

One must turn for consolation to the markets of Damascus, where the men bargain with Teutonic bluntness and the women's faces, framed in their mediaeval wimples, often show retroussé noses and astonishingly blue eyes. After a few weeks in Damascus or in the Druse Mountain in the south, one reverts fancifully to the Crusader hypothesis; for scarcely seventy years after the Druse religion was formed, the First Crusaders—a horde of Norman and Frankish bachelors, sitting inside the walls of captured Jerusalem—must have contemplated more subtle triumphs. Few of the spear-wielding German women who accompanied the army of Conrad on the Second Crusade survived the battles of Laodicea. The barons were virile and bored. Long intervals of peace and alliance brought them into close contact with the Moslems, and they intermarried. Their children became known as *Pullani*, 'young ones'.

When Saladin recaptured Jerusalem, he permitted its refugees to settle peacefully in Palestine. For months they trudged disconsolately on the roads to the Christian princedoms of

* A jealously-guarded golden calf or bull is perhaps kept by the Druses, but the origins of this furiously-denied creature are not known.

Tripoli and Antioch, but the gates were closed against them. Many found hospitality amongst the Saracens and in the Lebanese mountains. Some of the Alawi mountaineers are suspiciously pale-skinned. In Bethlehem you may still see fair-haired women in the steeple head-dresses of mediaeval France, and Lebanese families are proud of names like *Faranjiyah*, 'Frankish', or *Salibi*, 'Crusading'.

As for the Druses, it is impossible to know the truth; only that over the centuries their community became more compacted, embalming as it did so a vestige of Lorelei beauty. Now they form a clan of soldierly severity, vowed to each other's support. Momentarily drunk on blue eyes, one might see in them an ironic wraith of all that the Crusaders should have been and were not, an eidolon of fair women and brave men.

15. The Fleece

And wealth is like the fleece of the
little sheep—men make sport there-
with: at one time it is abundant on the
sheep, at another shorn away; . . .
Alqamah ibn Abdah

THIN, CROOKED STREETS, flanked by open shops and
overhung with clothes: the bazaars of Damascus—a scene which
dazzled centuries of travellers. The Damascenes, who are
businessmen, are still proud of them. Westerners, demanding of
Eastern wares what they would never expect of their own, are
disappointed.

As in most Middle Eastern cities, every bazaar, even whole
sectors of the town, are limited to certain products. The
Christian quarter is distinguished by shops for wood-mosaic, but
the art of true inlay has died, and left behind a bastard craft
without delicacy or durability. Long strips of walnut and apricot
wood, camel-bone and rosewood are glued together, and a thin
cross-section shaved off, laid on the wooden surfaces and bedizened with slips of mother-of-pearl from Kuwait or Australia.
The result is a nacreous array of decorated coffee-tables, tric-
trac boards, boxes and the polygonal stools called *kursi*. For
centuries no trace of new imagination has disturbed the old
designs.

The Damascene love of inlay has lingered in her copper,
veined with silver or brass—a craft monopolised by the Jews.
But the art reached its meridian in late mediaeval years,
and now the heavily inlaid trays and table-tops, with their
repoussé texts and figures, seem clumsy and pretentious for
their medium. Brass lends more beauty than copper to the
minutiae of Islamic decoration. I recall, in particular, an old
man in a shop in Keimariye.

'Praised be God, my ancestors have always been metal-
workers,' he averred, chipping at a brass bowl, and I remembered
the mediaeval law in the city which obliged a son to carry on
the trade of his father as a surety for good craftsmanship.

The old man's chisel-point niggled out the curves of black
designs painted on the metal surface. Sometimes he took fifteen
days to finish a small plate.

'My fathers were all metal-people,' he repeated, with such proud familiarity that one could half-believe they were peering over his shoulder, or worked with him in a recess of the shop. So ancient is the history of Damascus metal-work that his claim did not embrace a mere few centuries of dead craftsmen. In the shop's darkness he had resurrected millennia of metal-workers, succeeding one another down the eras like the spectre-kings in *Macbeth*. Their ghostly hammers began to tap in the room: moulders of pernickety table-tops for Ottoman cafés, of cups and braziers for the slave-kings. In Crusading years their mattocks slashed through the flush and sparks of foundries; they proliferated beyond the parvenu Arabs until they hammered out helmets and *clipei* in the forges of Diocletian, and squatted, a thousand years before, in the wattle huts of the Amorites, among an offspring of arrow-heads.

It has all been to no avail. The consummate patterns tapped out by the brass-worker's chisel are prostituted by inlaid rivers of silver and gold. Only rarely is a piece wrought with anything of the old excellence. Trays and vases glimmer along the walls of a hundred shops, and seem to have caught a mineral jaundice from one another.

For foreigners, there is little hope of avoiding purchase. The Christian vendors adopt tourists as their own, and overcharge them with charm and élan. 'Our prices are the very lowest in Damascus,' each shop-owner insists. 'You will save up to fifty per cent by buying here. You see, we are really wholesalers. . . . And we post orders all over the world. You are English are you not? Only February last year we sent two opaline jars to Lady B— in Surrey. . . . What about brocades? Two pieces of Damascus silk went as a gift to your Queen last year.'

The rolled damasks tumble along the shop counters, be-musing the eye with a bonfire of colour, and woven with silver- or gold-threaded patterns in the style called *damassin*. The loveliest are hand-loomed in pure silk, exquisitely-designed and delicate to the touch. Their dyes are imported from Germany, but their designs claim lineage from early Ottoman years and before. European *grandes dames* donned them for three centuries before taffetas and corded silks became the fashion. They regaled the jaded fancies of Mameluke sultans, and clothed the rough shoulders of Tamerlane.

Wherever a stranger may acquire his brocade, all other sellers will assure him that he has been swindled.

'By God, you did not buy from Kassab? What did you pay

him? . . . For *one* metre? . . . Overcharged? . . . Plundered!' A despairing headshake embraces shame for his countrymen, the loss of a business deal for himself, and sheer incomprehension at foreign stupidity. Then he becomes circumspect and a little stern. 'Did you feel the texture of Kassab's silks? You know that sometimes people try to sell you artificial ones; coarse, machine-made stuff. Now look at this'—a river of flame-coloured damask courses over your hands. 'Give your girl-friend this and she will love you ten times more!'

West of the second Roman arch, the Street Called Straight narrows. The Christian quarter meets the Moslem at a shop which displays pictures of the Virgin Mary, Islamic heroes and charms against the Evil Eye. Stale *berazlik* biscuits stack the bakery windows in yellow pyramids, with slabs of *markouk* still pulpy and steaming. Then a corrugated roof bends over the street, shot through by sunlight. Under it stand the shops of grocers and sellers of rush carpets and candles for Islamic saints.

Other bazaars dip away to the north. Near the old silk market is the Suq el-Bzouriye for spices, perfumes and confectionery. Perhaps it is the crowds of scent bottles which give el-Bzouriye its happy leftover quality, the whiff of an apothecary's den. The perfumes of Grasse and Amsterdam stand side by side with Damascus rosewater, which sells for twice their price. It is the pure essence of crushed rose-petals, the same as once anointed the throats of Byzantine Augustas and Assyrian queens. It is, perhaps, a little sickly, and one wonders, appalled, how many fields of slaughtered roses haunt the tiny bottles.

The scent vendors sit quiet and smiling, as if overcome by their perfumes. But once you have approached them, they are Argus-eyed and Shiva-armed. There is a joyous uncorking of bottles and an eulogy on all aromas. Your wrists are dabbed with sandalwood, musk and amber, and the violet, jasmine and orange blossom scents extracted in Damascus. It will be twenty minutes before you escape, your pockets clinking with tiny phials, your hands drenched in redolence.

The coffee and sweetmeats of Damascus, which share the Bzouriye with the perfumes, may still be the finest in the world. Crystallised fruits are soaked so deep in sugar as to sate the sweetest oriental tooth, and are packed in round wooden boxes, successors to the 'pruna' and 'cottana' of Roman times. Beside them, even the jellied cubes and sugared almonds are bitter. Northward through the bazaar, the sacks of dried apricots and shelled walnuts, which stand in the homely street, disappear. Jewellers sit in tiny, glass-fronted stores. Their wares are almost identical, each window festooned with turquoise-studded bracelets, styleless brooches and agate and Alexandrite rings in sizes which would have inhibited a Mogul emperor. For 'the art of jewellery', runs a saying 'was born in Aleppo, grew up in Cairo, and came to Damascus to die'.

Further north, the bazaar meets a wall of the Great Mosque. On one side is the woodturners' *suq*; on the other side a street leads through the shoe-market to the porticoes of the mosque. Here, broad and high, stretches the Suq Hamidieh, the fashionable shopping centre of Damascus. In the chiaroscuro shed by its riddled roof, shops sell Western products, Syrian fabrics and a variety of cheap orientalia which is a comment on the taste of tourists: tinted lanterns, silver daggers, machine-made prayer-mats with cotton wefts.

The stock-in-trade of antique shops is in late Ottoman daggers and inferior opaline ware from China, but occasionally some once-wealthy family is forced to sell its silver or glass. Since modern silversmiths devote themselves only to filigree, antique silver is cherished. Pieces wrought sixty or seventy years ago— a few vases, a salver, perhaps some remnants of a coffee service —are often exquisitely-worked, etched with birds of paradise and flowers.

The Suq Hamidieh is criss-crossed with alleys. There is a bazaar for narghilyes and a street where carpets are laid across the pavements to be burnished by passing feet. Shop-owners collect pieces cheaply from the country people. Most of their carpets are fifty or a hundred years old, bought at a time when trade with Iran was more free, and some of them may have suffered from aniline dyes. But a good Dozar or Zaronim can be bought at less than its European price, and a few shops hide the mellow piles of Tabriz or a mulberry aristocrat from Isfahan.

The Suq Hamidieh is touched by an urgency which other bazaars disdain. Perhaps it is the effect of the tourist trade, for Damascenes say that hurry is written on the hoof of a donkey. Hawkers thrust garments at you; flute-vendors pipe in your ear. A man stands in the street selling trousers, which he vows are English twill. In summer, flower and nosegay sellers stand in the bazaar, suddenly swelling the noise with their shout, 'Make it up to your mother-in-law!' or wander the streets with their arms full of roses, singing 'O Fragrance! Odours of Paradise, your fragrance!' Sherbet-sellers attract attention by clinking two metal bowls together, like castanets. They straddle the street corners, pouring out lemonade or water from silver vessels strapped to their chests, or stroll through the alleys with a lusty, nostalgic cry, '*Berid 'alâ kalbak!* Refresh your heart!'

The Damascus markets are sadder than most, because the beauties of the past have degenerated rather than vanished. In the sickly contours of brass and copper sit the ghosts of the handsome inlay work from past centuries, and the long-remembered damascened blades; and the souls of hundreds of old glaziers must be looking down dismayed at modern glass-work. For two hundred years, change has meant the ebb of artistry, changelessness a stagnant clinging to the past. At best the work of the old masters is slavishly reproduced. The crafts themselves, no longer utilitarian, dwindle into tourist trade.

The integrity of the bazaars is upheld by their humbler streets, in the honest leather and saddlery of the Suq el-Surujiye, where Bedouin buy rope and bridles, then walk to the fruit and vegetable market beyond the walls. Here, in the sun's forge, the horse-carts crush their way through country people with mules and donkeys; men with trolleys of colossal cheeses; pressed folds of *kamreddin* apricot; trays of skinned goats' heads staring at each other, cloudy-eyed; and all along the side of the road, in open shops, the flicker of forges and the dinning hammers of ironmongers.

At the entrance of the Street Called Straight is the Suq el-Kumeileh, a 'louse-market' for second-hand clothes. Peasant families congregate here from all over the orchards. Other groups filter in from northern Syria, the desert, the Hauran and the Druse Mountain. The orchard peasants and the Syrian Bedouin are a distinct racial type, with long faces and prominent noses, chins and low foreheads sharply receding—a Mediterranean face, which they share with the Arabians.

The features of the Damascene townsmen are more complex and various. Their bedrock is the brachycephalic aborigine and Amorite. Then came Hittites and Arameans, Philistines (an early Greek people), the Mesopotamian conquerors and occasional Phoenicians, who brought back a racial confusion of wives from all over the Mediterranean. Bedouin drifted in from the desert over several millennia. Out of such a *mélange*, with a dash of plundering Scythian, came the pre-classical Damascene. Through Hellenistic and Islamic times, a hundred strains of Asiatic, African and European blood were absorbed into the arteries—from the rape of the Mongol and the marriage of the Turk to the influx of Palestinian refugees.

Probably no other city nourishes such a farrago of human-kind. Woman may look at you with hazel or pale-grey eyes, or with the dusky stare of frescoed Copts; a man's cheeks may be sallow like the Mongol or dark as a Saudi Arabian, his hair bright red, his children blond as angels. Negroes are descendants of Bedouin slaves or the Nubians of the Turks. Upper-class girls, heirs to the walk and look of Circassian odalisques, still flaunt the harvest hair of their grandmothers.

Against these faces the louse-market by the Street Called Straight threw into relief the lineaments of the peasants and the Bedouin—narrow heads and fuliginous eyes. The people might have wandered out of bas-reliefs and into the market; every-where I saw profiles like those of terra-cotta Arameans, and the rigid noses of the Persian bodyguard from Susa friezes. The millennia seemed to have shuffled into confusion. Jostling and jabbering came Assyrian ministers stepped hot-foot from the carvings of Nineveh (leaving their stone beards behind them) and tribute-bearers returned from a long incarceration in Pharaonic tombs. Sumerian divinities demanded huge sums for second-hand vests, and a king of Babylon sold sherbet in the streets.

While countrymen wear the keffieh, *cheroual* pantaloons and western jacket, the costumes of their wives vary from village to village. Women from the near orchards dress in black and ultramarine cotton, their hair and necks veiled, their eyes out-lined with kohl in emulation of the gazelle. From the Barada valley they arrive in flowered dresses, slashed at the neck, with tight-fitting pantaloons frilled beneath the ankle. From other villages come women in pink and blue check mantles; all that may be seen of them are their bangled wrists and their wooden sandals which are painted, even on the insides, with tiny blossoms. Women from the near-desert regions round Hijaneh walk in saffrons and shocking pinks, their foreheads bound with serried gold discs—a man's wedding-gift to his bride—or in bands of chain-mail like the trappings of a Saracen helmet. And Hauran girls put on metal headbands drawn to a point above their brows, and thick, striated bracelets, whose design des-cends to them direct from Roman times.

The peasant women ripen and wither early. The young wives are erect and handsome in a heavy-featured, irregular mould. The town girl, in contrast, is soft and olive-skinned, her face often covered in a triple veil of black nylon, which is only lifted a few inches to gain an advantage during a bargain.

From the desert itself come the Bedouin of the Roualla, a vigorous people who once raided an enemy tribe by using twenty American taxis. Damascus has always been open to their influence; she is their harbour and arsenal, and they have given her a wild strain. But now it is usually the tribe's semi-nomadic groups who frequent her markets, people who have exchanged the arrogance of the sands for lives which are poor but no longer free. The men sell wool and buy coffee, and the women follow them in silence, often standing taller than their husbands, their chins tattooed in blue stars.

The farmer is no longer jealous of the herdsman. Cain accepts Abel without malice, and pays him a pittance for his wool.

16. Faces and Things which were Passing

> The life of clouds is a parting and
> a meeting. A tear and a smile.
>
> *Khalil Gibran*

I T I S H A R D to know how important personal experiences may
be, or if they are important at all, to the picture of a city. But
from the limbo of a shabby diary which I kept in Damascus,
incidental encounters and stray findings have been arguing for
their inclusion among things of more moment.

Diaries, I suppose, are selfish. But sometimes they capture
the mild disarray attendant on happy living, and Rahda, who
periodically rearranged my room, convinced me that confusion
is the natural state of man, editing my diary herself by tearing
up a part of it.

It begins, I see, midway between Paris and Istanbul, with a
night on the Orient Express, in which a Yugoslav woman woke
up suddenly and spat orange-pips over the rest of the carriage—
an ancient Croatian rite perhaps; and it progresses to my first
Damascus entry—an October day spent searching for a mosque
which must have vanished under the French bombardment.

The mosque had been furnished with a charitable revenue, or
wakf, for the feeding and housing of cats. A *wakf* was the legacy
of a rich and pious man, and was often devoted to the building
and preservation of a mosque or *madrasa* around his tomb.
Moslems like to feel that prayers and Koranic chanting will
attend their grave, but cat-purrings are a less usual fancy.

Damascene households feed and keep cats as a half-supersti-
tion, which nobody could explain to me. The opprobrium in
which dogs are held does not apply to them. They are occasionally suspected of harbouring djinns, but that provokes wary
respect, and it is even claimed that Mahomet liked them, and
that when one fell asleep on his cloak as he was finishing his
prayers, he did not disturb it, but cut away a part of his robe and
left it sleeping: an act which has been a great boon for generations of Moslem cats.

Cat mosques are few. There may still be one in Damascus, although I never found it; but there is one in Aleppo and another at Trablus. You may walk into these mosque courtyards and apart from a few sunbathing cats, mostly in a state of swollen-eyed marasmus, you notice nothing strange. But at a fixed hour someone brings a bucket of unidentifiable food.

The shadows stir with feline confluence, with palsied shapes, in fuscous, black and adulterated white. The whole courtyard starts to creep forward to the pannier of food. The window-grilles drop mildewed tabbies. Congeries of backstreet, dust-coloured kittens, with faces like marmosets, squirm through the doors. The food is overlaid by desperate mouths and suspicious eyes; long-bodied toms such as you see in Istanbul; hard, fierce catamounts like those of the Naples docks; and a sort of *minimum* cat, a cat shorn of all but the vitals, its half-furred hide drawn tight as a drum over its tent of flexuous bones. There are blind cats and tailless cats, cats with a tittle of tortoiseshell or a smack of Persian, and jaunty cats—compulsive gipsies and tramps. Occasionally comes some patrician, demoted from a marble courtyard, or mild-eyed creature with the facial discs of an owl—a ghost of the English cottage pussy. But most are turbulent and jealous, with ears like tattered wheat and coats in states of *délâbrement* which only nine lives might survive.

There is also a *wakf* in Damascus for the sustenance of two roosters. This is a very pious institution, for the crow of cocks traditionally wakes the faithful for the early morning prayer. Fleas* perform the same sacred office, with the advantages of closer contact. 'Thou shalt not vilify the flea, for he awakeneth the faithful to prayer' runs a tradition. Yet in all the annals of *wakf* I have been unable to discover a charity for fleas. Considering the disparity in numbers between roosters (which are few) in Damascus, and fleas, this seems ungrateful.

October 22nd I returned home to find a pigeon installed in the shower-room: a white, celestial creature which Umm-Toni had bought near the Gate of St Paul for almost nothing. It is to be fattened for some day's dinner, but the youngest son wants to

---

* I find an analysis of the flea from a Moslem biological lexicon: it is apparently 'in its greatest vigour towards the end of winter and the beginning of spring. It is strongly inclined to be hump-backed at the time of leaping; it is said to be of the appearance of the elephant, and to have canine teeth with which it bits and a trunk with which it sucks. . . .'

keep it as a pet. Horrible row. The boy in tears; Elias glowing
red like a half-erupted volcano; the bird making messes in the
shower-room, which was once a sanitary place.

October 24th The pigeon forced me to look for a public bath.
There are forty-one still operating in Damascus, and a few
retain fine plaster mouldings and tilework. If a cloth hangs over
the doorway, the bath is only open to women, who used to have
their eyebrows plucked here and their hands and feet hennaed
with little green stars and crescent moons.

The Hammam el-Jozé is the second oldest bath in the city,
and was built soon after Saladin's time. But its mediaeval sob-
riety has disintegrated into rococco: a congestion of chandeliers
and a mural in the Istanbul style.

On either side of the main room a railinged dais with divans
supported a benign row of pipe-smokers and coffee-sippers,
trussed in dressing-gowns. A Sudanese folded up my clothes and
wrapped me in towels and a turban. As I clattered across the
tiling in stilted wooden *kabkabs*, a narghilye-smoker looked up.
Mouths were disengaged from amber stubs and coffee-cups
temporised between saucers and lips. 'God is merciful! An
infidel in a towel!'

'The sky will fall next.'

'God knows best.'

I was pushed under a low door through a series of chambers
whose steam grew hotter and thicker. The paving under my feet
was oil-smooth and coloured in grey and muted reds. Water
runnelled away over the tiles along channels only faintly dinted,
and a greenish light fell from glass-stoppered holes in the dome
of the *chauderie*, illuminating white-paunched figures sprawled
in foggy recesses. The chambers were full of slapping and
gasping sounds, the cracking of joints, and groans. Attendants
in loin-cloths stood waxwork-like in a jubilee of steam.

As I entered the hottest room I was seized by a substantially-
muscled Turk, who smothered me in soap. I was washed and
scrubbed with a camel's-hair glove, and dowsed in scalding
water. Then the Turk began tugging my limbs in many strongly-
resisted directions and pulling my fingers out of their sockets—
an organised purgatory which may have lasted five or fifty
minutes. But I was comforted by the sight of a number of
uncomplaining men in other malbowges of the inferno, until I
was led away in my towels.

The happy part of a Turko-Syrian bath is the immediate

aftermath, when you may lounge on divans and be served with coffee. A feeling of relief and accomplishment alights on you. Not only is every grain of dirt expelled from the pores of your skin, but the pores have probably gone themselves. You dress tenderly. You pay a shilling. There are salaams and insinuations about backsheesh. As you turn the corner of the passage, the steam lifts its siege and the clatter of *kabkabs* dissolves. The natural world draws round at last—an elysian place, wonderfully dirty.

As for *kabkabs*: these are stilted wooden shoes, like those the geisha of Kyoto wear. They were part of the wardrobe of every woman. A slave-girl had to content herself with a six-inch *kabkab*, but for a lady of high birth a twelve-inch one, perhaps encrusted with mother-of-pearl, was the minimum. I was once asked if we had *kabkabs* in England, and I answered No with sudden regret. A woman of no standing, I suppose, would have to wear emaciated, plyboard *kabkabs*, crudely decorated. Middle-class girls would be allowed to ascend six inches or so, whereas nobility could move through a rarefied atmosphere on beautiful mahogany *kabkabs* with emblazoned stilts, generously vaulted to allow lesser folk to pass freely underneath.

October 30th Night-walk in Damascus. In the desert the richness of the stars seems a just recompense for the penury of the land. But here nature has been prodigal, and the lamps of Salihiye glitter close beneath the stars over Lebanon. The narrowness of the streets, the arches over them, and the walls dimpled with doors in the moonlight are at first unnerving. Every loitering figure becomes a *fedai* of the Assassins. But at street corners sit soldier-watchmen with rifles, and faces like stubbled Rembrandts in their firelight, spitting and snoring but comfortingly substantial in their heavy boots and overcoats.

Dogs, which sleep in fields and ruins during the day, are now everywhere. They are ownerless, for angels do not enter a house where dogs live. Every night they glide in through the gates after the town is silent, long-muzzled like wolves, and clean up the mounds of rubbish which are left along the alleys. Tonight I watched four or five of them flit in together through the Roman arch at the end of the Street Called Straight. Like other Damascenes, each band has its own quarter of the city, and sometimes there are battles under my balcony because the dogs from the Jewish quarter have dared enter the Straight Street. They rarely attack men, but they sometimes give the alarm from pack to pack as one walks down a street, so that always they are waiting baleful-eyed in gutters and the doorways of empty khans.

For centuries, even though hundreds of glass lamps might hang in the streets, a man had to carry a lantern in Damascus or he would be arrested as a robber. Big lanterns, the size of Victorian carriage lamps, were born by slaves before the emirs, and lesser citizens sometimes carried flames which glowed through coloured glass like nocturnal butterflies.

The streets of the Christian quarter are quiet, except for the dogs, and sometimes the bray of a donkey, which is a very sad sound in the silence. The old style of wedding appears to be dying out. I never saw one. But once the alleys would flicker with tapers, and a procession creep along so slowly that it seemed only to feign movement. From a distance the drums and cymbals were muffled by the lanes. Then the first shadows wobbled along the walls before the flush of candles. A buffoon cavorted in front; sounds of chanting and talking, and the screams of the women, like sea-birds. Friends carried the bride's dowry before her in an inlaid chest, while she, bowed beneath a canopy, a cloak and a red veil, passed by in glorified anonymity. As the procession vanished into the passageway of the bridegroom's house, the song of his mother flooded the streets.

> Who said that you are brown, oh face of the full moon,
>   Oh peeled sesame, oh honey-comb?
> Let me put my back for you, let me take you across the
>   river.
> Oh beloved of my heart, oh daughter-in-law forever.*

Inside, the girl, shedding her izzar, stood in a rich velvet jacket, jewels and flowers glinting and tumbling over her hair and veil. 'And at midnight,' says St Matthew's gospel, 'there was a cry made, Behold, the bridegroom cometh; . . .'

The streets of the Moslem quarter were brimful of moonlight. Outside the walls, by Chouhada Square, the last of the chestnut-vendors had rolled his trolley over the cobbles and into the dark. Between here and the Kassioun Mountain, the earth is thick with the bones of holy men. Some believe that seventy thousand saints crumble away under the tarmac and concrete of the modern city. Others say that these seventy thousand are martyrs

---

* The bride will probably come to live with her husband in his parents' household; the songs sung are traditional, and not necessarily felt. There is a hoary Arabic saying: 'It is written on the doors of Paradise: Never does a mother-in-law love a daughter-in-law.'

and that the saints are seven hundred. But, as the Damascenes wisely prevaricate, 'God knows best'.

It was cold climbing the mountainside through Salihiye. The wind blew sharp out of Lebanon. In the Kurdish quarter, rats flew into the drains like chips of shadow. The moon had halted over the desert, bending a shoulder towards the Euphrates. During night eclipses the Kurds used to run out of doors clashing kettles and pots, for they believed that an animal was eating the moon. The Kurds are mighty warriors, and the beast would slowly release its prey. The quarter was shuttered now, and there was only blackness where sixty years ago the fires of the Baghdad caravan-camps burnt in the desert.

The houses fell behind as I ascended. I heard rocks grating loosely under my feet, and the shrill scrape of thistles and artemisia. Damascus, pricked out in many lights beneath, was drowned in cold winds. The moon discovered a serrated harshness in the mountain, and splayed its white veins into shadow. On such a night, say the Arabs, a group of prophets climbed its steep slopes, their garments phantom-white, and from the mountain-summit stepped into heaven.

November 2nd I visited the Armenian church again to look at the frescoes, which are unexceptional. Damascus is starved of representational art.

The Koran does not expressly prohibit the portrayal of animal life, but the Islamic traditions, which are the second source of law, are specific. Angels pass by the house which keeps images, and at the Last Day 'Woe to him who has painted a living being!' Those whom he has portrayed will rise up and demand their souls of him and he, unable to invest his works with life, will perish eternally.

This façade covers an old unease: the primaeval fear that to portray a man is to possess his soul. And it is a reaction against pre-Islamic idol-worship. But these fears did not confine the art of earliest Islam. Dancing-girls with painted toe-nails adorn the panels of Ommayad hunting-lodges; beasts and kings strut across Hellenized mosaics. Only by the ninth century had the troupe of houris and bacchanals been expelled. Thereafter, the labours of Arab decorative artists were turned to floral and geometric designs.

The Damascenes, anarchic in all things, inveigled natural motifs into their minor work: astrological symbols on manuscripts and brassware, animals in ivory. Their museums contain stubby clay lions and horses, homespun cows and blunted birds; heraldic eagles and other fabulous beasts on Mameluke pottery; delicate, animal-shaped padlocks, whose mouths are quaintly and eternally open in expectation of a key; faience vases trodden by fantastical peacocks.

I remember a pair of crude and jaunty lions on the Tomb of Sukeina; the birds on the doors of the Mezzeh mosque; the menageries of the Persian carpets at Sitti Zeinab; the harmless overgrown cat of the Azem Palace. But although animal life lurks stubbornly in peculiar lairs, there is scarcely a human being pictured in the whole Moslem city.

November 8th Today I sent an inlaid box to England. The shop-owner was convinced that I was sending it to a girl-friend.

'You will give me the address and I will post it to her,' he said. He gazed at the name 'Miss E. Horn'. 'So she lives at Oxford? Is she a student there?'

No, she was not a student. In vain I told him that she was my eighty-year-old nanny.

'How old is she really? Is she beautiful?'

'Yes,' I said. Certainly my nanny is beautiful.

'Then I will send her a little souvenir in the box. Perhaps I will write something.' He stuck a pen between his teeth. 'Miss E. Horn' he repeated, and the words took on an added rapture through the Damascene accent. I left him humped behind his counter, wondering what sort of note he would enclose in the box. A number of lavish Arab precedents have become standard. Nanny might smell like ambergris or have the eyes of a young gazelle. Perhaps she would rival the full moon or shine like anemones. It was all very satisfying.

November 13th I never discovered where the first British consulate had stood. Evidently it was a handsome place with a marble-paved courtyard forty-eight yards long, planted with passion flowers and Indian honeysuckle, and incongruously ringed with Koranic inscriptions.

Flecker, I think, was the last person to note an old-style Damascene diplomat. The French consul appears to have spent his time playing *écarté* with the daughter of his Greek landlord —a girl who dressed in flame-coloured satins. The English consul haunted his house in a 'strangely undulated' felt hat, looking after aviaries of expatriate birds. And in his door-keeper's lodge stood an ostrich, which vetted all visitors (ostriches being notoriously bad-tempered with strangers).

I wondered how the British consul had fed his ostrich, and sifted through encyclopaedias in the Arab Academy to discover. There was little to be learnt, except that the ostrich, as the type of the family Struthionidae, possesses a head and neck comparatively destitute of feathers, that he can outstrip any horse, and that his third toe is wanting. Then at last: 'The ostrich has long been celebrated for his propensity for swallowing curious and heterogeneous substances such as pieces of iron and glass, large stones, and other objects of like anomalous description.'

It was clear now. The consul had returned to England in a hurry during the Great War, while the Turkish empire allied itself to Germany. The ostrich could not be brought to England as 'war effort'. It must have been locked up in the consulate to destroy the archives. Breakfast: two glazed tiles and some stucco inlay. Lunch: flagstones à la Carrara watered down with H.E.'s begonias. Gradually, resistlessly, as Gallipoli and Ypres rose and fell in tragic uproar, glass and iron and Koranic verses disappeared down the Struthionidan throat. By 1918, just as the British forces reached the Damascus oasis, the ostrich must have dismantled the consulate and exposed himself to the public gaze. Ostrich flesh is forbidden to Jews, but not to Syrians; and Allenby arrived too late.

November 18*th* Elias burst in and threw himself down on my bed.
'I've sold the house!'
Handshaking and shoulder-slapping. He had been trying to sell for months. And he had negotiated a fair price, he decided; more than he had paid for it. 'We'll be moving in the new year! Everyone will have a room of his own!'
'Where are we moving to?' I asked, and at once regretted a question to which I had already guessed the answer.
'I don't know. There isn't anywhere.' His lips pouted ruminatively. For a moment I thought I had spoiled everything. Then he spanked his knees and shouted: 'We'll find a place! God will make room for us somewhere! Perhaps we'll get a house in Kassaa. But there's one thing . . .' He looked at me like a truant child. 'Umm-Toni doesn't know yet. She may not like it.'
'You must tell Umm-Toni.'
'I must tell,' he murmured miserably to himself, 'Umm-Toni.'

She received the news quietly, but afterwards behaved with a compound of outward resignation and silent reproach which must be an international weapon in the armoury of womankind; although silence, in Umm-Toni's case, was relative.

November 19*th* Today I saw a complete set of Roman dental instruments, and a glass tumbler, light as a cobweb. But few antiquities come to Damascus to stay. The government insists upon seeing all pieces and commands an option to buy them at its own valuation; so a quiet stream of *objets d'art* trickles into Beirut. Most Roman pieces come from Bosra and the Druse Mountain. There are incense-burners, many coins and occasional crudely-worked bronzes.

I have searched for stray pieces of glazed tiles in the oceanic blues, greens and violets for which Damascus was famous. The kilns where they were manufactured have been discovered not far outside the eastern gate. The best tiling in Damascus may still be seen in the Mosque of Dervich Pasha near the entrance to the Street Called Straight, and in the Sinaniye Mosque. The Mameluke tiles, like those of the Teyrouzi Mosque in the Meidan suburb, are often fussy and show a Chinese influence; but those of early Turkish times—a distant gift from Persia—are among the most beautiful wall decorations ever conceived.

It did not seem too much to hope for: a fragment from the patterns of a wall or a lintel: some almond blossom perhaps, or a mauve tulip petal, or a frond of hyacinth. But I found nothing for sale in the whole city, and none of the early painted earthenware. There may be more Damascus tiles in the Victoria and Albert Musuem and Musée des Arts Décoratifs than in all the city mosques.

November 22*nd* Elias came in, beaming all over his face.

'I'm not selling!' he shouted. 'I decided we're staying here!'

I affected surprise. Had he not signed a contract?

'I asked to see the contract again, and when they showed it to me—I tore it up!' His fingers scissored the air. 'Shrrt! Shrrt!'

Umm-Toni was sitting on the divan looking dutiful. Was it really good to stay? she kept saying; perhaps they should have gone after all. God might not give them a second chance.

Elias was adamant. 'I've decided,' he interjected from time to time. The conversation was, I think, ritualistic. Umm-Toni emitted doubts and gasps and worries, and Elias crushed them with patriarchal finality until they re-emerged in curious guises, such as how to escape the Armenians downstairs, should the pigeon be eaten and was Rahda getting thin.

I heard them talking late into the night, like a piano sonata: Umm-Toni tinkling passionately in a plaintive octave, Elias rumbling conventionally below, until their voices swelled and diminished in a last crescendo, and ended with one of Elias's decisive and resounding kisses.

November 29th Bicycled into the orchards through plantations of fig trees, which the Arabs call the trees of heaven, so intelligent that they are almost animal. November is a time when the farmers start to mutter about rain and the will of God. Clouds stir over Lebanon and load half the sky with a saturnine pall, while the sun bends through perfect blueness in the south. For the first time I noticed the scarcity of birds. Only occasionally a magpie, a jay or a thrush filled some exotic copse with English minstrelsy. The peasants shoot them for food.

I reached Djisrin in the eastern Ghuta: a drowsy village through which a Roman road used to run. Ancient columns prop up its mosques. The larger mosque is part of the village girls' school and encloses four big pillars with deeply-carved Corinthian capitals, which stand in its gloom portentously, almost fiercely accomplished.

Strange that the coarse acanthus plant should be so immortalised. Greek history tells that once, when a beautiful girl died, her nurse gathered up her jewellery and placed it in a basket over her tomb. She covered it from the weather with a tile. When spring came, an acanthus plant pressed up beneath the basket, curled around it, and bent back its fronds against the tile. The Athenian sculptor Callimachus, passing through the graveyard, fell in love with this strange, harmonious shape and perpetuated it in stone.

I was the first European to visit Djisrin for many years. The schoolteachers deserted their girls and pummelled me with questions. Who had put the columns there? How old were they? What was Imperial Roman? One teacher thought they might be a hundred years old, another ventured a thousand. A third looked as if he had been about to say that his grandfather had carved them.

We sat all afternoon under a freak mulberry tree, which had outgrown its strength and clambered over the village graveyard. Pools of wax glimmered where candles had been put on the graves at night, and there was a broken cage in which birds were once placed to sing and cheer the sad spirits. We exchanged information. There were Byzantine sarcophagi in the village, unaccountable inscriptions and stray carvings. The shrieks of the teacherless schoolgirls reached us from quarter of a mile away. Nobody stirred. Sweetmeats and bonbons were carried out to us by a man in a near-by house, and we lay under the mulberry tree until dusk, relaxed in the Arab belief that it is not worth destroying a present hour by thinking about a future one.

December 3rd Surrounded by soldiers in the desert east of Dumeir, where I was taking photographs of the Roman city. Two miles beyond, humped in a haze and obscured by sand dunes, was a military camp: registered as a non-photographable object.

I sit in the guardroom while a sentry telephones for an officer. Nobody can speak any European language, but it is every soldier's duty to read through my passport upside-down. Inside the room they smile at me and apologise. Outside stands a corporal with a sten-gun.

Various officers arrive, but each proves too junior to cope with the situation. Stars and insignia multiply on each successive pair of shoulders, ribbons and medals and lanyards appear. Finally, the sign of an omnipotent military personage—boots which shine. He turns out to have been trained at the Warminster School of Infantry. He is desperately sorry, but my film will have to be developed in his military laboratories. It will take half an hour; meanwhile, he asks about Stourhead and the weather on Salisbury Plain and what is the point of Stonehenge?

After an hour a sergeant appears with the negative of my film. There are only two exposures: a poorly-focused picture of the Roman temple at Dumeir and a blotchy landscape which arouses immediate suspicion.

'What is this object?' an officer asks.

'A sheep's head.' I had photographed a desert landscape with a sheep's skull, for melodrama, in the centre.

Everybody returns to scrutiny. The sheep's head is held up to the light. It had been half-buried under the sand and looked, in its formless squalor, very like a Syrian military camp in the desert. The negative was turned upside-down and diagonally, placed under fierce lighting, held against the sky and magnified many times. Finally the Warminster officer picked it up and came over to me.

'This,' he said—and everybody fell silent for the monstrous revelation—'is a sheep's head.'

December 10*th* I have been trying to write all day without success. Every hour, Umm-Toni comes in with a tiny cup of coffee, or a dish of sugared beetroot, and starts to kiss the paintings of the Madonna on my Christmas cards: first the didactic Child of Filippo Lippi, then a pensive Virgin from Woolworths. The coffee is spilled over my diary.

This has become too much of a ritual to matter, but during the last few days Rahda has been escaping school. She sits outside my door pretending she is a cat, miauling and purring. Whenever I let her in, she reorganises my notes on an olympian scale behind my back. She tinkers endlessly with my possessions and asks me if I will give them to her. After a while she leaves the room with a little pile of expired biros, paper-clips, English pennies and a pencil-sharpener in the shape of a sad-eyed dog. An hour or two later I hear Umm-Toni's voice, very angry for her, or the long thunder of Elias. And the sad-eyed dog and the English pennies are pushed back inside my door by a disconsolate hand.

Then the mewing begins again. Work becomes impossible. Any errors in this book are the fault of Miss Rahda Bahena, Straight Street, Damascus.

December 11*th* Today, a visit to the museum—one of the most interesting in the Middle East. Built in 1936, it is a sparsely-inhabited tourist province—Syrians do not enjoy museums—a spacious, sensible building, set in a garden of eucalyptus trees and basalt statues.

Several remarkable reconstructions overshadow its smaller exhibits. The synagogue frescoes from Dura-Europos on the Euphrates, discovered by accident after seventeen centuries under the sand, are the earliest known paintings of biblical figures; gauche, lovingly-drawn people with ebon eyes and exclamatory hands. Their dress ranges through all the guises to which the hybrid city of Dura-Europos was susceptible, so that even as sober a figure as Ezekiel begins his sequence of panels dressed in Persian pantaloons and ends them in a Greek chiton.

In the garden stands the gateway of the Qasr el-Hair palace built by Hisham in the desert north-east of Palmyra. The bareness of its Roman-style towers has been covered with stucco moulding; foliated pilasters flaunt the busts of dancing-girls and its dog-tooth machicolations make no pretence at strength. Inside, the loveliest features must have been the limestone balustrades and window tracery; for the palace friezes —lions and simian faces painted in ochre—show an idiosyncratic transition from Byzantine to Islamic styles; and the walls of the rooms, decorated waist-high in rivers of black and brown, must have lent a pernicious, intestinal feel to the palace halls.

The museum is full of minor surprises. In the resurrection of an eighteenth-century Damascene house interior, fountain-water bubbles from concealed holes and skates like light over marble walls beneath dark painted ceilings. In another room is the earliest known alphabet—from the fourteenth century B.C. in the classic Phoenician lettering—inscribed on a stone tablet the length of a man's index finger. There is a Roman lamp in the shape of an elephant with its trunk extended to receive oil; some finely preserved mosaics; and the ghost of a circular ivory table from the royal palace at Ugarit, which must have been exquisite.

On an upper storey is a silver-coated mask-helmet from a Syro-Roman grave near Homs. And there are alabaster statuettes from Mari, from a beatific world of men with big eyes and contented smiles, like minor Assyrian gods. Their beards are long and wedge-shaped, their hands clasped over gratified stomachs, and they are dressed in cascading skirts.

The Palmyra room displays a peculiar blend of Hellenistic and oriental influence. In a vault of the museum, the Palmyrene tomb of Yarhay has been reconstituted as it was found: a sumptuous sepulchre from the second century A.D., belonging to an Arab family grown rich and Hellenised on the trade routes of Imperial Rome. A pair of stone doors swings open into the crypt. From its walls stare more than seventy sculptured faces—portraits of people whose remains were sealed up in the stone behind them. Yarhay's statue reclines like a king at the back of his tomb, his relatives seated round him, a bowl of wine in his hand. The expressions on their faces are identical and extraordinary. It is as if their eyes, raised in awe from some family conference, had fallen on a celestial Medusa. But the features are capable and business-like; some could almost belong to senators, others are fiercely oriental, drivers of shrewd bargains. They are robed like Greeks, but the ponderous jewels and starchy, veiled head-dresses of the women betray them. A few of them died young and soft-faced, but most seem to have passed away in a responsible middle-age: matrons of some presence, and respectable merchants.

It can only be a rigid artistic formula which gives them their startled look. But its massed effect confounds analysis. Their expressions, indefinably, are alarmed but not afraid: the court of a worthy king which has retained something of its dignity in the face of the divine.

December 13*th* 'You are always looking at tombs, Colin. Don't people die in London?' Razouk wiped kebab off his mouth and added, 'Do you want to see a film?'

Films here are generally American, Indian or Egyptian. The self-styled 'Society of the Friends of Virtue' has been militating for some years against their corrupting influence, and attempted to have them prohibited to women. There have even been virulent sermons in the mosques. But since the Second World War, a small, state-controlled Syrian film company has been formed. Until recently it only produced newsreels and documentaries, but now a trickle of feature films has appeared, with rambling plots and sequences of dance and song.

'You won't understand anything,' Razouk said, as we sat down in a bare, very modern cinema among a crowd of sheeted women. The theatre was filled with the rustling of paper, crunching of chickpeas and the shouting of advice to people on the screen. It was not necessary to know Arabic in order to follow the plot. It centred on a heroine who strolled through the desert singing songs in a chiffon dress, and who was pursued by six villains animated by the understandable wish to murder her. And as yet again a sheikh's dagger poised above the chiffoned head, Razouk would shout 'Now he wants to kill her' and the lady at my side would jump and spill chickpeas into my lap and a great sigh escape the audience as the sheikh failed.

December 20*th* Mustafa's mother, Hayat, came down from Ashrafiyeh to arrange a hearing in the law-courts for the case of the old man's taxi injuries. I had promised to meet her, but only recognised her by her eyebrows, since she always came veiled to the city. She walked four or five paces behind me, from the bus station to El-Nasr Boulevard and glared at every taxi she saw, not because it might contain her husband's assailant—he was in prison—but because taxis had become collectively guilty.

The Palace of Justice did not inspire confidence. On the steps we collided with a flock of Bedouin, whose heads were thrown back, canvassing God for the justice denied by man. Two soldiers were marching a peasant in gigantic handcuffs down the corridors. Black-veiled women crammed the halls, like a deluge of litigating widows, and Druse mothers squatted against the stairs, breast-feeding their babies.

Hayat and I reversed our positions. While she pleaded with a variety of officials, I stood a few paces behind her, like some threat of vast and nameless international jurisprudence. What she said about me I shall never know. Several of the officials cast panicky glances in my direction. I tried to assume the appearance of the positions to which she had no doubt promoted me: a steely Russian advocate, perhaps, or some litigious dignitary from the United Nations.

We left the Palace an hour later with a date for the hearing a long time hence. I never heard the outcome.

December 23rd It is Ramadhan, the month of fast. From sunrise to sunset, a Moslem must abstain from food, drink, smoking and women. It is a month of frayed tempers and the possibility of rebellions, and is worst when it falls during the long summer days. In the country a man may not eat until it is so dark that he can no longer descry a hair held between two fingers.

Clocks and bells have replaced the Ramadhan sunset gun in the city. A few minutes after sunset I visited a friend, who refused to break his fast until I had shared his meal. His approach to Ramadhan was a mixture of reverence and displeasure, reminding me of the Moorish song which Gide heard:

> If Ramadhan were a man,
> I should myself break his legs;
> But Ramadhan came from God;
> You and I accept his sufferings.

December 30th Somebody said that it might snow today. Snow! I had heard that it sometimes drifted down from Lebanon, but had never expected it. In Ottoman years the mail-diligence used to pick up travellers frozen rigid on the road to Beirut, and during a few freak winters the snow had broken down the roofs of the Damascus bazaars. But it seemed scarcely possible today: snow on the corrugated roofs of Straight Street; snow like muslin on the tomb of Saladin, tumbling in seams between mosque colonnades. And the muezzins, raised up on their minarets into this illness of the sky, would suffocate their songs in it. Snow did not seem possible. And it never came.

December 31st New Year's Eve. Feel sad, which Elias says is a disorder recurrent on the new year. We crouch round the oil-stove. Most of the children are in bed, but six-year-old Senah lies asleep on the floor, with her hand, like a bird's claw, in mine. Rahda is trying to knit, which is not a success, and Umm-Toni sighs on the sofa and mutters reproaches at her, extorting only a litany of giggles.

I ask Elias what he hopes to do in the new year, but he takes refuge in the will of God. The will of God is a depressing thing in Damascus and this, with the late hour, makes me tired. The Bible, I tell Elias cantingly, says that where there is no vision, the people perish. 'Some time,' he answered, half asleep, 'we will have another house. Maybe next year. Maybe after. Everybody will have a room of his own. . . .'

17. The Mandate

Turn with thy times, oh wise and
knowing one, and live. For thy
house is given to destruction. . . .
'Alā' al-dīn ībn Aybak,
on Damascus

DURING THE FIRST year of the Great War, Damascus was
the base of the Fourth Ottoman Army Corps under Djmal
Pasha, and became the headquarters for the combined
operations of the Central Powers in the Near East. Djmal's
administration was efficient but brutal, and his hanging of
twenty-one patriots in the Chouhada Square is still remembered.
Damascus had already become the centre of those secret societies
for Arab freedom which won over the emir Feisal to the cause of
the Arab revolt.

When the city was evacuated in September 1918, the war
was over for the Arabs. Huge bands of Turkish soldiers had
already been rounded up in the orchards. Arab forces entered
the city on the first day of October, and found an Arab flag flying
from the Town Hall. They were followed a few hours later
by the 3rd Australian Light Horse, who were greeted with
boisterous jubilation, and General Allenby arrived on October
3rd with Feisal, who entered on horseback at a full gallop.

The aftermath is famous. Lawrence conferred governorship
on a senior Sharifian officer on Feisal's behalf, honouring the
1915 Protocol of Damascus—the agreement with Sharif Husain
in Mecca that independence be granted to all Arab territory
except the areas of Alexandretta, Mersin and 'portions of Syria
lying to the west of the districts of Damascus, Homs, Hamah,
and Aleppo'.

Even such a fossil of imperialism as the Sykes-Picot Act,
which was not revealed to the Arabs until 1917 (and then by
mistake), granted independence to inland Syria. But France
repudiated both acts. She claimed that her old Capitulations for
protecting Roman Catholics in the Levant, and her social and
educational works in Syria, gave her a right to supervise the
country's development. The statesmen at Versailles thought

that Britain was purposely thwarting their ambitions by supporting 'a bedouin and his horde of bandits' in Damascus.

Feisal, meanwhile, was collecting together the remains of Turkish organisation to build the kingdom of Syria, with Damascus as capital. Life in the city became sufferable again. But in Versailles imperialism had taken its time-dishonoured course. Despite the findings of the American Commission that the Syrians wanted no intervention in their country, France extended an 'invitation' to Feisal to accept her mandate. Feisal, who was a politician, realised that his cause was hopeless. But Damascus rushed to arms. A band of demobilised soldiers and peasants faced the French army at Maysalun Pass eight miles from Damascus, and was there vanquished. General Gouraud's troops entered the holy city on July 24th 1920, 'the Year of Catastrophe', and the kingdom of Syria was ended.

The French mandate, which endured to the end of the Second World War, faced its giant problems with good-will, but with the intention of delegating power into Arab hands as slowly as it could. Civil service training scarcely existed. Syria, even when part of the decrepit Ottoman Empire, had benefited from a delta of free trade whose streams extended all over the Middle East. Now, from Jordan, Palestine, Iraq, Egypt and Arabia the barrier of the pound sterling rose up and isolated the devalued franc. France, violating her mandatory agreement, allowed Turkey to seize Alexandretta in 1938; and her own separatist policy cut off the rich coastal strip of Lebanon from the inland. Damascus was more isolated than she had ever been. Her ancient role as the middle-city of the Levant foundered. Her local crafts declined and even the lovely silks, although fostered by the French, became almost extinct.

France prepared the city for a new future. Factories were developed and modernised, and most of the present-day industries stem from the mandate: cotton-spinning, the cement works at Doummar, a cannery, cigarette manufacture, and the Kadem glass-works set up in 1945 with American equipment.

Communications spreadeagled from the main cities. A narrow-gauge railway, financed by the French, had connected Damascus to Beirut and the Hauran as early as 1895; and in 1908 the Hejaz railway had reached Ma'an and Medinah. A French company had gained a concession to run tramways in Damascus (although the old city was impenetrable) and to gird her with electric lights—phenomena hitherto unknown in the Ottoman Empire except in Beirut. But new roads now radiated

from the city, electrical power was developed, the telegraph repaired and extended, and in 1932 drinking-water was channelled
to Damascus direct from the Fijeh fountain.

Even in the nineteenth century, Damascus had extended
beyond her walls over the Merjeh fields and up the slopes of
Kassioun towards Salihiye. Along the shoulders of the Barada,
where violets and roses had bloomed, the Turks had built
baroque headquarters for military and civil staff, a post-office,
the Palace of Justice, and the Hamidiyya barracks, which were
overhauled in 1945 and turned into the Damascus University.
Suburbs had filled out the al-Kanawat, Suwayhat and Sarudja
districts beyond the western walls. Salihiye had crawled westward along the mountainside and formed the new quarter of
Mohajirine, peopled by Kurds and Moslem émigrés from Crete
and Roumelie. And Ottoman aristocrats in search of clear water
and fresh winds, had built handsome houses and gardens there,
away from the fever of a Damascus summer. Midhat Pasha had
even cut a few paths through the fetid jungle of the old city,
widening the Street Called Straight, turning the road to the
Great Mosque into the two-carriage thoroughfare of the Suq
Hamidieh, and filling in the redundant citadel moat to make way
for *suqs*.

Now, with French development, the throat which joined the
city to her head at Salihiye thickened into the suburbs of Djisr,
Chouhada and Arnouss. In 1929 the French town-planner
Danger, and the architect Écochard, started to rationalise this
bull-neck into the harmony of tree-lined streets. Soon Damascus
shared with Saigon, though less deservingly, the epithet 'Paris
of the East'.

In education, the religious propaganda of the late-nineteenth-
century mission schools was supplanted by institutions which
taught French language and history. Public services were
developed, and for the first time the cultural and historical
inheritance of Syria was systematically studied—by the French
Institute of Damascus—and enshrined in the new museum.

The Damascenes adapted themselves guardedly to new conditions. For a time they refused to drink the fresh water from
Fijeh, saying that it gave them kidney complaints and made
them impotent. The innovation of bicycles caused chaos. The
Damascenes tumbled off their machines at the meanest excuse,
collided with camels, ricocheted off mausoleums and bowled over
French soldiers on the pavements.

The ague of Syria was not cured by the development of her

cities. The country people, exploited and impoverished since the days of the Roman *coloni*, saw little change in their condition, although crops were slightly improved and areas of cultivation extended. Probings for mineral resources found the country fatally poor, and only asphalt, in the Latakiyeh district, was discovered. Oil-drilling failed; and the giant and beautiful forests of Syria were too long a memory to be resown.

Damascus, always fiercely political—I rarely met a Damascene who was not prepared to take over the reins of government instantly—remained a scorpion's nest of nationalism. In 1925 an appalling riot greeted the arrival of Lord Balfour and a few months later, French treachery to some Druse leaders detonated a revolt in which Druse insurgents and the city mob partially destroyed the Azem Palace and ran amok through the suburbs. Without warning, the French guns in the citadel shelled the orchards, the Meidan quarter and its northern outskirts, killing indiscriminately. But the rioting continued, and in early May 1926 the guns were again heard from the citadel, with aircraft overhead and a deployment of field artillery. The tombs and warehouses of Meidan disintegrated into obscure humps and sinews of the land. Even today the mosque domes look as if they would crack into pieces at a touch. The Ghuta was only cleared six months later, after several villages had been destroyed and over eight thousand soldiers, with tanks and field guns, had combed the orchards and diverted the irrigation channels.

Concessions to Syrian nationalism, like the conjoining of a parliament in 1932, seem something of a charade. Power always lay with the French. In 1936 there were more riots, and a promise of independence which was rescinded by new ministers in Paris. On the eve of the Second World War the fate of Syria was undecided, her economy stagnant, her people angry.

The battle for Syria against the Vichy French was an unexpectedly hard one. The Free French General Catroux dropped leaflets over the country, promising independence. The Vichy French tried, and failed, to save Damascus in a battle twenty miles to her south near Marj-as-Saffar, almost exactly where the Byzantines had made a stand against the Arabs one thousand three hundred years before.

On June 21st 1941, General Catroux reached Damascus at the head of a fleet of six ancient taxis, escorted by Circassian cavalry. Momentarily the cars were abandoned for the ditches while they were strafed by enemy aeroplanes. Then, with pomp diminished by the loss of two taxis, the procession advanced into the streets of the old city, where it stalled. It was met by a delegation from the Syrian government, politely enquiring about independence.

The assurances of Generals Catroux and de Gaulle, who officially announced the end of the mandate amid scenes of exultation, were sufficient for the delirious townsmen. But Syrian statesmen, grown long-toothed in disillusion, received the promises with scepticism. General de Gaulle was rigid and uncomprehending of Arab psychology, and slowly it became clear that the French planned to retain effective control of Syria. For four more years, in painful trickles, power was wrung from their hands. At the end of May 1945, the shells exploded in Damascus again. British troops intervened, and by 1946 Syria, for the first time since the dynasty of the Ommayads, was her own mistress.

18. The Moon on the Marble

> Lay your hands *now* to that in which
> we are engaged, and leave alone To-
> morrow, for it is not yet come, and
> Yesterday, for it is past.
>
> *Ma'ari*

I<small>N A TIME</small> a little earlier than grandfathers remember, and a
little later than the creation of man, Satan alighted on earth with
seven bags of lies. After his impartial fashion, he planned to
distribute these evenly over the surface of the world; but he fell
asleep in Syria, and here the bags fell open.

> If God made a land sink whose inhabitants lied,
> Then would Damascus be sunken with us because of
>   our falsehoods,
> If God crushed the mountains with a lie—
> Then would the mountains of Syria be crushed.

'*Shami shoumi*,' other Arabs alliterate. 'The Damascenes are a
wicked race.'

'By God, yes,' Razouk once declared. 'They say other men
walk like this'—he threw out his hand in a karate punch—'but
that we in Damascus go like this'—here his fingers undulated
and seemed to hatch a dynasty of air-born snakes.

'But we do not lie like the Iraqis,' said Toros, a melancholy-
faced Armenian sitting opposite us—a table in an empty
restaurant. 'Nobody can lie like the Iraqis.'

'Except for the Lebanese,' swore Razouk. 'They cheat you.
Phew! They strip you. My father went over to Beirut once to
sell some silk. . . .'

The Damascenes, when talking of other Arabs, seem at their
most tribal and anarchic. 'All the Arabs are brothers,' they swear
over the coffee-cups, but when asked what they think of the
Egyptians:

'By God, they are no good. They are not to be trusted. They
are like stones.'

What of Jordan?

'Primitive. They live like the pigs. My uncle was in Amman two years ago and . . .'

Of Lebanon?

'May God consume the bones of their ancestors!'

Of Iraq?

'They are more abominable than a black beetle which rolls forth dung by its nose.'

Ask a Lebanese about the Damascenes and he swears that they are backward and dishonest, and laughs at their politics with the shrug of an Englishman hearing of a new regime in a Central American state. 'The Damascenes?' a Jordanian or Iraqi sighs. 'They are tainted with the Turk!'

Since Ottoman times the café has been the accepted forum of political intrigue and debate in Damascus. The cafés over the Barada gyrate with nodding heads and muttering mouths all summer. In winter these parliaments convene in restaurants and private houses. Tric-trac boards and narghilyes (and perhaps hasheesh) accompany them. The dream of pan-Arabism, which touched them with caducean lightness in the late nineteenth century, now mesmerises the whole Middle East. Its desirability as a concept goes unquestioned. All Arabs are brothers. But the way it might be effected has, in Damascus, some six hundred and fifty thousand different interpretations; a little more or less depending on fluctuations in population.

Razouk and Toros were engaged in a sing-song half-argument, which is typically Damascene; the lilt of the last words uttered by one person decides the tone of those first spoken by the next. But sooner or later most discussions are darkened by a stygian sound—Israel: 'Eez-ra-heel,' as it is pronounced with perfectly elocuted ugliness. The effect of these syllables is invariable. There is a crashing of knives on plates, a waving of spoons and a discharge of eggplants over the table. Arms are extended in squally denouncements, fingers contorted into shapes which a Cambodian dancer might covet. Passion displaces thought.

For long evenings we would sit around miniature cups of sweet coffee (a Turkish beverage—true Arabic coffee is very black and bitter and Bedouin) while a transistor radio saddened the café with the cadenzas of Oum Qoulthum or Fairuz. At these times Arab manifestations seemed to be burlesqued in the Damascenes: the intoxication of language; the joys of contradiction; explosions of hurt pride; the omniscience of all present on affairs of state; suspicion; bouts of fearful stubbornness. But from time to time the debates were shot through with charm and humour—an old, aristocratic mood, which conceals, rather than modifies, a dangerous effervescence; for Damascus is a desert oasis, steeped in prejudice, chronically impatient.

Over the last twenty years a long series of governments has strutted into, and been dragged out of, her ferocious coliseum. Between 1949 and 1966 there have been fifteen *coups*, and the army has become so entangled in civilian government that it can no longer conceive itself as an un-political body. Statesmen search for military allies and vice versa, but decisive power always rests with the army. Generals and colonels fumble with politics like bears spinning wool, as the Arabs say, and *Yegallek Allah!* See where we have arrived!

The most powerful party to have emerged since the war is the Baath (resurrection) party, which is strongly nationalistic and socialist; but it is fragmented by left-wing and moderate sub-groups. The *coups* are often bloodless—the Syrians are not fond of fighting although they enjoy talking about it—but each year brings incidents and trials. In 1958 a nominal union with Egypt was achieved, and broken by a revolt in 1961. 'The Voice of the Arabs' still bombasts out of Cairo Radio, and the Syrian air is heavy with Egyptian vapours.

I remember driving from Damascus to the Hauran in the winter of 1962. Not far from Deraa I heard gunfire. Groups of people were running towards the road across the desert. I thought it must be a military exercise, until the bullets puffed up the sand.

A minute later, and a mile further back, I found a taxi driver, waiting. I asked him what was happening. He threaded and unthreaded his fingers violently, in gestures of conflict, and said: 'They are shooting students.' He did not seem to think this required embellishment, only lit a cigarette and leant against his taxi.

The firing petered out and we were allowed to drive on, over a village street littered with stones. The students were being forced into army lorries and taken back to Damascus. One was dead, and some women were bleeding by the roadside. They had rioted in favour of reunion with Egypt.

The affair was tragic because so futile: rebellion by a few village youths and their mothers. But the fever flushed by Radio Cairo had been contracted long before in the fading of traditional society into a half-educated people, with no jobs on which to expend themselves. 'The head of an idle man,' they say 'is the workshop of Satan.' The concrete tenements of Damascus are filled with such men: university graduates in humiliating jobs, living a travesty of Western life, attracted to socialism, flirting with Communism, but suspicious of foreign intervention. The government, whatever it does, is certain to attract rabid discontent, and to smack of favouritism, a rebirth of tribal nepotism. Change is generally seen in terms of a new dictatorship. A strong man, even if he be Yezid of the Wines, may be followed with faith.

For three years before 1966, Syria had a Baathist government in Damascus. Socialist ministers curbed the initiative of once-powerful businessmen, and redistributed the estates of the old landowners, whom the French patronised. So the lot of the peasant has become a little more tolerable. He is no longer hopelessly in debt to an absentee businessman, to tractor owners or irrigation pump proprietors; but he is still a serf to the land. Farming does not prosper. Penniless peasants seek the meanest urban job, and townsmen complain that the socialist government favours them. Socialism, like the doctrines of most past Syrian governments, persists in a void of economic and political xenophobia—'thy country's tares better than strange wheat'.

'By the way,' Razouk wrote to me two weeks after I had left Damascus, 'we have a new regime here.' This was after the *coup* of February 1966, a butcherly revolt by an extreme leftist faction, which described its achievement as 'a revolution to purify the March 8th revolution' of 1963. The Palace of Reception, said Razouk, had been shot to pieces; otherwise there was no change.

*　　*　　*

The modern town gnaws impatiently at the old, but wherever the tenements meet bazaars and palisades, the businessmen mingle with half-veiled peasant girls, and coiffured Lebanese ladies in American cars grind to frustrated halts among merchants and mules.

The periphery of the old city abounds with hybrid life: knife-grinders and sherbet-sellers; men wheeling trolley-loads of trinkets from China; glassblowers; a cripple holding guinea-pigs which select pieces of paper with fortunes inscribed on them. Bedouin squat in the shadow of office-blocks, and behind the aridity of a public park or a bank rises the dome of a Mameluke tomb.

The Chouhada, or Merjeh, Square is still the centre of the modern city, and is distinctive for a peculiar monument which commemorates the completion of the telegraph line to Mecca. Here, for a few pence, a juice-seller will crush a pile of lemons or carrots under a vice, until the liquid dribbles over the glass. '*Allah yahfazek!* Drink the fruit of Damascus and you can make love five times a day!'

From Chouhada Square the Beirut road follows the bed of the Barada westward. With the Boulevard de Baghdad, which runs parallel to it in the north-east, it is the largest of the city streets. In the shadow of the baroque-Moorish offices of the last Ottomans sit public scribes and street photographers. Further on, there is a froth of domes from the Suleimaniye; the rococo building of the Ministry of Education; the Damascus Secondary School. One arm of the road curls through eucalyptus trees to the university. The other points to Lebanon past barracks and sauntering sentries. In the south, the pavilions of the city's International Fair, which are only open one month in the year, loom depressingly.

To the north, residential quarters scale the Kassioun Mountain, ascending past Chouhada and the mongrel Parliament Building to Salihiye. Here and there, an Ottoman mansion with balustrades and timber overhangs the road like a disdainful and mellow effendi; and the wealthy still seek refuge in summer from the lower city in the houses of Mohajirine. Aristocratic families are impregnated with Turkish blood, Circassian and Georgian good-looks; but their old hegemony is already usurped by a new class of wealthy Syrian, who surrounds himself with a tasteless parody of European life, much as his ancestors once accepted the baroque fashion of Constantinople. Defenceless against Western bad taste, the streets are shabby with concrete offices and cinemas. Tourists, after their day in the old city, retire to the orange hull of the Semiramis Hotel or the New Ommayad, or seek out 'belly-dancing' in a rash of night-clubs.

The eastern extremities of the city are sad. In the desert beyond Mezze half-finished tenements prick the sky with steel joints, and erupt again at Kafr Sousa, once famous for olives, but now the centre of the motor-car trade. Buses—the last denizens of the trade routes to the east—clatter into depots, brown with Iraqi dust; and on the quarter's rim glimmers a gigantic graveyard for cars, where gutted Mercedes taxis have thrown down steel roots into the dust.

Industry spreads into the orchards. Where growth used to create beauty, it now destroys. Paradise is trampled under stone, and man has dealt with the Barada as he does with most of his great rivers: begins by worshipping, and ends by polluting them.

Doummar has its cement works, Kadem its chemical and metallurgical firms, glass and metal factories. Beyond Bab Charki new tanneries hum where once the Barada was fetid with refuse and arsenic; and in the suburb-village of Qaboun industries produce textiles, nylons, rubber, chocolate, conserves and important food products. This area is now the largest industrial centre in Syria, and with the cotton-growing area of Aleppo, the grain-harvest of Hauran and the oil transit dues, it has become a key factor in the economy.

As the craftsman forsakes his trade and takes a bus to the factory, the social strata reshuffle themselves with pain. The master-craftsman, who was always a co-worker with his men, is replaced by a factory-chief, unsoiled and remote. The protection of friendship is supplanted by the insurance of a syndicate. Old skills turn into mechanical habits. Even the once-famous Damascus soap, compounded of olive-oil and the *chinane* plant, has been replaced by a block of vegetable oil and caustic soda.

This modern revolution finds a city which has grown lean over several centuries, the wells of her creativity run dry. It is difficult to grudge men the extra wealth it will one day bring, or wish them harnessed, against the tug of progress, to the personality of the Damascus which is dying.

*   *   *

The room was quiet, except for the little girl Senah, who played with her boots. Umm-Toni, slumped in unbecoming silence, knitted very slowly. I was busy feeling sorry for the chicken I was eating, which must have led a very tough life. But chicken was special: a farewell meal. Usually we only ate rice and beetroot, stuffed vine-leaves and a little chopped mutton sunk in goat's milk. Restaurants were distant and offered many ways of death: *kobieh* pastries of spiced meat and onions; vegetables and beans of many kinds; chopped meat and mushrooms called *kama*; and macaroni and *kaftah* meat-balls, herb-flavoured. Shawrmah (pieces of meat wedged between leaves of fresh bread) and shish kebab were sometimes compensations, but little by little Umm-Toni had weaned me to beetroot and vine-leaves.

'You will speak well of us in England? You will say that we are good?' she suddenly asked.

How could I not?

Later that evening Razouk asked me the same question. 'What will you say of us in England? You must be glad to be going back. Some day I will leave here too.'

Razouk's house was one of the handsomest in the Christian quarter. The rooms were enormous and marble-paved. Painted ceilings echoed the design of Persian carpets, and showered down chandeliers. In the sitting-room, where nobody ever sat, a violin and an encrusted 'ud lay together on a divan.

I remembered an autumn night here, with smells of coffee and honeysuckle, the sky spread above the courtyard in a cold rectangle of stars; and Razouk's brother tinkled on the zither-like *kanoun*, singing 'O night, stay with us always'—a trick to pass the night away. These houses are like streams or tracks. Placed around courtyards, which are their essence, their lines are altered only imperceptibly by the nudging of centuries. This court, conceivably, was roughed out by some Aramean mind before the fall of Nineveh. Perhaps a Greek merchant refined it, or a Roman civil servant shaded it with porticoes. Gilded columns upheld its galleries, and across its mosaic paving gambolled fauns and satyrs.

Momentarily, it seemed ridiculous to leave. Then Razouk grated: 'I wish I could leave here too. I don't want to see my friends any more. I can't bear the sight of everyone.' His house was often filled by students, worrying about their degrees, or wondering whether they might earn enough marks from high school to reach university; or have to join the army; or after university, how to find free education in the Balkans, or perhaps —*in shah Allah!*—training in Munich or Paris.

'Whenever I see them I think "Failure, failure, failure". We sit about. We talk politics or women. We can't do much about either. The girls here are stupid and prim. What's the point in having beautiful women if . . .'

Razouk's eldest brother had been married, by family arrange-ment, to a woman he had met for two minutes. He had said that there was nothing unusual in this. His parents had chosen well,

Good birth, in Damascus, is of great importance. And the woman had recently borne him a son.

With the introduction of compulsory primary education and free secondary education the position of women is changing. More than a quarter of the Damascus University students are girls, mostly studying the liberal arts. The veil is being gradually evicted, and the Moslem view of women as inherently inferior beings 'brought up among ornaments and contentious without cause' is waning. Yet most marriages are still contracted arbitrarily—Moslem girls are often betrothed at the age of twelve or thirteen—and a woman does not command equal rights in practice, or even by law.

'I'll find a European wife,' Razouk said. 'Some day you will see me in England. It will be easy to get a job compared to this place. I will take anything; sell things in the streets. Just so I can be rid of here.'

It had grown late. I rose to go, walked to the doorway, and stopped in unbelief. In the courtyard the moon lay on the marble like a phosphorescent sea, pallid and miraculous. One dared not tread on it.

'Look at that, Razouk,' was all I could say.

'You should see it in summer. Then the vines hang so far over the courtyard that the light scarcely comes through.'

'And you want to leave?'

'I love this place. But what can I do? There's nothing here. The whole city is empty.'

We shook hands. Delicately, like violating snow, I stepped across the lake of frozen moonlight and into the alley.

Later I tried to feel glad that I was leaving Damascus, and hung over my balcony to deplore the striplights along the Street Called Straight. The wolf-dogs had long ago stolen into the city through the Roman gate, and were dragging refuse along the gutters with rasping and swishing sounds.

I had packed my case, but the children had unpacked it again. Elias and Umm-Toni had been forcing rice and chicken into me all day, and kept saying, Was I not afraid of the aeroplane? By God, they had heard of an aeroplane last April which . . .

'You will speak well of us?' Elias asked yet again, scratching his chest with a noise like tearing brambles. 'You have taken our photographs. So people in England will see that the Arabs are good and that we look like they do in Europe. We do not all live in the desert. Of course there are some who do, but there are people in the English desert too. It's the same everywhere.

. . . And babies are the same!' he shouted, kissing the child with a noise like the uncorking of a jeroboam of champagne. 'By God, yes. You can't change babies.'

They were asleep now. Soon Elias's snores would pulsate through the partition. One of the children was humming in her dreams. The neon cross on the Armenian church flickered out.

Elias woke later in the night and thumped downstairs in his pyjamas to find me a taxi. It was still dark when we said good-bye—I leaving through the Roman gate with a wail of tyres in the silence; he enormous and solitary in the biblical street.

The modern suburbs on the airport road passed by without noise or light. As the desert succeeded them, I realised how lonely Damascus is. It was hard to believe that the flats could be symbols of any future, but already they have pierced the walls of the old city. True to history, the enemy entered by the Eastern Gate. The Straight Street widens here, and there is an upheaval of new apartments in the south. In time, a distressing logic will creep into the streets. The summers will be purged of fever. Each of Rahda's children may have a room of his own. And the traveller will not wake again in a jasmine-scented night, to hear the sherbet-seller calling for him to refresh his heart.

Chronology of
Main Events in the
History of Damascus

1157	Earthquake damages city
1176	Saladin rules. Start of the Ayyoubid dynasty
1237	Fire destroys part of city
1260	Mongols under Hulagu capture Damascus and end the Ayyoubid dynasty. The Mamelukes defeat the Mongols at Goliath Springs, and occupy Damascus
1260–1277	Rule of Baybars
1299	Mongols under Gazan take Damascus. Salihiye sacked
1400	The devastation of Tamerlane
1468–1495	Rule of the Mameluke Kaitbey brings tranquillity
1516	Ottoman Turks under Selim I take Damascus
1520	Damascene revolt fails. One third of the city razed by the Turks
1555	Tekkiyeh of Suleiman built
1654	City burnt and flooded
1749	Asaad Pasha builds his palace
1832	Ibrahim Pasha of Egypt occupies Damascus. Improved conditions.
1840	Ottomans retake city
1860	The Christian massacres
1878	Midhat Pasha governor
1918	Damascus liberated from the Turks
1919	Damascus the capital of the kingdom of Syria
1920	French occupation begins
1925	Riots. French shell the city
1941	Damascus falls to the Allies
1946	Syria independent, with Damascus as capital
1958	Union with Egypt
1961	Break with Egypt
1966	Baathist government of General Ameen Hafiz overthrown and replaced by a left-wing regime.

SELECT BIBLIOGRAPHY

Abdul-Hak, Selim. *Aspects de l'Ancienne Damas* (Direction Générale des Antiquités, Damas).

— *Catalogue Illustré du Départment des Antiquités Greco-Romaines au Musée de Damas* (Damas, 1951).

Arnold, Sir Thomas, and Guillaume, Alfred (ed.). *The Legacy of Islam* (Oxford University Press, 1943).

Bagh, Adib Souleiman. *L'Industrie à Damas entre 1928–1958* (Imp. Université de Damas, 1961).

Battuta, ibn-. *Travels in Asia and Africa 1325–1354*. Trs. and selected by H. A. R. Gibb (George Routledge & Son Ltd., London, 1929).

Berchem, Max van. 'Notes Archéologiques sur la mosquée des Omeyyades.' *Bulletin d'Etudes Orientales*, Tomes VII–VIII (Institut Français de Damas, 1937–8).

Besnard, Lieut.-Colonel G. 'Damas, son oasis, ses habitants.' *L'Asie Française*, No. 286, January 1931.

Bouchier, E. S. *Syria as a Roman Province* (B. H. Blackwell, Oxford, 1916).

Bukhsh, S. Khuda. 'Damascus and the Court of the Omayyads.' *Journal of the Moslem Institute*, Vol. 1, No. 4 (Imperial Press, Calcutta, 1905).

Butler, Howard Crosby. *Early Churches in Syria* (Princeton University Press, 1929).

Castle, Wilfrid T. F. *Syrian Pageant* (Hutchinson & Co. Ltd., London, 1948).

Charlesworth, M. P. *Trade Routes of the Roman Empire*. Rev. edn. (Cambridge University Press, 1926).

Creswell, K. A. C. *Early Muslim Architecture*. 2 vols. (Clarendon Press, Oxford, 1932, 1940).

Dussaud, René. *Topographie Historique de la Syrie Antique et Médiévale* (Librairie Orientaliste Paul Geuthner, Paris, 1927).

Écochard, M. 'Le Palais Azem de Damas.' *Gazette des Beaux-Arts*, No. 140 (Paris, 1935).

Écochard, M. and le Coeur, Charles. *Les Bains de Damas* (Institut Français de Damas, 1942–3).

Elisséeff, N. 'Dimashk.' *Encyclopaedia of Islam*, Fasciculus 27. Ed. B. Lewis, Ch. Pellat and J. Schacht (E. J. Brill, Leiden: Luzac & Co., London, 1963).

— 'Les Monuments de Nūr ad-Dīn.' *Bulletin d'Études Orientales*, Tome XIII (Institut Français de Damas, 1949–1951).

Farley, J. Lewis. *The Massacres in Syria* (Bradbury & Evans, London, 1861).

Fedden, Robin. *Syria, an Historical Appreciation* (Robert Hale, 1955).

Harrer, Gustave. *Studies in the History of the Roman Province of Syria* (Princeton University Press, 1915).

Herzfeld, E. 'Damascus: Studies in Architecture.' *Ars Islamica*, Vols. IX, X, XI–XII, XII–XIV.

Hitti, Philip K. *History of Syria*. 2nd rev. edn. (Macmillan & Co., Ltd., London, 1957).

— *The Origins of the Druse People and Religion*. Columbia University Oriental Studies, Vol. XXVIII (Columbia University Press, 1928).

Hole, Edwyn. *Syrian Harvest* (Robert Hale, 1956).

Hourani, A. H. *Minorities in the Arab World* (Oxford University Press, 1947).

Huxley, Henry M. 'Syrian Songs, Proverbs and Stories; collected, translated and annotated.' *Journal of the American Oriental Society*, Vol. 23 (New Haven, Conn., 1902).

Irving, Washington. *Mahomet and his Successors* (James B. Millar & Co., New York, 1884).

Jazari, Muhammad ibn Ibrahim al-. *La Chronique de Damas*. Trs. J. Sauvaget (Bibliothèque de l'École des Hautes Études, Librairie Ancienne Honoré Champion, Paris, 1949).

Jubayr, ibn-. *The Travels of Ibn Jubayr*. Trs. R. J. C. Broadhurst (Jonathan Cape, 1952).

Kennedy, Pringle. *Arabian Society at the Time of Muhammad* (Thacker, Spink & Co., 1926).

Khoury-Sarkis, G. and Kamal, Ribhi. 'Maalola's Syriac and Differences between Syriac Dialects.' *Syria*, No. 5 (Government Press, Damascus, 1965).

Kremer, Alfred Von. 'Damascus and the Court of the Omayyads.' *Culturgeschichte des Orients*. Trs. S. Khuda Bukhsh. Extract: *Journal of the Moslem Institute* (Imperial Press, Calcutta, 1905).

— *Mittelsyrien und Damascus* (P. P. Mechitharisten, Wien, 1853).

Lallemand. *Jérusalem-Damas* (Ancien Maison Quantin, 1894).

Lammens, Henri. *L'Avènement des Marwānides et le Califat de Marwan 1er*. Mélanges de la Faculté Orientale, L'Université Saint-Joseph, Beyrut, Tome XII, Fasc. 2 (Imprimerie Catholique, Beyrut, 1927).

— *Études sur le Règne du Calife Omaiyade Mo'awia 1er*. Mélanges de la Faculté Orientale, L'Université Saint-Joseph, Beyrut, Tome I, Fasc. 1; Tome II, 1907 (Imprimerie Catholique, Beyrut, 1906–7).

— *Études sur le Règne du Calife Omaiyade Mo'awia 1er. La Jeunesse du Calife Yazid 1er. Le Califat de Yazid 1er*. Tome III, Fasc. 1; Tome IV, 1910; Tome V, Fasc. 1, 2; Tome VI, 1913; Tome VII, 1914–21 (Imprimerie Catholique, Beyrut, 1910–21).

— *Études sur le Siècle des Omayyades* (Imprimerie Catholique, Beyrut, 1930).

Laoust, Henri (Trs.). 'Les Gouverneurs de Damas sous les Mamlouks et les Premiers Ottomans.' *Traduction des Annales d'Ibn Tulun et d'Ibn Gum'a* (Institut Français de Damas, 1952).

Lassus, M. Jean. 'Note sur les Mosaïques de Jerusalem et de Damas.' *Bulletin d'Études Orientales*, Tome III (Institut Français de Damas, 1933).

Lerner, Daniel. *The Passing of Traditional Society* (Free Press of Glencoe, Illinois, 1958).

Lewis, Bernard. 'A Jewish Source on Damascus just after the Ottoman Conquest.' *Bulletin of School of Oriental and African Studies*, Vol. X (University of London Press, 1939–42).

Longrigg, Stephen. *Syria and Lebanon under French Mandate* (Oxford University Press, 1958).

Lorey. Eustache de. 'L'Etat Actuel du Palais Azem.' *Bulletin d'Études Orientales* (Institut Français de Damas).

Lorey, Eustache de, and Wiet, Gaston. 'Cénotaphes de Deux Dames musulmanes à Damas, Syria.' *Revue d'Art Oriental et d'Archeologie*, Tome II (Librairie Orientaliste Paul Geuthner, Paris, 1921).

Lucian. *The Syrian Goddess*. Trs. A. M. Harmon (William Heine-mann, London, 1925).

Mackintosh, Mrs. *Damascus and its People. Sketches of Moslem Life in Syria* (Seeley, Jackson, & Halliday, London, 1883).

Majlisi, Mohammed Baqir. ''Ali in Shia Tradition.' Trs. Rev. James L. Merrick. *The Moslem World*, Vol. IV, 1914.

Margoliouth, D. S. *Cairo, Jerusalem and Damascus* (Chatto & Windus, 1907).

Maussion de Favières, J. de. 'Note sur les bains de Damas.' *Bulletin d'Études Orientales*, Tome XVII (Institut Français de Damas, 1961–2).

Muir, Sir William. *Annals of the Early Caliphate from Original Sources* (Smith, Elder, & Co., London, 1883).

Mukaddasi. *Description of Syria, including Palestine*. Trs. Guy le Strange (Palestine Pilgrim's Text Soc., London, 1892).

Munqidh, Usāmah ibn-. *An Arab-Syrian Gentleman and Warrior in the Period of the Crusades*. Trs. G. R. Potter (George Routledge & Sons, Ltd., London, 1929).

Olmstead, A. T. *History of Palestine and Syria to the Macedonian Conquest* (Charles Scribner's Sons, New York, 1931).

Porter, Rev. J. L. *Five Years in Damascus, with Travels and Researches in Palmyra, Lebanon, The Giant Cities of Bashan, and the Haurân* (John Murray, London, 1870).

— *The Giant Cities of Bashan and Syria's Holy Places* (T. Nelson & Sons, 1872).

Qalānisī, ibn al-. *The Damascus Chronicle of the Crusades*. Extracted and translated by H. A. R. Gibb (Luzac & Co., London, 1932).

Rosebault, C. J. *Saladin, Prince of Chivalry* (Cassell & Co. Ltd., London, 1930).

Rostovtzeff, M. *Caravan Cities*. Trs. D. and T. Talbot Rice (Oxford University Press, 1932).

Sadeque, Dr. Syedah Fatima. *Baybars I of Egypt* (Oxford University Press, Pakistan).

Sasrā, Muhammad ibn Muhammad ibn. *A Chronicle of Damascus 1389–1397*. Trs., ed. and annotated by William M. Brinner (University of California Press, 1963).

Sauvaget, Jean. 'Une Ancienne Représentation de Damas au Musée du Louvre.' *Bulletin d'Études Orientales*, Tome XI (Institut Français de Damas, 1945–6).

— 'Le Cénotaphe de Saladin.' *Revue des Arts Asiatiques* (Les Éditions G. Van Oest, Paris, 1930).

— 'La Citadelle de Damas.' *Syria*. Tome XI, 1930.

— *Les Monuments Historiques de Damas* (Imprimerie Catholique, Beyrut, 1932).

— 'Remarques sur les monuments omeyyades.' *Journal Asiatique*, Tome CCXXXI (Librairie Orientaliste Paul Geuthner, January–March, 1939).

Sauvaire, H. (Trs.). 'Description de Damas.' Traductions de l'Arabe. *Journal Asiatique*, 1896.

Seale, Patrick. *The Struggle for Syria. A Study of Post-War Arab Politics, 1945–1958* (Oxford University Press, 1965).

Servier, André. *Islam and the Psychology of the Musulman* (Chapman & Hall Ltd., London, 1924).

Shamir, Shimon. 'As'ad Pash al-'Azm and the Ottoman Rule in Damascus (1743–1758).' *Bulletin of Oriental and African Studies*, Vol. 26, Part 1 (University of London Press, 1963).

Shukri, Ahmad. *The Handicrafts of Damascus, Syria*. (The Islamic Review, Woking, December, 1954.)

Somogyi, Joseph. *Adh-Dhahabī's Record of the Destruction of Damascus by the Mongols in 1299–1301*. Ignace Goldziher Memorial Volume, Part 1 (Budapest, 1948).

Sourdel-Thomine, J. 'Les anciens lieux de pèlerinage damascains d'après les sources arabes.' *Bulletin d'Études Orientales*, Tome XIV (Institut Français de Damas, 1952–4).

Suyúti, Jalálu'ddīn a's. *Works*. Trs. H. S. Jarrett (Bibliotheca Indica. J. W. Thomas, Calcutta, 1881).

Thoumin, R. 'Deux Quartiers de Damas.' *Bulletin d'Études Orientales*, Tome I (Institut Français de Damas, 1931).

Tourneau, Roger le. *Damas de 1075 à 1154*. Traduction annotée d'un fragment de l'Histoire de Damas d'Ibn al-Qalānisī (Institut Français de Damas, 1952).

Tower, J. Allen. *The Oasis of Damascus* (American Press, Beirut, 1935).

William, Archbishop of Tyre. *A History of Deeds done beyond the Sea*. 2 vols. (Columbia University Press, 1943).

Woodsmall, Ruth F. *Study of the Role of Women in Lebanon, Egypt, Iraq, Jordan and Syria, October 1954–August 1955* (International Federation of Business and Professional Women, New York, 1956).

Wulzinger, K. and Watzinger, C. *Damaskus, Die antike Stadt* (Walter De Gruyter & Co., Berlin, 1921–4).

—— *Damaskus, Die islamische Stadt* (Walter De Gruyter & Co., Berlin, 1921–4).

Zāhirī, Khalīl Az-. *La Zubda Kachf al-Mamālik.* Trs. *Venture de Paradis* (Institut Français de Damas, 1950).

Zaydān, Jurjī. *History of Islamic Civilisation.* Part 4: *Umayyads and 'Abbāsids* (Luzac & Co., Leiden, 1907).

Ziadeh, Nicola A. *Damascus under the Mamlūks* (University of Oklahoma Press, Norman, 1964).

— *Syria and Lebanon* (E. Benn Ltd., London, 1957).

Index